Turning Tides

ANDREW PHELAN first skippered an ancient rowing boat on the River Suir at the age of ten. Later he acquired cruising experience on coasts from Norway to Spain, and frequently wrote and broadcast on sailing and Irish history. A native of Co. Waterford, he practiced at the Bar in England, and his book, *The Law for Small Boats*, was published in 1974.

Retirement allowed Andrew to cruise more widely in his thirty-two foot sloop *Sarakiniko*. His circumnavigation of Ireland resulted in the book *Ireland from the Sea* (Wolfhound Press), an exploration of Ireland's seafaring culture and the fascinating history of its coasts.

As *Sarakiniko* became a familiar sight in the west of Scotland and the Hebrides, the boat's frequent passages through the Irish Sea inspired her skipper to look at the communities bordering that sea and the links between them. *Turning Tides* is the result of these journeys.

Andrew Phelan has lived for many years in West London, by the Thames. He skippers his grandchildren on the local dinghy, and promises promotion to *Sarakiniko* once the crew is seaworthy.

To my grandchildren – a promising crew

Turning Tides

A Voyage Around the Irish Sea

ANDREW PHELAN

WOLFHOUND PRESS

Published in 2003 by
Wolfhound Press
An imprint of Merlin Publishing
16 Upper Pembroke Street
Dublin 2
Ireland

Tel: + 353 1 6764373
Fax: + 353 1 6764368
www.merlin-publishing.com

A CIP record for this book is available from the British Library

ISBN 0-86327-908-2

5 4 3 2 1

Cover Design by Graham Thew Design
Printed and bound by Nørhaven Paperback A/S

Foreword

RATHER LIKE crossing and recrossing the Irish Sea, putting this book together has been a complex journey, but what follows is, for better or worse, both a sailor's account of confronting the sea and a historian's attempt to make sense of its history. I have tried to carry both the sailor and the landsman on an adventure along the coasts of the Irish Sea, where a seaward approach forces one to realise how clearly this sea has moulded the peoples around it and drawn their destinies together.

I needed, and had, a patient and cheerful crew. I thank them for these qualities, even as I loitered in libraries or seemed to waste time in persistent chatter with harbourmasters and many others.

I have had kindness and help on every shore, from Elizabeth Balcome of the Skerries Historical Society to Ernest Evans of Bardsey Island and Simon Glyn of the Bardsey Island Trust. Ron Rowan, guardian of the Isle of Man Maritime Museum, and his colleague John Kerr, gave their valuable time during my tour of the museum and our subsequent correspondance. I also had extensive help from Patricia Griffiths of Manx National Heritage, Douglas.

Submerged for many months in paperwork ashore, my morale was maintained by the comments of a good friend, Wallace Clarke, of Northern Ireland – author and veteran of many Celtic voyages. Winkie Nixon and Cormac McHenry of the Irish Cruising Club gave me timely encouragement in Dublin.

Many others who were so generous with their time must remain nameless. I think of the staffs of the Greenwich Maritime Museum, the Public Records Office in Kew, the National Library, Dublin, the librarians of the Royal St George and the Royal Irish Yacht clubs at Dun Laoghaire, and the library of the Royal

Cruising Club in London. Need I say that the voyage would not have progressed very far without the splendid sailing directions of the Irish Cruising Club and the many charts available from the Royal Cruising Club.

My wife Joan gets special thanks. While crew could often escape to a saner life ashore, she lasted the course to the end, often turning shipboard meals into mini dinner parties. And for many months she urged me to keep faith with a computer which I love to hate. I would not have survived the trial without her.

Finally I thank my publishers and my patient editor, Peter Malone.

Andrew Phelan
London, April 2003

Contents

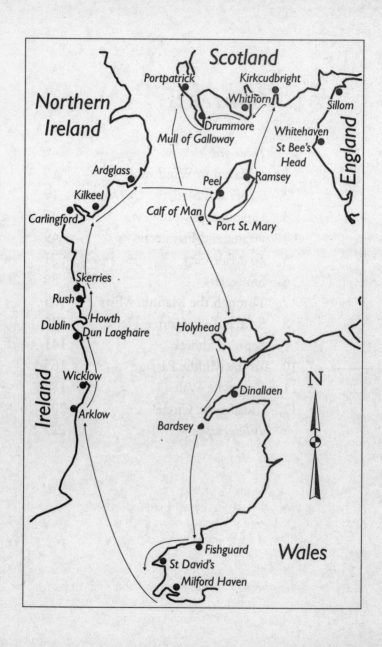

ONE

A Haven to Windward

ERNEST'S FACE TIGHTENED in concentration. He clambered past me, ducking from a fan of salt water.

'Got it?'

'Yes.'

He grabbed the tiller and squinted into the darkness. The wind, cold for early summer, chased across the mouth of the Bristol Channel. We were well reefed down, *Sarakiniko* surging forward, gunwale submerged whenever she was rolled by an occasional crest.

It had been a tiring two-hour watch, but I didn't go below at once. Night sailing tightens the nerves, and just now I needed conversation even more than I needed sleep.

Ernest had his legs braced against the cockpit locker, his safety harness clipped on. I stood on the step of the companionway, sheltered by the sprayhood as the yacht shuddered at the impact of another sea on her port bow.

'A nasty sea,' I called, 'wind against tide.'

'We can't have it every way,' Ernest said. 'We got the north-making tide around Land's End. Now that it's turned we have to pay for it.' He followed my gaze astern, where a light flashed intermittently.

'Hartland Point in north Devon?'

'No. It's one of the Lundy Island lights; one flash every twenty seconds. We're sinking it now. And about time.'

'So we were pushed a good way east earlier on?'

'Yes. Strong tides.'

Ernest adjusted his seat and his grip on the tiller, taking charge of the boat as she sailed into the weather. 'You should turn in,' he said. 'I'll wake Tony when he's on.'

I went below and pulled the hatch across, marvelling as I always did at this sudden transition to domestic comfort – upholstery, a shelf of books, a net of fruit swaying to the roll of the boat, and the swinging oil lamp, turned low to save night vision. It was a household sustained on a skin of plastic, somehow actually within the sea. Staggering, I crumpled my oilskin trousers down around my seaboots, stepped out, found the hook for my dripping jacket and rolled into my sleeping-bag.

We had sailed from Plymouth on *Sarakiniko*, my thirty-two foot sloop, bound for Milford Haven and on a course that would take us clockwise around the Irish Sea. Before us were Wales, Ireland, Scotland and England, four countries linked for centuries by the travels of boats under sail. Dependent on winds and tides, they carried news, goods and people, and navigated within sight of land whenever they could. Their journeys created a web of connections between the different coasts, all of them bound together by the Irish Sea.

We would sail across St George's Channel, the sea route linking southern Wales and the south-eastern tip of Ireland. Ernest and Tony, however, would have to leave the boat at Milford Haven, where my wife, Joan, and Martin Wemyss would join us. As another gust laid us over and a dollop of the Bristol Channel rattled on the sprayhood, for a moment I envied Ernest and Tony the home comforts which would soon enfold them, but I knew that even now neither would wish to be elsewhere. What a curious paradox that discomfort and the keen edge of apprehension should be key elements in our enjoyment.

Ernest Howes was an ex-farmer whose life altered when he and his family had to leave Zimbabwe, a beautiful country he had grown to love. Arriving in Britain, he trained as a restorer of antique furniture and now lives among his customers in a lovely corner of the Welsh countryside. He had apparently adjusted to British bureaucracy and the welfare state, but I thought he missed the stimulus of Africa's outdoor pursuits, and while life on *Sarakiniko* might not offer the excitement you get hunting snakes from your sheds or ambushing baboons marauding in your cornfields, it was the best substitute I could offer him. Moreover, he had fingers that moved with ease around engines and pumps, a talent that made him an asset on board this particular ship.

Tony O'Gorman, from Clonmel in Ireland, I had lured away from his own boat on the coast of Co. Waterford. As a native of Waterford myself, Tony and I can reminisce about both town and county until the cows come home. Tony was the man in mind when the term 'laid back' was invented, but combined this ease of manner with enviable energy. He helped *Sarakiniko* to make a circumnavigation of Ireland a few years ago, and brought a delicious contribution to the galley, barm brack, an Irish speciality which I describe inadequately as a cross between bread and fruit cake. Its thick, buttered slices do wonders to refuel a hungry crew. When he was not at sea, Tony was likely to be exploring the Irish mountains. Now he was being hoisted and dropped in the low cubbyhole of the forepeak. I hoped he was getting some sleep.

It did not come readily to me. I lay mulling over some recent reading, especially a volume of *Sailing Tours: Land's End to the Mull of Galloway – a Guide to the Western Seas*. It had been written by a nineteenth-century sailor, Frank Cowper, who sailing alone and without an engine produced five pilot books on the British, French and Irish coasts, harbours and anchorages. His books are still of absorbing interest and practical value. I have a neighbourly regard for him because he built what he called his ideal yacht, *Undine II*, on the foreshore of the Thames at Strand on the Green, Chiswick, close to my home. It was forty-seven feet overall, drew just over five feet, and Cowper did much of the work on it with his own hands.

For me he is the most congenial of the crashingly hearty Victorians who took to single-handed sailing off the British coast in the nineteenth century, the sort that perhaps Thomas Arnold's Rugby would have been proud of. Still, they were very few – in the 1870s, Cowper found but one yacht in each of the Isle of Wight harbours of Bembridge, Keyhaven and Yarmouth, and only three in Lymington – and the yachtsmen's stories make fascinating reading. One, John MacGregor, handed out Bibles to fishermen and bargees and produced a bestseller, *The Voyage Alone in the Yacht Rob Roy*. Another, Middleton, in *The Cruise of the Kate*, brought to sea his sense of loneliness, and found in the sea comforting detachment from a world which would not accept his propositions that heaven was located inside the sun and the earth was not in fact a globe but saucer shaped. Last of a curious trio was MacMullen, who wrote in his book *Down Channel*, 'in language too mild to express my real sentiments', that he disliked 'a sloven' – 'a slovenly reef, a slovenly furl and a dirty mast look disgraceful on a yacht of any pretensions'. An authoritarian through and through, he felt England itself was no longer a tight ship. He died of a heart attack in 1891 while sailing alone in the Channel and was found by a fishing boat off Cherbourg setting west under full sail, still gripping the tiller.

Cowper's firm views on the Bristol Channel occupied my thoughts: 'Not in my opinion a suitable place wherein amateur sailors may practise cruising. The tides are too strong, the coasts too exposed and the harbours of the poorest description, few and far between. The prevalent winds blow up and down and the seas are choppy and heavy.' Of the entire Irish Sea, he added, surely with undue gloom, 'from Falmouth to the North Channel there are only the harbours of Milford Haven, Holyhead, Kingstown and the dubious shelter of Belfast Lough wherein one may take refuge in case of a really hard blow'.

Soon we ought to reach ample shelter in the drowned rivervalley which is Milford Haven. I fell asleep reflecting that *Sarakiniko*, at any rate, has twin keels which give her the freedom to sit upright in tidal harbours that dry out, an asset which Cowper did not have when he castigated the Isle of Man, central island of the Irish Sea, for not having a single harbour 'where a yacht can be afloat and be in comfort and safety from every wind'.

But in the Isle of Man on a clear day, you can see four countries – England, Wales, Scotland and Ireland – and understand how the Irish Sea was small enough to yoke them together, each to the other, in challenge and invitation.

TO A modern eye water is a barrier. Our perception of travel is land based, the sea an impediment to the urgent movement of our cars and commercial vehicles. Giant ferries, their interiors a cross between an hotel and a shopping mall, are designed in many cases to prevent passengers from ever going on deck. Fewer and fewer people actually experience the pleasures and frustrations of winds and tides, unless they work on boats for a living or use them for recreation. For most people, the sea has become a second-hand experience.

Yet the commonplace that geography shapes history applies as much to water as to land, to the seas and great rivers as to a plain or desert. The folk wanderings of ancient times were westward from the European mainland into the islands of Britain and Ireland. The waves of peoples who landed on the southern shores of England pushed through pathless forest or worked up the rivers until they met natural obstacles, the mountains to the west and north. And if those mountains had not existed, if Britain had been lowlands right to the western seas, racial differences might never have persisted. There might be no discernible differences now between the peoples of Wales, the Scottish highlands and the Saxon east.

Take it further. The primitive Saxon invaders might have swept on and colonised Ireland in the sixth century, whereas the Norman arrival was delayed until the twelfth. Or – put another way – if there had been mountain ranges along England's south and east coasts, they might have restricted the tribes which invaded these islands and limited the extent to which more ancient peoples were pushed west to become the 'Celtic fringes' of Cornwall, Wales and Scotland.

The Irish Sea's distinctive character has been recognised for a very long time. After all, the first known map of the island of Ireland was drawn by the Greek cartographer Ptolemy in the second century AD, and his information came from Phoenician mariners who had trading contacts on each side of the Irish Sea. In 1527 a cartographer called Humphrey Lloyd published the first individual map of Wales, with 'The Yrish Oceane' off the coast and sketches of three-masted ships around the margins. His artistry was outclassed by a contemporary, Michael Drayton, whose map of Wales depicted nude ladies bathing in rivers, shepherds and shepherdesses disporting on hilltops and Neptune (without his trident) rising from the estuary of the River Dee. No more fanciful in its way than the names 'the British

Mediterranean' – used eighty years ago by the geographer Halford MacKinder – or 'the Celtic Mediterranean', a term favoured more recently by the archaeologist Lloyd Laing.

In prosaic terms, the Irish Sea lies between 52 and 55 degrees north and 3 to 6 degrees west. For good or ill, these limits made it small enough to be traversed in daylight hours, a Middle Sea where the earliest mariners could steer by reference to the surrounding summits, creating a criss-cross pattern of routes linking four countries with one another.

St George's Channel in the south, stretching some forty-four sea miles from St David's Head in Wales to Carnsore Point in Wexford, is the wider of the two channels that give entry to the Irish Sea. To the north, Scotland's Mull of Kintyre and Torr Head in Co. Antrim stand a mere eleven miles apart. This relatively enclosed sea has its own currents and tides, even its own distinctive winds and waves. It is classified separately in broadcast shipping forecasts, and no submarine commander bound in or out of bases in the Clyde forgets that it is also rather shallow, mostly under 170 feet.

Its tides are quite distinctive. The waters of the Mediterranean, which has only one outlet to the Atlantic, have a negligible rise and fall, but in the Irish Sea the ranges of the fortnightly spring tides, which alternate with the fortnightly neaps, vary greatly – not by much along Ireland's east coast, in places under two metres, but over off Lancashire by around seven metres. The billions of tons of water which surge in and out to the Atlantic every twelve hours enter through a relatively wide passage in the south but by a narrow one in the north, and these short routes between Britain and Ireland tend to be the most hazardous when the wind runs against the tidal flows and roughs them up.

There is a further oddity. Where the Atlantic surge coming from the south meets that coming around from the north, the opposing flows mean that tidal streams grow weak. As a result, sea levels between the Isle of Man and the Irish coast rise and fall, but the actual tidal currents here are negligible. This means that a smart sailor can carry a favourable flood tide down from the Scottish narrows and into the Irish Sea and then collect another favourable tide when he reaches the ebb running south.

Winds dictated the journey in the days of sail. They blow generally from the west or south-west, so that a passage from Ireland to Britain was generally faster than one the other way. A shift from westerly to south-westerly could shape a virtual trap for vessels attempting to beat south to the freedom of the Atlantic. As a young man, in October 1938, the travel writer Eric Newby joined the *Moshula*, the largest sailing ship in the world, as she left Belfast to load grain at Port Lincoln in South Australia. *The Last Grain Race* tells the tale:

> For five days we staggered about the Irish Sea, now beating up to the coast of Co. Wicklow, now fetching up on the other tack by the South Stack light on the Welsh side [near Holyhead]. We tacked ship so many times that I lost count. I have never been so tired in my life ... we were far too done in to appreciate the pyramids of gleaming white sails towering above us ... By Saturday the captain gave up trying to beat down the Irish Sea and finally decided to turn and clear into the Atlantic round Ireland's north coast.

SUNLIGHT WOKE me. I had slept through the change of watch. I pulled on some clothes, climbed the companionway steps and found Tony at the helm.

'Sleep well?'

'Indeed,' I said. 'The sea's going down.' The water was a glorious blue-green in the morning light, flecked with white horses. We were going well, about 5 knots.

'I sailed up near a lobster-pot buoy to see what the tide was doing,' Tony said, 'but there was no pull to it. We must be near slack water.'

'I'll get the GPS.'

I held up the little unit, a global positioning system smaller than a mobile phone, pulled out the aerial and waited a few moments as it probed for satellites. Longitude and latitude flashed on the tiny screen. I sat at the navigation table, laid the parallel ruler on our chart, traced in faint pencil the horizontal and vertical lines of latitude and longitude, inserted a small circle where they crossed and measured the distance from this to Milford Haven.

'Twenty-seven miles,' I called, 'and the entrance bears 325 degrees, near enough north-west.'

I glanced at the cabin clock, opened the tide tables and found we were three hours after high water at Dover. A chartlet showed the scatter of little arrows which marked the flow around Milford Haven.

'The new tide is heading us now. I'm afraid there's not much we can do. Can you still fill the sails if you turn a bit more west? It might compensate for the way we're being pushed.'

'Another five degrees maybe,' Tony called.

'Right, but only if we can still keep the speed up. It never pays to cut speed for a fractional improvement in the course.'

Ernest woke up and rose, rubbing the bleariness from his eyes. He lit the gas under the swinging kettle and soon we were having first breakfast: a glass of orange, tea, and bread spread with marmalade. Presently Ernest pointed away on our beam.

'I can see a lighthouse.'

'Impossible,' I said, but I knew he had hawk's eyes.

'In fact, I see two lighthouses now.' He reached for the binoculars, but before he raised them we spotted pencil-like shadows on the very edge of visibility. They were oil refinery chimneys, the tallest a remarkable 218 metres high. So we held our course, and the wind, determined to obstruct us, now came head on so that the sails flogged and rattled. Anxious to wrap land around us, we turned on the engine, got the mainsail tied on the boom, rolled the jib on its stay and thudded into the adverse tide. Far away on the port bow, a tanker was pushing its enormous tonnage towards Milford Haven.

By afternoon the coastline was slowly thickening and taking shape, land surfacing lazily out of the sea. At the two-mile-wide entrance to the great haven, we left the foam-streaked waters behind and turned east, raising sail once more. The wind which had headed us was now astern, a good sailing breeze that wrinkled the water. A few miles further up, tankers lay alongside jetties only reachable by walkways running across the shallows, hardly touching Wales at all. We slipped past the remote, apparently lifeless vessels, flexible pipelines hanging from their great gantries. On green country slopes cattle grazed, indifferent to the flame hissing from a chimney-top, the gleaming oil-storage drums, the whole convoluted mechanism of the refineries.

At a village petrol station next day I saw a notice, 'Support your local refinery.' I believe the refinery produces some nine million gallons of oil which are shipped out of Milford Haven every day, but every little helps.

Milford town and its marina drew past. Sir William Hamilton, husband of Nelson's mistress, Emma, was the local landowner. Its terraces – one is called Hamilton – still seem pleasantly nautical. Hamilton and his nephew developed the town almost from scratch. It was at his invitation that whalers from Nantucket came here, and though the first spluttering oil industry they helped develop did not last, for a time the sperm oil they processed was used to light London's streets.

Nelson stayed here at the New Inn. It is now the Nelson Hotel, spreading in Georgian grace above a harbour which he described as the finest he ever saw outside Trincomalee in Ceylon. I expect he was in benign mood, the guest of Sir William and Emma.

The huge bulk of an Irish ferry closed on our stern so quietly it startled us, but we waved dutifully to a line of cheering children all the same. It crept towards the terminal at Pembroke. Here in the nineteenth century the Admiralty constructed a dockyard from which several hundred warships were launched. The elegant yards, interspersed with small mansions built to house the navy's admirals, have since been left to rot.

Almost opposite lay our destination, Neyland marina. Neyland started life as a planned settlement, and when the railway was completed in 1856 and a huge hotel erected on the waterfront, its future seemed assured. A fine statue of the legendary engineer Isambard Kingdom Brunel, holding a toy-like ship in one hand, a locomotive in the other, greeted us from the waterfront. He built his South Wales Railway to serve a terminus here and intended to establish a passenger service to New York on his mammoth steamer, the *Great Eastern*. The Great Eastern Terrace in the village perpetuates the memory of the ship, which helped lay the first transatlantic cable. But Brunel's plans ended in failure, and the *Great Eastern,* which cost £600,000 to build, was eventually sold for its break-up value, £16,500.

The mail steamer to Waterford also left from here. It set out at 2.30 AM and returned to Neyland at around midnight. When the Irish service was transferred to Fishguard in 1906, Neyland settled into a gentle decline, though its vigour has now been restored by the arrival of modern yachting.

Outside Neyland creek we rounded up into the wind to drop sail. The tension of the passage drained away as we went about our chores, setting and coiling the mooring warps at a pontoon, re-stowing the mainsail more neatly, lashing out the lines so that a night breeze would not start them slapping against the metal mast, and then we stripped off our damp oilskins and washed our salt-stiffened faces. We had refilled with diesel at the fuel point. It was time to refuel our personal tanks at the nearest pub.

TWO

Saints and Settlers

ERNEST AND TONY had to leave *Sarakiniko* at Neyland, but time flew as I waited for my new crew: my wife, Joan, and Martin Wemyss.

I had sailed past this corner of Wales the year before, feeling that here, the point closest to the Republic of Ireland, I should learn more about how two communities had looked at one another from their opposite shores.

A fanciful eye can imagine the sea chart of west Pembrokeshire, or Dyfed, as the profile of an angry animal's head. See him as the Red Dragon, the national beast of Wales – which some say is descended from the purple griffin of the Imperial Roman banner.

At any rate, I see him with a mouth opened wide as a bay, facing the Atlantic. This bay, St Bride's, was named after St Bridget of Kildare, even though she probably never came here. Up to the north-east, Strumble Head, Fishguard behind it, projects as a sort of ear, while the animal's upper lip spews out a mass of reefs and islands, the largest of them the island of Ramsey. From that comparatively large island, some three miles long, you look back across Ramsey Sound to the cliffs on the mainland and a long sandy beach called Whitesands Bay.

It is eight miles south across the beast's open mouth to its lower jaw, which curls into frothing reefs and two more islands, Skokholm and Skomer. The sea rips between Skomer and the mainland, a perilous corridor called Jack Sound, where the tide rushes like a weir.

While I waited for Joan and Martin, I explored the coastline by car. The road atlas was intriguing. It showed the 'Porth Mawr' – Great Port – at Whitesands Bay, and indeed the nearby hamlet has the same name, though one can no longer trace any remains of a port from either land or sea. In his classic book, *The Cruise of*

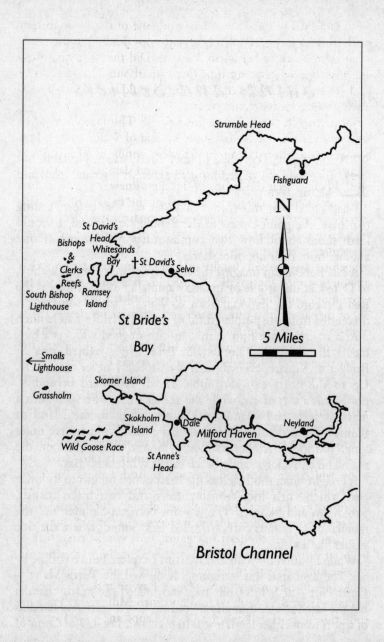

Strumble Head

Fishguard

N

St David's
Head
Bishops
Whitesands
&
Bay   † St David's   Selva
Clerks
Reefs
South Bishop   Ramsey
Lighthouse   Island

St Bride's

Bay

5 Miles

← Smalls
Lighthouse

Skomer Island
Grassholm

Skokholm
Island   Dale   Neyland
Milford Haven
Wild Goose Race

St Anne's
Head

Bristol Channel

the Nona, Hilaire Belloc wonders why 'one of the most ancient roads in Britain comes down here and stops dead upon the sands at an open beach called Porth Mawr ... Did the Ancients throw out great breakwaters and thus form a harbour? That could not be, for surely, had that been done, there would be remains of such mighty work. I leave it unsolved ...'

But perhaps it is not such a great riddle. This lovely stretch of sand, sufficiently flat to have become one of Wales' fine surfing beaches, is sheltered from south-west winds by the bulk of Ramsey Island, and the tides of the Sound dampen the Atlantic swell. I believe that thousands of travellers knew it as a great port when vessels were still made of skins in the fashion of the Irish curragh or were galleys small enough to be hauled ashore.

Did Belloc's charts not show that from here boats could achieve the shortest crossing to Ireland, and avoid one of the most dangerous coastlines in Britain – the upper and lower jaws of that dragon, away to the south? Whitesands Bay lies a bare thirty-seven miles from the sentinel outcrop of Tuskar Rock, which juts out of the racing Irish tide streams as a waymark for the seven- or eight-mile passage through the sandbanks to the shallow harbour of Wexford. Moreover, Whitesands Bay is easily identifiable, lying beside distinctive hills – the modest St David's Head and behind it the prominent Carn Llidi – which are normally visible many miles to seaward.

By contrast, the coast for several miles each side of Whitesands Bay makes an unappealing landfall. To the north-east, beyond St David's Head, is a wild, lonely landscape where rocks and sea meet in uncompromising conflict; no sandy beaches here, but some which are dark and menacing. And a more southerly approach to the mainland would have been even more hazardous in primitive craft. Not only would the distance have been greater – to get down to Milford Haven involves a further fifteen miles – but craft without modern navigation aids would have had to negotiate those offshore islands and reefs I have mentioned, whose churning white water act as a bar to vessels trying to reach anchorage in the quiet of St Bride's Bay or make the further distance around St Anne's Head and into Milford Haven. One collection of horrors known as the Bishops and Clerks extends across four miles. They generate masses of spooling water, eddies, overfalls and shooting tides. I have found it but small consolation, coming down from Fishguard, that one can spot the four Bishops permanently above water. The seven Clerks are kept just below.

They were always dreaded by mariners. 'They preach deadly doctrine to the winter audience,' wrote the seventeenth-century George Owen, 'such poor seafaring men as are forced thither by tempest. Only in one thing are they to be commended,' he added, in a gibe at the clergy in nearby St David's, 'they keep residence better than the rest of the canons of that see are wont to do.'

The narrow sea between Pembroke and south-east Ireland was traversed each way by traders, raiders and colonists from when people first settled in these islands. Stone Age people traded in one of the toughest rocks in the world, the fine-grained stone called porcellanite. This blue stone was shaped into axes in Antrim and Rathlin Island, in the North Channel of the Irish Sea. They were much in demand for clearing forests and have been found in Ireland, Scotland, Wales and even in south-east England. Ireland also exported gold and copper, the workings conveniently located near the coast of Wicklow. Ancient Ireland was rich in gold; Dublin's National Museum houses the largest collection of gold ornaments from this period in northern Europe.

Trade, and raiding, between coastlands persisted for centuries. Settlements of people built up and migrated to follow new sources of minerals or shoals of fish. The Romans – famously – never crossed this sea as invaders. A pity, perhaps; if they had, Ireland's stormy history might have been superseded by a unified government and the spread of a common culture. There is a story in the *Histories of Tacitus* that Agricola, Tacitus' father-in-law, examined the crossing from Scotland to Ireland in about the year 80 AD and felt that an invasion could be achieved by one legion and a few auxiliaries. Roman seamen were certainly familiar with Irish waters and probably established trading stations in islands like Lambay. Roman pottery has been found on Rathlin Island.

When the empire which had ruled almost the entire known world for 400 years fell into decline, Irish raiders took advantage of their neighbour's weakness. As Rome's legions began to withdraw, the Scotti – called after Ireland's name: Scotia – laid siege to the west coast of Britain. The Irish Sea, the poet Claudian remarked, was 'foaming with their oars'. Tradition has it that between 380 and 405 AD raids on the legions' camps were led by Niall of the Nine Hostages, an honorific title, for the prestige of a king was increased by the number of his hostages. In the middle of the sixth century, a British monk, Gildas, recalled these raids: 'They [the Romans] were notwithstanding no sooner gone home but, as the brownish band of wormes and eamots which in the height of summer and increasing heat do swarming break out of their most straight and darksome dens, the dreadful routes of Scots and Picts aland out of their ships wherein they were transported over the Sythian Vale [St George's Channel].'

By the beach at Whitesands Bay, a notice tells you that an ancient trading route ran from here to Stonehenge and probably existed from around 1,500 BC. In a field a few yards from the sandhills, I found a distinctive mound some fifty yards long and, almost hidden in the encroaching weeds, a two-foot-square stone slab recording that here was the Chapel of St Patrick. No trace of any walls protrude from the mound now, but in an excavation of 1924 the skeleton of a young man was uncovered beneath the chapel floor.

Did St Patrick know the Great Port as slave or missionary? He wrote his *Confessions* about fifty years after he began his mission to Ireland – scholars say in ragged Latin with little of the grace of classical prose. At the age of sixteen, he said, he was captured along with many others by Irish raiders and spent six years in Ireland tending sheep, until he escaped and returned to his relatives in Britain. But here he had a vision – of a man, Victoricus, 'coming as it were from Ireland with many letters and he gave me one and I read the opening words which were "The Voice of the Irish" and I thought that at the same moment I heard their voice. They were those beside the Wood of Foclut which is near the Western Sea. Thus did they cry out as with one mouth: "We ask thee, boy, come and walk once more among us."'

The urge to give St Patrick an anchorage in place and time has generated sharp dispute among medieval biographers and modern scholars. Some suggest that there may have been more than one missionary saint. The *Confessions* only tell us that he was a Roman citizen: all else is speculation. His mission in Ireland lasted some thirty years, and we can only be sure that it began in the second or third quarter of the fifth century.

Anglesey, Cumberland and other places have been suggested as Patrick's home, while a dozen villages in Ireland could lay claim to have had the name Foclut. However, Whitesands Bay, lying at the end of a famous highway, would have been a beach familiar to Ireland's national saint. If Pembrokeshire was his homeland, he would most likely have returned there when he escaped from Ireland, and later, as a missionary, departed from the same place.

As the missionary activities of the Celtic saints began to grow from about 450 AD, austere hermitages and small churches became common in remote localities in Pembrokeshire. Voyaging to and fro across the Irish Sea, the holy men must often have been driven ashore, happy to offer thanksgiving for their safe delivery. Thus the small chapels all around these wild coastlines and islands. Near muddy Bannow Bay in Wexford, scene of the first Norman landings in 1169, is Tintern Abbey, built in 1200 by William Marshall, Earl of Pembroke. A fine Cistercian edifice, based on the foundation's famous namesake in Wales, it owes its existence to a vow the Earl made when he was caught in a storm off the Irish south coast. Praying that he might be saved, he promised to build an abbey wherever his vessel came ashore.

As the paganism of old Wales was absorbed into the Christianity of the Celtic evangelists, the see of St David, the patron saint of Wales, came to be based near Whitesands Bay. Legends about him have left their traces all over this country, from his first hermitage, where he dieted on water and leeks, to the site of his death, where he lay surrounded by massed angels and choirs of celestial music. The famous cathedral of St David and its associated buildings are close to the shore, but you will not see even the pinnacles of the tower from a boat. When the Normans began to build the cathedral in 1180, they selected a hollow where it would have shelter from the Atlantic weather and be hidden from heathen warships. Viking raids were still a vivid memory.

In fact, the cathedral and the buildings that preceded it were sacked several times and painstakingly restored; it has a wonderful roof of black oak fetched from Ireland in about 1500. The cathedral became not only the mother church of Welsh Christianity but also a hub of the Christian world. Irish missionaries stopped here on their way to evangelise Europe. Pilgrims came here as to Santiago in Spain; the shrine was so famous that Pope Calixtus decreed that two pilgrimages 'in search of David' were equal to one to Rome 'in search of the Apostles'. In a small chapel in the cathedral, I saw the reliquary which is said to contain the bones of the saint of Wales.

Legend relates that St David was baptised by an Irish bishop from Munster, 'who by divine intervention was landed in Wales from Ireland'. He was educated not far from St David's but spent much of his missionary life in other parts of the Celtic world. Legend tells us that he roused the enmity of a heathen chief called Boia, whose wife told her maids to 'go where the monks can see you and, with bodies bare, play games and use lewd words'. The display is said to have had the desired effect on the monks; St David remained unmoved.

David's Breton friend and confessor, St Justinian, is supposed to have shifted across to Ramsey Island to escape the lax ways of mainland monks. Even there he was pestered by visitors, though, and he prayed to God to remove the causeway linking the island to the mainland, whereupon a giant axe appeared and chopped most of it away. The rocks left over now impede the sweeping tide in Ramsey Sound. I like to think that Justinian may have had a hand in naming them 'The Bitches'.

The local lifeboat sits ready on stilts at St Justinian, the mainland village which has the ruins of a chapel built in a later century, and a St Justinian's well. The lifeboat used to stand in the village square at St David's, though from there launching the boat involved pulling it with a team of horses for over a mile along country lanes. It was moved in 1888, not, I believe, because that system was considered inefficient, but owing to the cathedral Dean's opinion of what villagers got up to under its tarpaulins. Justinian might have agreed.

The Vikings burned the shrine of St David's several times on their Welsh raids, which continued from 844 to 1091. It is not known what ports and harbours they used, though Milford Haven has a tradition that a Viking chief, Hubba, wintered there with twenty-three ships and 2,000 men in 877. There are many placenames of Viking origin – islands like Ramsey, Skokholm, Skomer and Grassholm, and the harbours of Fishguard and Goodwick – but perhaps the most vivid evidence of Viking settlement is in blood grouping. The frequency of the 'A' blood group gene in the population around Narberth, Tenby and Pembroke is the highest in western Europe, reaching levels found otherwise only in southern Scandinavia.

The first Viking raiders appear to have attacked Iona, in western Scotland, in 795 AD. Their longships attacked Lambay Island off the Dublin coast that year also, and after that they struck again and again at settlements and monasteries all around the Irish coast, even at lonely Skellig Michael off Kerry. The Vikings were traders, merchants and craftsmen, but as the accounts of their deeds come largely from monastic records, they have had a very bad press. We get a chilling glimpse of the fear they inspired in the oft-quoted poem found scribbled in the margin of a monastery manuscript:

Since tonight the wind is high
The sea's white mane a fury
I need not fear the hordes of Hell
Coursing the Irish Channel

By 837 AD, fleets rather than single raiding ships had begun to appear off Ireland; 'immense floods and countless sea-vomitings of ships' as the chronicles record. Sixty were seen in the mouth of the Boyne and sixty in the River Liffey that year. By now the Vikings were beginning to set up permanent settlements. Dublin grew out of one of the 'long ports', the name the Irish gave to the defended bases which the Vikings established as they built stockades around their valuable ships. In 914 a great fleet founded the settlement of Waterford, a place which would later appeal to the Normans also, for the three river arteries of the Suir, Nore and Barrow were near by to feed invaders into the heart of Ireland. The Vikings developed Dublin, Waterford, Wicklow and Wexford, and launched a sea-going trade which brought Ireland into the market age.

In a land of many small kingdoms, no leader was responsible for the defence of the island as a whole, but by the late tenth century the King of Munster, Brian Boru, had emerged as a powerful figure, capable of claiming the kingship of Ireland. The Vikings began to play a more subordinate political role in the power struggles of the Irish kingdoms. The final trial of strength between Irish and Viking resulted in an Irish victory at Clontarf in 1014. The Norsemen brought great changes to Ireland, but as the historian Liam de Paor has concluded, the most enduring effect the Vikings had on Irish life was 'to shift the social and political centre of gravity once and for all from the midlands to the east coast – indeed, one might say, to the Irish Sea.'

MARTIN AND JOAN have arrived aboard. Lockers are restocked, stores refilled. Joan has said that the gas stove is as clean as a male crew can achieve but has threatened to throw our kitchen towel into the rubbish bin, even though it is a useful towel, patterned with a coloured sketch of the shipping forecast areas. Martin is unpacking at the triangular double bunk up at the sharp end, out of the line of fire. He emerges with an impish grin and a shopping bag containing a bottle of gin and a bottle of whisky. In a world of political correctness, I rejoice in a crew of agile mind and puckish, reactionary bent.

'This should get us across the Irish Sea,' he says.

Martin had retired from high rank in the Royal Navy, but when she is at the helm Joan can take us both to task if his opinion of sailing tactics, as seen from the bow, conflicts with her husband's, as seen from the helm. 'Admiral or skipper; which am I to obey?'

Martin had once commanded a squadron of nuclear submarines, each one displacing more water than a large cross-channel car ferry. Though I have reassured him that *Sarakiniko* can float in just four feet of water, I remember some years ago that he grew restless on a foggy morning in the English Channel when our depth-finder dial recorded a mere thirty feet beneath our keel.

Tea was ready. Joan cut a large homemade fruit cake.

'What have you been doing?'

I explained about the trail of St Patrick.

'But what about Tony and Ernest?' Joan asked, bringing things back to the present.

'Ernest got a train to Hereford, Tony the Irish ferry to Rosslare.'

'Poor things, they must have been worn out.'

'Not at all,' I said. 'In fact, the night we tied up here we walked two miles to a pub to have a meal.'

'Two miles?'

'Yes, it was the furthest one of three on this side of Neyland. The crew wouldn't settle for packets of pork crackles in the first pub, but the girl serving at the bar phoned ahead and we got there in time. She was called Carry, or Charlie, or maybe Caroline,' I added.

'A rose by any name,' said Martin.

'And we set off for Rosslare tomorrow?' Joan asked.

'Yes, this time on the trail of the Normans. The forecast is good.'

Starting from Milford Haven, as the Norman invaders did in 1169, our voyage would give us an insight into how they fared on that crossing. The sea, tides and weather, the rocks and birds, and the shapes of distant shorelines do not change over a thousand years.

The Norman invasion was the most significant sea link forged between Pembroke and Ireland – indeed, historian Goddard Orpen wrote that it was 'the most far reaching event that occurred in Ireland since the introduction of Christianity'. After that, things were never the same again. Yet, while we know of the invasion's impact on Ireland, it is easy to overlook Ireland's earlier involvement with dynastic struggles in England and Wales and its support for the inevitable resistance movements which came after the Norman conquest of 1066. Another island beyond another sea, it would for a time remain a refuge for fugitives and a source of aid for rebels.

When King Dermot MacMurrough of Leinster, having abducted (or, more probably, eloped with) the wife of O'Rourke of Breifne, fled his lost Leinster kingship seeking King Henry II's authority to recruit help from Wales, he was coming to no strange land. His forefathers had been involved in the struggles of Edward the Confessor, King Harold and William the Conqueror.

When Edward the Confessor – more saint than king – succeeded to the Earldom of Wessex in 1051, it had been with the help of Irish troops supplied by Dermot MacMurrough's great-grandfather. That last English king, Harold, died at the Battle of Hastings in 1066, and his three sons were driven out of England by William the Conqueror. They crossed to Dublin and obtained from the MacMurroughs and the Norse of Leinster a fleet of fifty-two ships, which they sailed up the Bristol Channel and the Severn, attacking Bristol and raiding into Somerset. They were repulsed, but the following summer, 1069, they came from Dublin again with sixty-four ships and sailed to the south coast of England, where they sacked coastal settlements, including Exeter. When their forces were again defeated, the sons of Harold escaped to Ireland once more.

Norman power spread throughout Britain. Wales was conquered by armed force, intermarriage and the planting of strong castles, a process which would later be repeated in Ireland. Just twenty-one years after Hastings, in 1087 the Prince of south Wales, Rhys ap Tewdar, retreated into Ireland, where he died in 1093. Seven years later, Arnuf, Lord of Pembroke, who continued to oppose Henry I and Norman rule, proposed an alliance with O'Brien, Ireland's High King, and married O'Brien's daughter, Lafrocoth, but despite the support of Irish troops he was later driven out of Wales, and became another refugee in Ireland. As the Welsh cause declined, his son also crossed the Irish Sea, where he remained concealed for years from the vengeance of Henry I.

It is too readily forgotten that the Norman invasion of England would for a time cement Irish and Welsh interests.

By the close of the eleventh century, Pembroke lay under Norman rule. English and Saxons were encouraged to settle there, and the area, 'little England beyond Wales', still has something of an English air, as in walled Tenby with its Georgian terraces. Flemings were also introduced to the region. William the Conqueror had used Flemish troops as mercenaries in his invasion of England and brought in more in 1108, 1111 and 1156. Flemish men-at-arms made a formidable force when they were combined with Welsh archers, whose longbows permanently proletarianised warfare, for the arrow shaft, like the bullet, 'made all men alike fall'.

In his recruiting drive through Pembrokeshire, Dermot MacMurrough secured many offers of support, notably from the Earl of Pembroke, known as Strongbow. Giraldus Cambrensis, an eyewitness to the invasion, though neither wholly accurate nor without prejudice, pictures MacMurrough 'sniffing from the Welsh coast the air of Ireland wafted upon the western breezes and ... had no small consolation feasting his eyes on the sight of his land [in Ireland] though the distance was such that it was difficult to distinguish between the mountains and clouds.' Dermot had probably climbed the hills behind St David's Head, from where he could see the mountains which rose behind his castle at Ferns, Co. Wexford.

Satisfied with the support he had received, MacMurrough returned to Ireland. He landed at a place 'where he had many enemies and few friends', Glascarrig creek, about twelve miles south of Arklow and the same distance from Ferns. Giraldus states that he spent the winter in the Augustinian monastery at Ferns, planning the invasion, while some or all of his small group returned to Wales. It would need a sheltered anchorage, sufficiently remote to allow time to build on the initial bridgehead but within easy reach of the first target: fortified Wexford.

Preparations continued apace in Milford Haven, and in May 1169 the first invaders set out in three long Viking-type boats, each hoisting a square sail on a single mast and manned by pilots of great experience. The *Annals of the Four Masters* refer to 'seventy heroes dressed in coats of mail'; more detailed records refer to thirty knights, three score esquires and 300 men. Each ship could carry about 120 men with some horses and provisions. The mast was probably unstepped to get the animals aboard; the 'navier-hussier', a vessel with stern doors for loading horses, was not developed for another century.

With latter-day charts and tide tables, one can develop a fuller picture of this fateful voyage. The problem of loading horses and stores on to vessels far bigger than the traditional skin boats would rule out Whitesands Bay, that ancient port for Ireland, but the price of using Milford Haven, the likely departure point, was a longer journey, and the added difficulty of making safe passage through those many reefs and tide races when leaving the coast. The voyage had to begin at first light, so as to round Carnsore Point and the Saltee Islands off the Irish coast before darkness fell. An east wind would fill the square sails, but in the prevalent westerlies, with the course set probably a little to the north of due west, the oarsmen must have spent a long day at the sweeps as St David's Head faded astern. The helmsman, peering ahead, would have watched for the Blackstairs Mountains rising behind Wexford, then they would have set a course south of Carnsore Point to avoid Norse shipping in the vicinity of the fortified port of Wexford.

Bannow harbour, an inlet lying some fifteen miles from Ireland's south-eastern corner, had been chosen as the landing point. A channel led past an island in the bay into sheltered water and a fishing village on the mainland which was unlikely to offer resistance. The island itself would be a temporary defensive camp. Waterford, ten miles to the west, could be temporarily disregarded as its garrison was cut off by the wide estuary of the Suir. The target, Wexford, was sixteen miles to the east; not too near, not too far.

Bannow's suitability was not obvious when I made a visit there a few years ago. Silt and storm-driven sands have joined the island to the mainland and closed the channel for ships. 'This was a place of great trade in the times past,' a writer noted in 1684, 'until the sand filled up the ancient passage near the towne of Bannow.' A few decades earlier, the *Down Survey* published a map showing the shipping channel, so the silting probably arose in the mid-seventeenth century. It is said that exceptional storm-driven tides have been known to reopen the old channel.

The approach to Bannow bristles with reefs and a seaway with shallows and rips where the tide can run at 8 knots, giving the Norman force little time to cast a lead to take soundings. They needed daylight and clear weather here unless their craft kept well offshore. Turning in for Bannow, they faced the risk in onshore weather of being embayed. The two Saltee islands, eight miles east of the entrance to Bannow, and the high ground of Hook

Head some six miles to the west, were vital seamarks.

The three ships achieved harbour and were followed next day by two more bearing ten men-at-arms and about 100 archers. They waited in a temporary camp until MacMurrough heard of their safe arrival and came from Ferns, thirty miles away, with 500 followers. They attacked Wexford the following day.

A word-picture from Geraldus describes the impact of that fearful assault on the peaceful sea-traders in Wexford harbour. His older brother was in the vanguard, wounded when a rock was thrown down on him as he tried to scramble up the town walls. The attackers withdrew that evening, but renewed their efforts with more success next morning, and now 'they gathered in haste on the neighbouring strand, and forthwith set fire to all the ships they found lying there'.

With Wexford taken, an incursion which had started as a result of a local vendetta gave the Normans a bridgehead in Ireland.

THREE

Crossings

I LOOKED UP from the navigation table, my mind made up. 'We should leave at 0530.'

Two pairs of eyes swivelled as one. 'Couldn't we just wait for a civilised breakfast?'

'We'd miss the tide.'

'And then we'd never get anywhere.'

A well-worn rejoinder. The dialogue is a ritual of departure and usually ends in our agreeing that *Sarakiniko* must be the victim of a mysterious influence which dictates that cold dawns and demanding tides are malignly wedded. But the logic of tidal flow is inescapable. If you move through the water at 5 knots with a 2 knot tide in your favour, you cover 7 miles in an hour. With 2 knots running against you, this falls to 3.

We bent over the chart, South West Coast of Wales. I moved the points of the dividers.

'Nine miles down the Haven to the open sea at St Anne's Head; then we turn to starboard, right angles almost, to get through Broad Sound between Skokholm and Skomer. That's another five miles. So,' I finished, 'we need a good tide behind us from St Anne's Head onwards.'

'North flowing.'

'Yes, and for as long as possible. Broad Sound on to the South Bishop lighthouse is another eight miles – basically north-west and on our course for Rosslare. After that we're offshore and the tides grow much weaker. I think we should make the South Bishop in a little over four hours.'

Martin had been thumbing the tide tables. 'This rising tide up the Irish Sea flows up the Haven also, so it will be against us at first.'

'Indeed.'

'And to allow for that, we should really be off at 4 AM. Look,' he turned to Joan, 'we actually have a considerate skipper.'

A gin later we went ashore for supper, blaming the yielding pontoon for a tendency to roll. Some true yachtsmen sniff at marinas, but it is an advantage not to have to heave a rubber dinghy off the deck, roll up one's trousers and row ashore to collect groceries in cardboard boxes which invariably dissolve on the way back. I can readily ignore the impression one gets in a marina of being corralled in a watery car park.

Cradling cups of coffee in our cold fingers, we thud next morning down an almost deserted harbour, our wake a sparkling V in the early sunlight. The forecast for Irish inshore waters announced a high-pressure system for the day, and we thought we might look forward to a sparkling run across blue seas. So man proposes.

Soon after 0700 we were approaching St Anne's Head, the indecisive wind coming over our stern, hardly perceptible as we thumped ahead of it. We took turns to sit at the helm, all of us rather cold and stiff. 'All yours,' I told Martin as I went below to put the kettle on for second breakfast, adding as an afterthought: 'There are a few lobster-pot buoys around.' I wondered if this rather obvious spur to vigilance marked me out as a nagging skipper – still, they were a menace, especially as the tide had been pulling them half under.

Martin and I tend to use bad language on trifles, but as conditions at sea get worse he grows more cheerful. The wind had picked up a little, and this new breeze was a north-wester, dead on our nose, so we kept the engine on, motoring uncomfortably into a chop. As diesel engines go it was a stripling, just five years old. At a one-day diesel engine course I had been told that it should live to 150. It was cooled by sea water sucked in past a seacock in the hull and circulated until it was ejected warm from the exhaust pipe. If weed or drifting plastic interrupted its flow, the engine announced that it was overheating with some decisive hooting. The remedy was to remove and clear the obstruction from a cylindrical sieve – after, of course, shutting off the seacock. The reason I pass on these gems of knowledge will become apparent.

We worked gradually across Broad Sound through vast colonies of seabirds who scattered before our bow: kittiwakes, razorbills, guillemots, puffins, Manx shearwaters, oystercatchers, shags and cormorants. A few miles to the west was the small flat island of Grassholm, where over 30,000 pairs of gannets nest on twenty acres of rock. It is the second largest gannet colony in the northern hemisphere, second only to St Kilda in Scotland, and even at this distance we could see how the tightly packed throng of birds had turned the island white.

'Think of the noise and smell downwind of that lot,' Joan said.

Small whorls and pyramids of water slapped against our topsides as the Wild Goose Race, which lay to port, reminded us that it was just dozing, but not asleep. We edged further north, into the chop of Skomer's overfalls. The Smalls lighthouse emerged beyond Grassholm and drew slowly south-west as we progressed, passing beyond the last edges of Wales. I focused the glasses on the Smalls, an impression of black rocks in the sea, yet rising from them was a tower like the spire of some subterranean cathedral.

All lighthouses in Britain and Ireland have now been automated. The profession of lighthouse keeper has been eliminated by time and technology, the brasswork and polish by computer equipment which switches lights on and off, monitors daylight and calculates windspeeds. Perhaps what is really astonishing is that for so long into the twentieth century it required three men to tend a light bulb.

Three men. If that sounds like over-manning, perhaps the Smalls was responsible. The light had two keepers, and in 1802 was being served by a pair known to dislike each other intensely. It was a winter of atrocious gales, and for four months it was impossible to relieve them. One of the men, Thomas Griffiths, took ill and died, and Thomas Howell, fearing that he might be blamed for the death, decided to keep the body. He lashed the corpse to the outer balcony, where it was eventually spotted from the boat coming to relieve Howell, who was by now half demented. It is said that, from then on, Trinity House decided that all British lighthouses must have a crew of three men working together.

The first light tower on these reefs and jagged islets was built by an amateur engineer, Henry Whiteside. He decided to set the light on a kind of 'wigwam' of forty-six-foot-long oak posts through which the seas could run. The keepers reached their accommodation by climbing a rope ladder to the octagonal timber house on top. It was an astonishing achievement. Holes were drilled into the rocks by Cornish tin miners and great beams set in with molten lead. The construction was first tried out at the fishing village of Solva in St Bride's Bay and the sections then transferred to the Smalls. By January 1777 the reefs had a light.

A few years after Whiteside built the Smalls, he went out with a blacksmith to inspect it: the keepers had complained that its movement in gales tended to make them seasick. As things turned out, a gale marooned Whiteside, and the bad weather persisted week after week. As their food began to run out, in desperation Whiteside sent a message sealed in a keg, addressing it to Thomas Williams: 'We are in distress from a gale of wind from 13 January since which we have not been able to keep and light ... we prayeth for your immediate assistance ... or we fear we shall perish.' The keepers sent a letter too, asking the finder, in these calm and dignified words, 'to be so merciful as to cause it to be sent to Thomas Williams of Trelethin near St David's, Wales'.

Astonishingly, the keg was found two days later on the shore close to Williams' house and the men were rescued.

The Smalls became the most profitable lighthouse in the world. In 1829 it earned £6,700 in dues paid by passing ships, while its owner paid only £5 per annum as ground rent to the Crown, and his running costs, which included keepers' wages, were only £870 in that year. Seven years later Trinity House bought out the lease for £170,000. It must have seemed a good price. The owner would hardly have foreseen that as a result of the huge growth of shipping – much of it to expanding Liverpool – the annual harvest of dues would be over £23,000 by 1852.

Whiteside's achievement lasted seventy years. It was replaced by a stone-built lighthouse in 1861, but the stumps of the earlier building's oak legs lasted until recent years. I have seen the remains of some discarded in the grass at the entrance to the village car park in Selva.

Incidentally, it is at Selva that one finds by the beach the remains of seven of twelve limekilns and a plaque carrying lines of that seventeenth-century Pembrokeshire wisdom: 'A man doth sand for himself, lime for his son and marl for his grandson.'

Wales sidled slowly past on the starboard beam, the land receding north-east towards Strumble Head. Another lighthouse, the South Bishop, fell astern. We had run out of favourable tide, and soon it was pushing against us. *Sarakiniko* seemed to mark time as she bounced into an uncomfortable chop, all motion but little progress; the boat felt as if it were tethered to the seabed. Little black-and-white guillemots kept diving ahead – there one moment, gone the next, leaving a hole in the water as if drilled by a bullet. We hoisted the mainsail and bore off ten degrees so that the wind filled it and steadied us. A ferry bound from Rosslare to Fishguard went by, the only vessel we had seen today.

So, in a falling wind, we thud on until we are jerked from thoughts of lunch by the strident bleep of the engine alarm. Overheating. We turn off the motor at once.

'Weed,' I explain to Martin. 'Remember how it happened two years ago in the English Channel?'

'It doesn't take long to clear it.'

I propped up the mattress of Joan's bunk – which runs in a sort of tunnel under the cockpit – lifted the lid of the batteries' locker underneath and reached down to the little wheel of the seacock, turning it until it closed shut. I undid butterfly clips and lifted out the wire mesh strainer. Not a trace of seaweed. Perfectly clean. I looked up at two anxious faces.

'Perhaps it's plastic outside the hull,' said Martin. 'It can get sucked against the inlet hole.'

'Maybe. I'll have to open the seacock and wait for a torrent. Let's have some rags to protect the batteries.'

He dropped down some old towelling and I twisted the seacock wheel anti-clockwise. A jet of Irish Sea rushed in, arcing towards my face. I hastily turned the wheel back.

'It's obviously clear outside,' I called.

'Could it be lack of oil in the engine?' Joan asked.

'Surely not. I checked it yesterday. I'll look again.'

I removed the companionway steps, unclipped the engine hatch and knelt forward, blackening one ear against the sooty silencer padding, the other almost touching a hot engine casing, until I could make finger-tip identification and pull up the dipstick. I withdrew to daylight and applied some kitchen roll to the gleaming rod. Three-quarters full. I repeated the gymnastics in reverse.

'Try starting up again, Martin.'

The engine burst into life. So did the piercing alarm call.

We would ruin the engine if we carried on. The north-west wind was still with us, favourable for a return to Milford. 'But we might lose it altogether in those awkward tide races around the islands,' I said worriedly.

'Agreed,' said Martin, 'but the Irish coast is even further, and we might be closing on the shipping lanes around the Tuskar in the dark.'

'It will be dark anyhow,' Joan said, 'and at least the Haven entrance is wide and well lit.'

So we debated, finally deciding to retreat to Wales. The boom snatched to and fro in the gloomy silence, grating on our nerves, though Joan insisted cheerfully that it was peaceful enough now to hear the gulls in the distance. She turned out pizza hot from the oven, and with an increased ration of lunch-hour gin our spirits lifted. I told the crew to ignore my earlier threat that I might add *Sarakiniko* to the welter of small print advertisements in the yachting press ('Owner forced to sell beloved Westerly Fulmar') and told Martin that in the days of betrayal by our old engine we had once caught the ebb tide for nine miles down the Treguier river in North Brittany and made it the 150 miles to Portsmouth under sail. The passage was marred only by some hours becalmed in a shipping lane and a terse exchange with a nervous ferry captain in the narrow entrance to Portsmouth harbour: 'Where's your ruddy engine, mate?'

In our course now we were achieving about three knots from a light wind but doing rather better over the ground, as the weakening tide was still helping us on. The wind held as we idled through limpid water a few hours later; then the tide turned and ran against us. We watched our boat drift away from its destination and passed the time trying to calculate where we would end up. The tide reverses about every six hours, but the speed of its flow depends on how much it rises or falls in each hour and this varies a lot. You apply the Rule of Twelfths as a gauge. Take the example of a modest range of twelve feet between high and low water. In the first hour the rise (or fall) will be one foot, in the next hour two feet, in the third and fourth hours three feet each hour, in the fifth hour two feet, returning to one foot in the final hour. The current is never constant, but continually waxing or waning.

The tide returned. It was still with us but waning as a low red sunset glowed through a bank of clouds and sank away. Darkness closed in. The wind huffed and puffed as we edged away from the shoals around the islands. Soon buoys were blinking a few miles out to starboard, marking the shallows on the outer approaches to Milford Haven.

We remained inshore, turned an elbow of cliff and crept under the beam of St Anne's light. Then we bore north-east through the entrance and north for Dale Bay, five miles up in a sheltered corner of the haven. Joan glanced up from the dial of the depth finder: 'Four metres!' I called to Martin at the bow, spinning *Sarakiniko* to face and spill the breeze, and the anchor rattled down.

Joan was inside her sleeping-bag in minutes. Martin and I relaxed over a dram in the cockpit, calling down that we were just checking that the anchor was holding us fast to Wales.

John Richards' visit next day was brief and tactful; he is a very pleasant engineer. 'The solenoid, perhaps.' He unscrewed a unit on the engine not much larger than a thimble. 'It simply controls the alarm system,' he said; 'your engine is perfectly all right. You could have unscrewed this and carried on. I can probably find a replacement for you today.' He added kindly that the old system, where the dial on a clock pointed to red for overheating, had foolproof simplicity. The chastened wits on *Sarakiniko* readily agreed.

He screwed in a replacement unit, clearing the way for an evening ashore in Dale's convivial inn. Dinner would celebrate a kind of victory. Fate, surely, had relented.

'Perhaps we should move a hundred yards first,' Martin said. 'We seem a bit close to that other yacht.'

But the anchor would not shift. We started the engine, drove ahead, astern; rocked to each side. We tried hauling the anchor-chain using one of the deck winches. All our efforts failed. Joan and Martin went ashore to seek help in Dale's diving school, and soon a big, genial man called Dave and a mate of his swung a powerful dinghy alongside in a cascade of spray. They told us they had no doubt the anchor was trapped under a mooring chain, but Dave could not dive and release it as he had a head cold.

Instead, massive shoulders bent over our cable, *Sarakiniko*'s bow dipped down, and a mooring chain broke surface. Dave swiftly got a line around it and allowed our anchor to swing free.

It was too late now for showers or dinner ashore, and as the merciless tide would run north tomorrow from 0530, we ought to be away by 0600. We moved to a vacant buoy, captured it with the boat hook, and hoped the owner would not return in a few hours and ask us to shift.

Our schedule had slipped. We decided to omit Rosslare and run instead for Arklow, half-way up the east coast towards Dublin. It was a longer journey than we had planned – it lay seventy-seven miles from Milford entrance in contrast to fifty-five to Rosslare – but an early start with most of a north-going tide should soon place us well offshore, with a fair prospect of getting through the Irish sandbanks and reaching Arklow by last light.

FEAR, DISCOMFORT and fickle winds were for centuries the lot of voyagers between Britain and Ireland. One wonders at the persistence of John Curcie who, as Laud's *Annals* state, tried in 1204 to sail to Ireland fifteen times 'but was always in danger and the wind evermore against him, wherefore he waited for a while among the monks at Chester. At length he returned to France and there rested in the Lord.'

The sea had little respect for rank or station. In 1365 the Treasurer of Ireland was shipwrecked on passage from England; eminent ecclesiastics fared no better. The Archbishop-elect of Dublin lost his gold, silver, plate and jewellery as he crossed to take up his new see in 1450. A century before, in 1318, King Edward II had to write to Pope John XXII excusing the failure of the new

Archbishops of Dublin and Cashel to attend the papal curia 'because the Irish Sea is so very perilous and stormy in winter'.

Diaries from the seventeenth, eighteenth and early nineteenth centuries give informative, sometimes vivid accounts of crossing the Irish Sea under sail. Perhaps the most notable was that of Arthur Young. In June 1776, 'after a tedious passage of twenty-two hours from Holyhead', and having travelled around Ireland for a few months, he came to leave from Co. Waterford on 18 October. He drove his chaise and horses to the village of Passage on the River Suir, where 'twenty sail of ships gave animation to the scene ... I got my chaise and horses on board the *Countess of Tyrone* but found a difference between these private vessels and the Post Office packets at Holyhead and Dublin. When the wind was fair the tide was foul and when the tide was with them then the wind would not do. There was not a full complement of passengers and so,' he added tartly, 'I had the agreeableness of waiting with my horses in the hold by way of rest.'

After one 'beastly night spent on shipboard and no signs of departure', he left to stay with friends, and on his return found the ship was delayed once more.

The *Tyrone* had been inaugurated a year earlier as a packet service for passenger traffic to Milford Haven, a far shorter crossing than the long haul up the channel to Bristol. Established by John Congreve, of Mount Congreve, Co. Waterford, the Tyrone was a rare and interesting example of landlord investment in shipping, backed in this case by innkeepers in Waterford, South Wales, Bristol, Bath and London. The ship was built with a great cabin, two state chambers with two beds in each, and fifteen standing beds in all. There was space for horses and carriages. The service was in the hands of one James Wyse, and a kinsman, William Wyse, was the captain, and in good winds Milford could be reached in eight hours.

But the voyage could sometimes be contrary. Young set off on 20 October, but 'after being in sight of the lights on the Smalls [some fifteen miles from the Welsh mainland] we were, by contrary winds, blown opposite to the Arklow sands. A violent gale arose which presently blew a storm that lasted thirty-six hours in which, under a reefed mainsail, the ship drifted up and down wearing [tacking] in order to keep clear of the coasts.

'No wonder this appeared to me, a fresh-water sailor, as a storm when the oldest men on board reckoned it a violent one. The wind blew in furious gusts, the waves ran very high, the cabin windows blew open and the sea, pouring in, set everything afloat, and among the rest was a poor lady who had spread her bed upon the floor. We had however the satisfaction to find, by trying the pumps every watch, that the ship made little water.

'I had more time to attend these circumstances,' he went on, 'than the rest of the passengers, being the only one in seven to escape being sick. It pleased God to preserve us but we did not cast anchor in Milford till Tuesday AM at 1 o'clock.' It had been a forty-one hour voyage.

Young complained about the fact that packet ships regularly delayed sailing 'until there is such a number of passengers as satisfies the owner and captain'. Two years later he found the old system still in force. 'Having been assured that this conveyance had been put on a new footing, I ventured to try it again but was mortified to find that the *Tyrone* – the only one which could take a chaise and horses – was repairing but would sail in five days. I waited and got assurance after assurance it would be ready on one day, then another. In fact I waited twenty-four days before I did sail. All this time the newspapers had advertisements of *Tyrone* sailing regularly instead of letting the public know it was under repair.' Young thought, 'The owner will probably give up unless assisted by the Waterford Corporation with at least four ships more.'

In 1778, the year of Young's second crossing, Wyse did introduce a second vessel, the *Lord Milford*, but the tendency to delay sailing in the hope of luring more passengers persisted. The missionary, John Wesley, who crossed the Irish Sea regularly, advised passengers never to go aboard until the captain did, not to send one's luggage ahead of one's self, and never to part with cash before sailing.

Travel by road was so underdeveloped in Ireland that as late as 1807 Sir Richard Colt Hoare felt the tourist would do better to bring his own carriage and horses across with him. He warned that a traveller 'must not expect to find post-chaises and post-horses ready at a moment's notice ... these accommodations are to be found only on the great roads of communication ... On the crossroads he must bear in patience the delays of post-boys and the indifference of postmasters.'

The *Travels* of Sir William Brereton give us some idea of the trials faced on a ship with horses aboard. He left from Portpatrick, Scotland, in 1735, on a passage to Carrickfergus in Belfast Lough. He had five horses, and five Yorkshiremen joined with five more. These were more than enough, but the captain ignored their protests when an Irishman and his wife arrived with their three animals, and then four more horses were hoisted aboard. Brereton's comment – 'We had not every man his own length allowed to be at ease' – is quite an understatement, because the equine passengers lacked even stalls, and it was up to their owners to control them.

A gale developed and the gaff-rigged boat blew north along the Irish coast until the master and his son got their open craft, packed with horses and sick passengers, into some slight shelter at a small recess called Port Davey near Larne. 'Hereby we were sheltered all night from most cruel, violent and tempestuous storms which did much affect and discourage us though we lay at anchor under a large hill,' Sir William wrote. 'All the horses were first thrown into the sea and did swim to land and climb a good steep rock.' He landed probably in worse shape than the animals. 'The sea wrought effectively and plentifully with me; more vomit when I was at sea than ever formerly.'

In good weather the Irish Sea crossing was tolerable; in bad weather, whether travellers took the short route or a long one, they faced delays, hunger, seasickness and danger.

Two women have left us accounts of their travails in the Irish Sea. Mrs Freke, who made several crossings in the later seventeenth century, seemed prone to accidents, whether getting lost in the dark when disembarking from a small boat or barely escaping capture by French privateers. Dorothea Herbert, one of nine children born to a well connected couple in Carrick-on-Suir, near Waterford, wrote her *Retrospections* in the first decade of the nineteenth century, leaving an intriguing personal record which lay undiscovered for a hundred years.

She described a family voyage across the St George's Channel in

1776, after her mother, who was in poor health, had been ordered by her doctor to drink the waters at Bristol. The family committed themselves to the sea passage with misgivings. 'Never,' wrote Dorothea, 'was there a more dismal parting. The neighbours wept about us, sure that we would never return alive. On my side, I thought that to leave house and home and cross the seas was an affair that could never be got over by any of us. The night before our departure I walked about like a ghost, crying over everything, kissing everything and bidding each dear haunt a last goodbye.'

The crossing to Milford Haven was uneventful, and they went on by coach through Haverfordwest, Carmarthen, Abergavenny and across the Usk ferry at Newport. This took them on a ten-mile crossing of the River Severn to Bristol. They had earlier attempted to shorten the long road by cutting across the Pendine sands – on an inlet of the Bristol Channel – but 'had like to be lost in crossing the Bar' and were forced to put back. So, after a week living near by in 'a wretched hovel and literally famished', they found food and shelter in Carmarthen. Dorothea wrote about the meal with relish. 'Two Courses of Seven Dishes, tarts, pies, sweetmeats, ham, honey, bread and cheese and cyder all for four shillings for five people and wine proportionately cheap.'

They decided to return to Ireland three months later, 'having engaged one Captain Cleveland's vessel, a Trader returning by the Long Sea [a name for the Bristol Channel]. After waiting three days, he got other passengers and put to sea unknown to us in a violent storm.

'Vex't to death by this disappointment we hired a boat and followed him three long leagues, the tempest increasing every moment and the seas mountainous high. We had a mad woman with us who roared in our ears "blow ye winds, blow," our oars broke and the boatmen gave us up for lost. However, as my mother's white handkerchief floated astern, the brutal Captain Cleveland tacked his ship about and picked us from the waves, half dead with terror and fatigue.'

The next stage of their voyage is more remarkable still.

'His ship, the *Two Brothers*, was a dirty, dark vessel laden with rotten eggs for the sugar house, had a quantity of stinking meat aboard and a corpse to make it more delectable. This last article was hid under our bed for neither the sailors or we would have relished such a shipmate, the former being always superstitious on such occasions. The stenches became so intolerable altogether that we kept our beds from nausea and only found relief in embrocations of vinegar. I was seized with a vomiting of blood which was near ending my existence. From thence I grew quite heavy and stupid. The honest tars, however, forced my mother much against her will to pour down my throat a whole bowl of their brown pottage, which stopped the vomiting and cured me. This brought the pottage into high vogue amongst the quality and was a most seasonable discovery as all our hamper provisions grew putrid.

'We now got sight of the Irish coast but the captain would not put in without a pilot. The winds were fierce and changeable, the shore uncertain and dangerous, and the whole ship short of provisions. After a horrid bandying about amongst the billows we got into Passage, from thence to Waterford and on 11th June arrived at dear dear Carrick-on-Suir.'

And, remarkably, her mother was restored to full health.

We had lost time on our own journey, but I may say we did not give way to 'sick hurry and divided aims' as we lay in Dale like many frustrated sailors before us. We fared better, in any case, than that light-hearted young Breton, the emigré royalist de la Tocnaye, who, dressed in silk stockings and dancing pumps, his swordstick-umbrella slung over his shoulder, set out in 1796 to tramp across Ireland.

'Tired of waiting for the wind at Bristol I went after it,' he wrote, 'and with as little ceremony as was accorded to the mail bags, rattled along to Milford Haven past Swansea and Carmarthen, noting at Carmarthen salmon fishing from a boat, or rather a basket covered in horse skin. They sit in the middle and preserve equilibrium very cleverly, and, fishing over, they carry the boat home where it serves as a cradle for the children.'

BUT THE age of steam was not far ahead. In 1815 the engineer, William Dodd, built in Glasgow an eighty-foot paddle steamer, the *Thames*, intending to make the first ever crossing of the Irish Sea and proceed around Land's End to London. He made a hazardous voyage to Dublin in poor weather, taking shelter twice before he made the Irish coast. In Dublin he encountered Isaac Weld, a man of wide interests, of which steamboats was about to become one.

Weld, who later became president of the Royal Dublin Society, was the author of the *Survey of Co. Roscommon*, the finest in a series on Irish counties; he arranged exhibitions to promote Irish arts and agriculture; and even had the zest to invent a paper boat for the Killarney lakes. Weld joined the *Thames* and wrote of his experience in the French *Journal des Mines* and the *Scots Magazine*. More significantly for the future of transport on the Irish Sea, he gave evidence to a parliamentary committee in London set up to examine how the Irish mail service could be speeded up. 'I found the *Thames*,' he wrote, 'more seaworthy than any vessel I ever was in. She is fully capable of going head to wind in violent gales and over high seas.'

When Weld heard of the *Thames*' arrival at Howth, he and several others joined it to see how it would deal with the short crossing of Dublin Bay to Dunleary. 'Some naval officers who were on board,' he wrote, 'agreed in thinking that this vessel could not long sustain a heavy sea and that there would be great danger in venturing far from the coast.' However, after reaching Dunleary, Weld and his wife decided to remain on board for the voyage to London. They were the only passengers

Clearing the Irish coast they found a heavy swell. 'In fact,' Weld wrote, 'the movement of the vessel differed entirely from that of one pushed by sails or oars, the action of the wheels upon the water on both sides prevented rolling; the vessel floated on the summit of the waves, like a seabird. The most disagreeable movement took place when the waves struck the ship crossways; but here too its particular construction gave it a great advantage, for the cages which contained the wheels acted like so many buoys.'

When smoke was seen pouring from the steamboat's chimneys as it sailed off Wexford next morning, pilot boats, thinking that the vessel must be on fire, put out at once. 'Their hopes of salvage were happily frustrated,' Weld remarked. After a night ashore while the brave Mrs Weld recovered from seasickness, the craft went on to Ramsey Island near St David's, where boats again put out on seeing the smoke. They carried on and near Milford Haven saw the Waterford packet boat. Weld decided to send a letter to his anxious Irish friends and got the *Thames* to give chase to the packet, and, to general astonishment, they not only overhauled the sailing ship but motored twice around it.

Crossing St Bride's Bay was unpleasant. 'A great swell was produced by the meeting of the spring tide with the current which came out of Ramsey Passage. The turbulence of the waves, when we were in their power, was truly alarming; we were often so low between two of them, that we lost sight of the coast, though [it is] very high, but the vessel made its way across all these obstacles in the most alert manner and we left far behind us a fleet of merchant vessels which attempted to follow.

'We now opened a very dangerous passage called Jack Sound. Our situation at one time would have been very perilous on board a vessel which had only sails to trust to, but our powerful and indefatigable wheels soon drew us out of this danger and brought us safe and sound into Milford Roads.'

The paddle steamer reached St Ives and later Plymouth, where a naval court martial was abandoned to enable the court to inspect it. Crowds gathered to look at this strange ship. A Plymouth newspaper reported that, passing the Cornish coast, fishermen seeing a craft 'vomiting forth flame and smoke, conceived her to be a she-devil and made a precipitate retreat'.

On their next halt, at Portsmouth, snooty naval officers said that a steam vessel might one day have a future in towing men-of-war in and out of port. They got that one wrong. Within a few years of the *Thames* reaching its destination in London river, the Age of Steam would usher in a new era on the sea, and little 100-ton steamers would be plying to and fro between Holyhead and the fishing port of Dunleary.

FOUR

Pirates and Privateers

W E TURNED IN early, and I enjoyed some hours of that deep, deep sleep which neither dream nor reality can penetrate. I woke to the clatter of rain on the sprayhood. It was 12.40 AM, close to the time when an unfeeling BBC invites one to listen to the shipping forecast. Not every yachtsman carries a radio equipped to record weather prophecy automatically and deliver it with the breakfast toast.

The faintest glow of light moved to and fro across the cabin table, the reflection of our riding light, a small paraffin lamp tied to the boom end, which warned trawlers and yachts of *Sarakiniko*'s presence. As quietly as possible I rolled from the sleeping-bag and tapped the barograph with a knuckle; the glass dropped a fraction. Stealthily I climbed the five companionway steps, clambered to the foot of the mast – the boat rocked: I hoped it did not wake the crew – and tightened the elastic on that damn halyard beating a tattoo on the metal spar.

The rain had ceased. A gentle breeze came warm and soft from the tree-lined shore and the fields of the headland, carrying the scents of farms and wet grass, sheep and seaweed. Wild geese flew honking overhead. A few miles to the east some lights twinkled, the indistinct mass of Milford Haven town. The breeze also carried a faint hum, the generator of one of the monster oil-tankers that lie to a jetty but never sleep.

Bare feet now chilled and wet, I descended quietly and sat on the edge of the bunk and plugged in the radio earpiece. The forecast was for freshening easterlies and fog patches. The high-pressure system seemed to be holding. I snuggled back into my sack and lay reflecting on how shipping forecasts have a certain poetry, a kind of mantra or litany that holds one suspended between anxiety and reassurance. I like the names of coastal stations: North Utsiré, Tyree, Royal Sovereign, Ronaldsway, Valentia. They suggest something exotic or recall the familiar. I remembered from a few years back the hushed efficiency, winking computer screens and chattering fax machines of gale-blown Valentia, Europe's most westerly met station, and the welcome we received from its director, Gene O'Sullivan. Subsequently I had been at Tyree in the Hebrides, where the world was enwrapped in a deep grey mist which lifted to show a sea in every tone of green and blue and purple running on to white sands. No wonder the Atlantic fringes drew the saints and hermits.

The music before the early morning forecasts adds atmosphere to the broadcasts, those timeless strains of 'Sailing By' and the 'Londonderry Air', interplayed with 'Annie Laurie' and 'What Shall We Do With the Drunken Sailor?' The stirring 'Men of Harlech' may merge into 'Scotland the Brave' and, finally, 'Early One Morning' gives way to 'Rule Brittania'. No wonder so many commuters who have to be on the roads early turn up the volume when the music starts.

I went back to sleep until dawn began to glimmer in the porthole and then switched off the insistent bleep of the alarm, struggled into seagoing kit and lit the gas. Joan groaned and turned sleepily in the cubbyhole of her bunk. A clatter in the forepeak indicated Martin was awake.

In the cockpit I took in the masthead burgee hanging limp from its stick. The early morning light was good enough, I thought, to allow us see any lobster-pot buoys before their ropes became entangled in our propeller. The kettle started to whistle. Tea and biscuits now and, before we had to face any rock and roll beyond St Anne's Head, there would be an aroma of sizzling bacon, coffee, then sunrise and perhaps that fair east wind. Joan came up, wrapped her arms around her chest and looked over the chill scene with some disfavour.

'I wonder what Dorothea Herbert would think of this?'

'You read some of the *Retrospections* last night?'

'Yes. I wonder if she exaggerated – that corpse in the cabin.'

'You can't exaggerate a body.'

'And poor Mrs Freke, almost captured by French privateers. It makes a voyage in *Sarakiniko* positively alluring, I suppose.'

Martin emerged, cup in hand. I bent to the engine button. Smoke jetted momentarily from the exhaust, followed by pulses of cooling water. Martin moved to the bow, the buoy splashed overboard, and we were on our way to Arklow. The time was 0430.

Once more we passed the holy islands of the Welsh – Skomer and Skokholm and Ramsey, the gentle mainland hills sweeping around them, gulls and gannets wheeling and crying above us and Manx shearwaters, so called because they skim across the water, following the heights and hollows of the seas. There are said to be 150,000 breeding pairs on Skomer. Towards the end of summer, the young take off and roam the oceans from here to South America.

By the time Ramsey lay some three miles to the east we were passing our last seamark of the Welsh coast, the forty-four metre high South Bishop lighthouse, outpost of the rough, surf-washed Bishops and Clerks. It was 0745. We had come seventeen miles on a north-running tide, and in the last hour we had made 7.2 miles over the ground. The morning calm had given way to a freshening easterly wind so we had cut the engine and we revelled in that easiest point of sailing, a breeze more on the quarter than abeam. They call it a soldier's wind, for even he can hold his course on this bearing.

I folded away the chart of St George's Channel, wondering why seas enclosed by Wales and Ireland should be called after a mythical English saint. In the early nineteenth century, and possibly earlier, this area was often called the 'Irish Channel'; why should my modern Irish ordnance road atlas now mark it as Muir Bhreatan – the British Sea?

Charts are a relatively new phenomenon. The British Admiralty began to produce them only in 1795. Before that they were drawn up by private individuals – Captain Cook prepared his own chart of the Pacific – and bought in coffeehouses and taverns. Apparently it was the Revolutionary War with France which induced the British to straighten out the confusion of maps, for at the Battle of Quiberon Bay in 1792, British captains used about eight different charts and all were inaccurate. Modern European charts did not achieve accuracy until John Harrison invented the chronometer in the eighteenth century and longitude as well as latitude could finally be calculated.

Presently the wind moved a trifle to the north-east, a rain shower passed over and the sun came out in a rather torn but beautiful cloud-filled sky. *Sarakiniko*, whose twin keels can trap air as they strike a choppy sea, began to pound noisily. Joan tried to ease the jolts by placing cushions in the cockpit, and as we settled in our seats as best we could, Martin wondered if the boost of a good gin and tonic was going to be deferred, as traditionalists say it should, until the sun was over the yardarm. 'That can't possibly happen going north in the Irish Sea,' he reminded the skipper. We agreed that tradition should not be taken to extremes and raised a glass to our progress.

While Martin and Joan collected bottle and glasses, I clambered along the side deck with the Irish tricolour and hauled it to the starboard crosstree. *Sarakiniko* must be properly dressed. First and foremost she had her ensign, her national colours, on a staff at the stern. The burgee of the Royal Cruising Club fluttered at the masthead. We were leaving British territorial waters and would soon enter Irish waters, so I sent the tricolour flying as a courtesy greeting to a new landfall.

Settling back in the cockpit, over the next half-hour we established that a gin at sea beats anything in a yacht club bar, a venue usually so noisy that one cannot hear the speaker and just laughs when he does. Mind you, if your hearing is particularly sharp, you tend to acquire a fund of stories, and at a later stage some can be retold to the speaker, who is left wondering where he lifted the tale to begin with.

Twenty-two miles from the North Bishop is the forty-feet-high Arklow Buoy. It would still be ten miles into Arklow, but it boosts morale to break a voyage into sections. The buoy is one of many that mark the string of banks, shoals and overfalls along Ireland's east coast. It stands at the south end of the Arklow Bank, which stretches the length of fourteen miles about six miles off the coast. 'A remarkable phenomenon,' declared my pilot book, 'as any skipper will tell you after he has suddenly seen the seagulls walking six to eight miles out from the shore and found himself aground within seconds.'

The winds that blow across the sea from Ireland may be

'perfumed by the heather as they blow', but they are soon likely to be generating electricity also. There are plans to build 200 wind turbines out here, standing 300 feet above the sea, spinning day and night, their vanes bigger than the wings of a jumbo jet. The managing director of Eirtricity, developer of the Arklow Bank project, has written that it will be the world's largest offshore wind-park and generate five per cent of Ireland's electricity. Ireland has twenty land-based wind-farms already. Opponents of the project say that these restless objects, visible from the shore, will spoil the serenity and beauty of the coast, and that conventional plants should be built or expanded instead.

Now, however, and without doubt we must find and leave the Arklow Buoy safely just to our north. Normally one sees it a long way off, but I was looking at a horizon where the line between sea and sky seemed to have lost its sharpness. I had little doubt that if fog did close in our GPS would get us a reading from the satellites accurate to within 100 metres. More to the point, the wind was stiffening and swinging into the north-east, and I had read with some attention that the narrow entrance to Arklow was unsafe in strong north-east onshore winds, when the waves break on a bar and there is a nasty sea in the approach. It should, noted the book, be 'attempted only with care and in full control' when the winds were Force 5 or more.

We were sailing splendidly, close hauled, the wind a good Force 4. The alternative to Arklow was Wicklow, fourteen miles further north and hidden behind Wicklow Head. There was nothing else really on a coast notoriously short of emergency havens. The tide would soon turn against us, and if the wind shifted further into the north, we might have it on the nose on a course up to Wicklow, together with a tide hard against us as it flowed in a channel between the banks and the shore. The longer one left a decision now the more into the wind our final course for Wicklow would be. I decided to hold on for Arklow; if eventually we had to turn for Wicklow, the long slog would probably be more comfortable inside the banks.

I put the dividers and ruler away and heaved myself up to the cockpit. Joan had the helm. Poor visibility had deteriorated to mist. Martin was peering over the sprayhood, wiping his glasses.

'Nothing yet. Misleading visibility. It could be a few hundred yards or over a mile.'

'Bless the GPS,' I said, 'one of our few concessions to the electronic age.' I called up the satellites and in a few moments got a position which placed the Arklow Buoy three miles off, bearing 308 degrees. We were off course by about twelve degrees – set down by the tide – so we turned the bow to starboard and soon Martin spotted the dark shape emerging. To assess the tide we thrashed close by and found the sand-tinted tumble now running against us and rather stronger than expected. It was 1550.

'Ten miles to the entrance,' I called, 'and the next buoy is six and a half miles ahead. We mustn't miss that – there are more shallows just inshore of it. No trace of the coast yet.'

Martin went to put the kettle on, and bent over the chart table, thoughtfully spreading the tea towel to catch drips from his oilskin sleeve. 'This tide is still setting us down and off course. We'll need to come up even more to starboard,' he said.

'Yes, a good fifteen degrees, I'd guess.' I knew we couldn't sail that. *Sarakiniko* finds twin keels useful, for obvious reasons, but they mean that, to get moving, she needs the wind fifty degrees off the bow. 'Let's have the engine,' I called. 'The sail will flog about, but we might drop it. It's been a long day.'

'Yes,' Joan agreed, collecting our empty mugs in a plastic bowl. 'We are supposed to be out here for fun. I want to reach a restaurant tonight.'

But to spite us, the pin of a shackle on the boom end worked loose and fell out. The mainsheet – the line which controls the angle of the boom and sail – fell into the cockpit, and both boom and flogging sail began a merry waltz across the decks. Joan cut our engine speed right down and held the bow into the rising wind to reduce pitching and rolling, while Martin and I clipped our lifelines to such deck points as we could find, swearing unreasonably that their six-foot scope hampered us as we tried to tie the billowing canvas to the swinging boom. A few tugs on the mast slides brought the white canopy down around us; the next job was to reach up and get a controlling line on the end of the boom which was swinging wildly. I blamed myself for not checking that shackle. It had been an accident waiting to happen.

A dawn start had made one forget the daily routine of looking for trouble, particularly any weakness in load-bearing components like shackles and the bottlescrews that secure the stays of the mast, as well as checking for traces of chafe on sails or rigging.

I wondered if the wind had topped Force 5 and decided maybe not, but the adverse tide was remarkably strong, more than the pilot book suggested. I agreed with its comment that 'the simple elegance of pure sailing is at a discount over this piece of ground'. We pushed up the throttle a little more. The coast had to be at most two and a half miles off. We were near shallow water, but we could see nothing. Nervously we edged a little offshore, and the buoy emerged just after I had taken another GPS fix. Then we saw the low, grey line of the coast. It was another hour, with the tide still falling over that bar ahead, before I aimed the boat midway between the harbour piers at the narrow entrance to Arklow, with all my senses on full alert, the engine thrusting at full power as steep-sided waves took *Sarakiniko* over the shallows, and we were suddenly in the calm, pulled by the ebbing south-east current towards the dark slimy sides of the narrow gut. Then the waves were mere ripples chasing up the Avoca river and we eased power right off and turned into the deserted-looking dock.

A cheerful husband and wife crew on a quayside motor cruiser, *Carrick Trader*, took our lines and told us they were bound for La Coruna in north-west Spain. Martin, who is not invariably the soul of tact, suggested that their cruiser could be in for some rolling in the Biscay seas. At this they showed us a device they would use to offset their boat's rolling, long metal booms which could be deployed on each side and alternately dipped as a form of water scoop into troublesome seas. On the upswing, we were told, they dampened a roll.

We did not absorb all the details, for Joan, transformed at speed into shore-going elegance, was reminding us that it would be a mile-long walk this dank Saturday night to the nearest restaurant. We followed her along the dockside.

'Perhaps she was not very interested in those booms,' Martin muttered.

'You could be right.'

How old is Arklow? In 1966, Pat Walsh discovered part of a

dug-out canoe in the river silt, the wooden bung still secure in the bung-hole. The craft may have had a Viking origin; they built their sea bases at anchorages like this along the east coast, and at Arklow erected a stronghold on a hill overlooking the deepest part of the Avoca river. But Arklow predates the Norsemen who raided and then settled here. In the second century, when the Greek cartographer Ptolemy made his map of the world, one of the settlements marked on Ireland's east coast was named Manapi. Historians agree it was almost certainly located here.

Arklow's river provides a waterway through the poet Thomas Moore's 'Sweet Vale of Avoca', all the way to Glendalough. That lovely spot among the hills was one of Ireland's greatest centres of pilgrimage, a complex of church buildings by two mountain lakes for ever associated with the fifth-century St Kevin and St Lawrence O'Toole of the twelfth century. Thousands of pilgrims used the harbours of Wicklow and Arklow on their journey to the site. Arklow's waterway led directly to the Glendalough lakes and would probably have been readily navigable – in the lower reaches at any rate – by small craft such as a canoe.

Arklow's significance was enhanced by having holy Bardsey, the 'island of 20,000 saints', lying off the Welsh mainland just across the Irish Sea. In Pembroke I had learnt that two pilgrimages to the shrine of St David were proclaimed as the equivalent of one to Rome. Glendalough had a rating of seven. Possibly a sojourn there was more pleasurable than penitential.

Arklow's estuary was always prone to silting. This was not a problem in the age of small fishing or trading vessels, as they could be hauled on to the sands at the river mouth. But as the years passed and the port proved unusable for much of the winter months, the local producers of copper, tin, zinc and sulphur in this mineral-rich area found their English markets at risk. Fortunately for Arklow, in 1840 the King of Naples put a heavy tax on copper exports from Sicily, and Arklow boomed for a few decades more.

In 1864 a notable family, the Tyrrells, opened a boatyard which is renowned for having built Francis Chichester's *Gipsy Moth III* and the training ship *Asgard II* for the Irish Naval Service. But its mainstay was in working boats, and the yard was the leader in

Irish shipbuilding for more than a century, while Arklow was one of the main ports trading between Ireland and Britain. When the four-acre dock where we lay was opened in 1911, some eighty trading vessels and 160 fishing boats filled the river. Arklow's decline came as a result of restrictions on normal sea trading during World War I. Some ships were sunk by U-boats. At least three were impounded in German harbours. Others were stripped bare and towed outside the port to be scuttled or allowed to be broken on nearby reefs, later to serve beachcombers as firewood. Many rotted in the Avoca river in a pool called 'the cemetery'; in later years, a local paper complained that they reduced the town's appeal to tourists.

Whatever about its decline as a port, Arklow's best-known skipper and sea trader should surely be a beacon for modern women. Kate Tyrrell, second eldest of four daughters, sailed with her father as a young girl, and when he died suddenly on board the family schooner *Denbeighshire Lass* in 1886, twenty-five-year-old Kate took over his work. She traded to and from Liverpool, Belfast, Carrickfergus, Dublin, Courtown and Waterford, was known in North Wales and the Bristol Channel, and traded as far south as Spain and Portugal. She usually sailed with just a mate and a cook and was responsible not only for navigation but for cargoes (her ship could carry 120 tons), port negotiations, insurance, and the repair and maintenance of her ship. She successfully invaded a strongly masculine world and won respect and prosperity as the decades passed.

When World War I broke out, however, coastal shipping faced enormous difficulties. The big Kynoch munitions factory in Arklow needed large coal imports, but U-boats were liable to sink any vessel flying the British Red Ensign. In 1917 a devastating explosion at the factory killed twenty-seven people, and its closure the following year was a further blow to the small community. There were other strains, too, as the rebellion of 1916 flared into a full-scale Anglo-Irish war.

A patriot, Kate resented flying the Red Ensign and kept an Irish tricolour locked in her cabin. By now her health had begun to deteriorate, and she was gravely ill when the truce was called in 1921. She did not live to see the new Irish Free State established, nor the Civil War which followed. After her death in October, her ship did not sail again until 1922. That year, or just afterwards, the *Denbeighshire Lass* was unloading cargo in the north dock in Swansea, with Kate's husband, John, as master and their daughter, Elizabeth, also on board. When John found Kate's flag, a 'specially folded and wrapped up nautical tricolour', he assembled the crew and hoisted it aloft. Some Italian sailors came over to the *Denbeighshire Lass* thinking she was flying the Italian flag; other crews gathered from the Irish, Russian and British ships near by. Elizabeth Tyrell recalls her father saying to her: 'There now, Kate's last wishes have been carried out. God rest her.' It was the first time a trading vessel of the new Irish Free State had flown its national flag.

As a matter of cold fact, it was unauthorised. Nothing in the Anglo-Irish Treaty had laid down a new status for Irish ships on the high seas. While the Irish Free State came into existence on 15 January 1922, Irish ships continued to be 'British' to the international community, despite President Liam Cosgrave telling the Dáil in 1923 that an Irish mercantile flag would be established. Ireland remained a member of the Commonwealth, and the country's position was to that extent no different from that of Canada or Australia. Irish ships continued to fly the Red Ensign and were administered from London by the Board of Trade – as was sixty per cent of the world's tonnage, a proportion which is hard to grasp today.

There were advantages to being linked to London, the world centre of shipping, chartering and insurance. As well as that, coastal rescue arrangements and the maintenance of navigation aids operated by the Commissioners of Irish Lights could continue under the supervision and financing of the British Board of Trade, while the British Post Office maintained – and controlled – the coastal radio stations at Valentia and Malin Head. But though the new Irish state had many urgent preoccupations, it is difficult to understand why maritime affairs were so generally neglected as the country sought international standing in the years between the world wars.

ONLY DUCKS seemed to be on the move next morning as we eased out of the rain-lashed dock, timing our departure to achieve a favourable north-going tide. Bouncing under motor against a drizzle and head to wind, we made heavy weather of it for thirteen miles until, off the great headland of Wicklow, the wind swung south-east, a perfect point now for the run to Dublin Bay. We hoisted the main, filled the jib like a white balloon, killed the engine and revelled in the quiet. The 180-foot-high Wicklow Head, the Republic's most easterly point, is a striking feature. Here vessels can cut in around the head, away from the notorious banks which sneak along offshore, and run safely in inshore water the remaining miles to Dublin Bay.

Navigationally safe, but in times past certainly not safe from marauders. For centuries, pirates or privateers lurked off Wexford in the south-eastern corner and off Wicklow Head in the Dublin Bay approaches. A scheme was arranged in 1457 for armed ships to patrol the sea from Wicklow northwards, the cost to be met by a levy on merchant vessels and fishing boats. It must have met with some success, as records show that the scheme was renewed in 1460 for a further three years.

The romantic glamour cast over piracy, the risks, the daring and, of course, the booty turned a nefarious trade into a romantic exploit. This illusion has been the stock-in-trade of a hundred novels, but in reality a pirate did not dwell in a glamorous island hideout. He dealt in tea and tobacco, ordinary goods in the main, disposed of by middlemen and distributed in the market. Piracy was, in many people's view, simply 'the trade'.

The pirate once existed in a kind of legal 'no man's land'. The early attitude of the law sometimes conceded that it lacked adequate jurisdiction over crimes committed at sea; at other times it tackled piracy through violent suppression. Pirates did not work within national boundaries, but they struck against mankind in general, and in time it came to be accepted that any state could try them; they could even be tried at sea. Eventually the courts sidestepped the problems of legal jurisdiction by handing pirates over to maritime courts, and so the courts of Admiralty came into being.

Pirates were lawless, with plenty of ruffians among them. In

1437, Breton pirates captured the official carrying letters from King Edward III to the Chancellor in Ireland – he spent a year as their prisoner until a ransom of £200 was paid for his release. The Archbishop of Dublin was abducted in 1454 in Dublin Bay and taken to Ardglass, some fifty miles north, but a fleet was mobilised, sailed to Ardglass and rescued him. Later, in 1467, the Dublin authorities planned to fortify Lambay Island near Dublin for 'Breton, French, Spanish and Scots are being harboured there', but this scheme gave way to one for building a fortified harbour near Skerries. In the event, neither was carried out. Henry VIII finally set up an Admiralty office across the Irish Sea at Beaumaris, in Anglesey, to modernise the trial of pirates, but his efforts do not seem to have been effective. In 1610 the Venetian ambassador in London was writing that pirates were safe in the seas around Ireland 'for there is no force in these waters able to give them battle'. Two years later, one John Hume of Plymouth, with help from a Wexford pilot, prepared a chart of Ireland and the Irish Sea as an aid to seamen plagued by Irish pirates and north African corsairs.

The Algerians were perhaps the most professional corsairs. Thomas Wentworth, the Lord Deputy in Ireland, had some success in driving them away from Irish coasts in the 1630s, but they returned. In June 1667, a Captain Henry Boyle wrote to his mother telling her that he hoped to cross to Minehead in the Bristol Channel without encountering any 'Algerians'. A few years earlier, in 1632, they had captured the ship in which Dr Edmund O'Dwyer was sailing to Ireland as the confidential agent of the Vatican, and sold him as a slave. He was bought back by a French Calvinist minister with £60 provided by Fr Luke Wadding. Wadding, the great Franciscan who founded the Irish College in Rome and published a sixteen-volume work on John Duns Scotus, was a central diplomatic figure in the complex aftermath of the Irish rebellion of 1641.

Wentworth was frustrated in his efforts to tackle piracy by the lack of co-operation from the Isle of Man, which had no laws prohibiting dealing with pirates. The island's governor, Edward Christian, released a notorious pirate, John Banks, in April 1631, excusing his decision simply by saying, 'nobody came to prosecute him'. Wenthworth's representative, Captain James, warned: 'This Island, if it be not governed by an honest and faithful person, may be a most dangerous and lurking place for Pirates, for a ship may ride round about it in all winds and from it you may see England, Wales, Scotland and Ireland and endanger all the Shipping that pass anyways in those Seas as being not twenty leagues from Dublin, Beaumaris and the Streight of Carrickfergus.'

Captain James was entirely accurate in his assessment. Pirates would continue to haunt the Irish Sea for many years to come, with the Isle of Man at the centre of 'the trade'.

IT WAS, I think, privateering which muddied the waters between criminal act and legal violence. The privateer plundered as much as any pirate, but he could claim authority for his actions.

Nothing was more firmly fixed in the Middle Ages than the institution of the mercenary soldier, who fought for the personal gain his skill at arms could win him. Why should a mercenary of the sea not be regarded in the same way? Commissioned by national authorities to use his ship against their enemies, the owner converted the ship at his own expense into a 'private man of war' – a privateer. His reward came from the ships he captured, after an Admiralty prize court assessed the legitimacy of his action and the size of the prize money the ship's company would share.

The shaky ethics of the practice were concealed by the elaborate verbiage in which such commissions – called letters of marque – were drawn up. In earlier times a mere proclamation was used to legitimise private forays against enemy ships; in the fourteenth century Richard III authorised his subjects to attack his enemies at sea; in the sixteenth, proclamations of Queen Elizabeth gave similar licence to any who assailed French ships. The wavering character of the law of the sea is well illustrated by that great queen's tendency to disown the seamen who did prey on her enemies. When French ambassadors raged in London, she would shrug and deny responsibility for such actions; when her subjects came home laden with booty, she took her dividend.

Ships' captains, often financed by well-respected merchants, moved chameleon-like between the roles of privateer, when they made war under authority, and pirate, when they became a law unto themselves. The qualities of discipline and leadership which made a good privateer could readily tempt him into piracy, and in the cargo-rich waters of the English Channel and the Irish Sea, the pickings could be tempting indeed.

Thus, the Lord Deputy in Ireland, Thomas Radcliffe, anticipating the outbreak of the French wars in 1554, appears to have supported the dispatch of the *Anne of Dublin* as a privateer to make war on the French. The ship belonged to two Dublin merchants, Thomas Borough and John Marsh, who had bought her for £50 from her Spanish owners. They effected repairs, collected sailors and soldiers, and sailed south. In Waterford they learned that the French war had started. The erstwhile naval officers began their mission by seizing several ships in the port.

After cruising the Irish Sea, they were boarded by one of the Queen's ships off Land's End and taken to Plymouth on suspicion of piracy. A court in London heard that they had behaved as 'mere piratts who set out to spoile and rob all such as they might overcome, were he Frenche man, Spanyard, Englishe or of anye other nation'. The Dubliners denied this, claiming they had followed Radcliffe's command to clear the seas of French and Scottish men-of-war. A cynic might find it significant that the matter was settled when the Lord Deputy's brother-in-law, the Vice-Treasurer in Dublin, mediated so successfully on the *Anne of Dublin*'s behalf that the Plymouth proceedings were dropped.

WHILE A privateer must claim that he acted under authority, the obvious question was: what authority? Normally it would be that of his government, but even here matters were often ambiguous. The *Anne of Dublin*'s voyage, one historian has suggested, while ostensibly a cruise against the French, may have been part of a broader, semi-official operation against the Scots in Ulster. And as Ireland entered the seventeenth century, the range of political interests grew ever more complex as events took a frightening, and tragic, turn. Only by the briefest summary shall I mention them.

Never reconciled to the Plantation of Ulster, the Irish of Ulster rebelled against the Crown in 1641 – an event which would condition attitudes for generations to come. Their leaders, Ulster gentry of Irish origin, fought to regain their land titles, but thirty years of resentment soon exploded into savage atrocities. King Charles ordered the insurrection to be crushed, while the Presbyterian Scots, who had themselves been at war with the King and emerged victorious in 1640, prepared to send their own forces to Ulster to protect the new landowners, many of whom were Scottish. The King faced an even greater crisis in England. On a blustery wet day in August 1642, he raised his standard at Nottingham and declared war against his own Parliament.

In Ireland the Ulster revolt gathered strength and spread south. The rebels made common cause with fellow Catholics, among them the Old English, long-time settlers in Ireland who still owned perhaps one-third of the land. They combined their forces in the 'Catholic Confederacy'.

The King's difficulties in England were seen as a chance to wrest concessions from him, such as repeal of the anti-Catholic Penal Laws. The King prevaricated on granting reform, but hoped nonetheless for Irish support for an attack on the Parliamentary forces in England. He appointed the Duke of Ormonde as Lord Lieutenant in Ireland, formally confirming that the government in Ireland remained Royalist, while the Catholic Confederacy raised some 15,000 men to invade England and crush the power of Parliament. Ormonde had already fetched about 4,000 Irish troops to Chester and others to Mostyn and Anglesey in support of the King.

The King's heavily armed vessel, the *Swan*, using Carrickfergus in Belfast Lough as a base and a link with allies in Scotland, patrolled the approaches to Royalist Chester and limited Parliament's naval control to the northern areas of the Irish Sea. She was a prize target for Parliamentary attack. When her commander John Bartlett, from a family of Dublin mariners, brought the ship to Dublin, a group supporting the Parliamentary cause entered the bay in a longboat, captured the *Swan* and sailed her to join the Parliamentary squadron in north Wales. The cutting-out had been well planned; the attackers even brought a spare set of sails. The loss of the *Swan* did incalculable damage to King Charles's cause. According to at least one source, its capture enabled Parliament to win the battle at sea and was decisive in their taking Chester from the King.

The Catholic Confederacy also assisted the Royalist cause by seeking to control the Irish coasts, authorising privateers to attack the ships of the 'Parliamentary Rebels'. Privateers were empowered to 'enrich themselves by the prizes taken up on our coast' and accost all enemies of 'the Catholic cause in Ireland as well as all adversaries of King Charles found at sea'. Letters of marque were granted from 1642 even up to 1649 under the authority of Viscount Muskerry, named by the Confederacy as High Admiral of Ireland under the Crown. Among the first to get a commission was a 120-ton ship, *St Michael the Archangel*, in 1643. The captain was ordered to bring all prizes into named ports like Wexford, 'or any of the other Irish ports which are now or hereafter in our possession, and none other'. A copy of a typical document is one to 'Anthony Undermacke of the frigate Marye of Antrime', who was authorised to 'secure the sea traffic, advance His Majesty's service and do his Rebbells and enemies damage'. Full power was given to furnish the frigate with warlike provisions and to 'cross the seas to take, seize and make prize of all ships of the Parliamentary Rebels and enemies of His Majesty and any ships bound to such enemies' ports'. The letter was endorsed by one Thomas Porter, Recorder of Waterford.

As early as 1641, agents of the Confederacy had been asked to seek 'able and honest men' in Flanders, and Catholic priests were appointed, one in France, one in Flanders, who were given blank letters of marque and the authority to issue them to 'such Catholliques as are likely to do us the best service'. The Confederacy also created its own naval ensign. A letter to the notable Confederacy cleric, Fr Luke Wadding, refers to an ensign 'which bears the Irish harp on a green field and should be flown on the main top'.

Wexford, on the strategic corner of Ireland, embraced the ideals of the Confederacy from the start, and within a few months of the insurrection in 1641, some 1,500 men were mustered in the county under the authority of the Supreme Council. The town opened its quays to privateers.

Ships of several countries fell victim to the Wexford-based frigates which roamed the Irish Sea and the waters of north-west Europe. Their targets were mostly English, 'ships of the Parliamentary rebels', but also, as the letters of marque put it, 'any ships bound for such enemies' ports'. German, Spanish, French and Turkish ships had their cargoes confiscated in Wexford, where the pillars of local society – among them an alderman, town officials, a collector of customs and a bailiff – were willing patrons of the privateering trade. The Mayor of Wexford, Nicholas Hay, a history of the town published in 1906 records, was 'a very active agent in procuring foreign seamen, fitting out and in instructing masters of Wexford frigates to capture English ships'.

To the Parliamentarians, the Confederacy's ships were simply pirates. John Rossiter, killed defending his ship the *Mary and John of Wexford*, was one 'who pillaged much goods taken away from ye English and brought into Wexford'. James Welsh, who lived in the town, was 'a pyrat in the ffriggot called the *Ffrancis* and brought in much plunder'; a part owner in that ship was described as one who would 'entertaine, harbour and relieve, in his house in Wexford, many seamen employed in the above [plundering] and pyrats who robbed the English'.

The Confederacy's ships certainly disrupted the seaways. The Venetian ambassador to London reported that the insurgents in Ireland had thirty well-armed ships at sea – and had recently captured a richly laden vessel. A few years later, it was said that the seas were now so infested with Irish pirates that the Newfoundland fishing fleet could not proceed without being in convoy. But it is difficult to find evidence that the Confederacy exercised effective control over this plundering or made much direct financial gain from it. There seems to have been little or no insistence that prizes be fetched in to ports under Confederacy control – a designation which in any case sometimes meant little. The captain of the *St John of Waterford* claimed in 1649 that he had captured so many prizes that he could not count them all and admitted that he had not sent any to an Irish port. On the other hand, the *Mary* sailed in November 1648 with a crew of 109 and thirteen pieces of ordnance, and in February the following year sent three captured vessels back to Ireland with prize crews. The Supreme Council of the Confederacy claimed one-tenth of the proceeds. By now, with the King defeated and the Crown abolished, the Confederacy could only have been acting on its own account.

After the fall of Chester and his defeat at the battle of Naseby in 1645, Charles's power had declined. The Confederacy, which had raised substantial forces during the ongoing wars in the three Stuart kingdoms, met military defeat in 1647. King Charles was executed early in 1649. Ireland, having lost tens of thousands of soldiers and thousands of civilians, now faced the vengeance of Oliver Cromwell.

Cromwell, leader of the Parliamentary revolution in England, saw Wexford – chief port of the Catholic Confederacy, with a tradition of Royalist sympathies – as a lair of pirates whose cargoes had enriched town and countryside. The signs were ominous. A report came to the Confederacy that a traveller saw twenty ships waiting to load in Milford Haven and that twenty- six more were on their way there.

Cromwell sailed for Ireland aboard his ship *John* with an armada of about 100 ships (some accounts say 95, some 130) laden with provisions, siege guns and horses, as well as troops. He heard of the fall of Dublin – 'an astonishing mercy, so great and seasonable' – off Milford, and with a fair wind in their favour, Cromwell's forces reached the city in two days. Drogheda fell quickly. Cromwell now turned south for Wexford.

IRELAND MADE slow recovery from the depredations of the Cromwellian wars, while the severity of his campaign and the subsequent land settlement, which gave many native Irish the choice of going 'to hell or Connaught', left an indelible impression on the national memory. But by the later seventeenth century the capital at least was making some headway economically. Dublin's population in 1670 – some 40,000 – would expand over the next century to about 80,000, and its sea trade would make it one of the larger ports in Europe – larger than Bordeaux, Cadiz,

Hamburg or Lisbon. Its sea approaches, however, remained a hunting ground for raiders.

Shortly after the Earl of Essex, Arthur Capel, landed at Dalkey as the country's new Lord Deputy, in June 1675 he reported on the menace of privateers, noting in particular a French ship 'owning herself to have commission to take any of the French King's enemies ... and is reported now to lie at Lambay, an island two leagues north from Howth. It is believed she attends the coming out of some Dutch ships now in Dalkey Sound, loading goods to return home.' Dublin merchants, he noted, 'are much disturbed'.

The Lord Deputy himself was 'a little apprehensive of some affront from these pirates, it being easy for them to come into the harbour at their pleasure and there plunder and fire what ships they think fit. Nothing can remedy this but His Majesty sending a small frigate (one of twenty or twenty-five guns will be best) to secure us. In former times this port was seldom without such and, indeed, considering the Customs His Majesty receives here, which is commonly £30,000 per annum, I think it may well deserve to be a little better looked after.'

But within little more than a decade, Ireland was once again caught in the grip of warring rivals for the English throne, playing a part in support of one faction or another. In December 1688, King James II fled England for refuge in France, supplanted by William, Prince of Orange, whose relatively bloodless 'Glorious Revolution' was to end the long rivalry of Crown and Parliament. The Siege of Derry and the landmark Battle of the Boyne lay little more than a year ahead, and the cycle of Irish involvement in British and European wars would continue through those years and into the future. Philip Walsh captained the ship which took King James II into French exile after the Battle of the Boyne in 1690; his son, Antoine, played a similar role when the Young Pretender, Bonnie Prince Charlie, the last Stuart heir, launched his daring campaign which raised the Scottish Highlands. Prince Charlie looked to Irish privateers operating out of Brittany to provide sea transport to Scotland, and found Antoine Walsh, one of many Irish men who served in the French navy, to captain the small frigate, *Du Teillay*, to the Western Isles.

Although many Irishmen operating as privateers under French authority had Jacobite sympathies, pro-British merchants in Ireland also sought letters of marque to legitimise their attacks on French and other foreign ships. When Britain's Seven Years War with France broke out in 1756, Dublin and Cork merchants got letters for eighteen vessels and petitioned the Lord Lieutenant in Dublin so that 'a sufficient number of musquets and old brown swords may be delivered out of His Majesty's stores for the use of a privateer to be fitted out'.

Fitting out a ship was a considerable expense, often undertaken as a co-operative investment. Dublin merchants wrote to a Belfast firm in July 1755: 'We are in daily expectation of a war [with France] and are here preparing the *Boyne* for a privateer to carry twelve guns and 120 men. If you choose to venture £100, in this way we fancy we can get you in for so much.'

The cost – and profit – was met from prize money. Agreements on the division of prize money varied greatly. One eighteenth-century Anglo-Irish document provided that no dividend should be paid before the costs of fitting out were covered, after which half the spoils went to the ship's owners.

The owners directed the captain to sail in the areas they selected. For officers and seamen it was a case of 'no prize, no pay', and there was always the danger that a mutinous crew could slip into piracy if they failed to gain legitimate prizes. The owners' agreement with the crew provided for loss of his due share of prize money if a crew member was found guilty of cowardice or mutiny – this in addition to the usual criminal law sanctions. There was compensation for loss of limb, disablement and so on fixed in a definite sum, and the first man to sight the sail of an enemy might, if it was captured, get a bonus of one guinea. The first five men to board might share ten guineas. Good behaviour was to be rewarded at the captain's discretion.

I have seen a copy of an agreement for the *Active*, one of the Confederacy ships that operated out of Wexford, which laid down that there be no stripping of prisoners, the clothes on their backs should not be touched nor any violence used on them. The agreement with the crew stood for three months. All undertook to serve for that time, and if the ship was not then back at her home port, it had to be navigated there and properly given up to its owners. The ship's company's signatures or marks were appended to the list of regulations and the figures of allotted shares. The document ended: 'God save the King and success to the *Active* and her brave crew.'

The *Dublin Privateer*, fitted out in 1744, was a 350-ton ship with thirty carriage and twenty swivel guns – an expensive range of ordinance. Another, the *Peter and Paul*, of only 100 tons, had ten carriage and fourteen swivel guns. A suitable privateering ship needed to be about 150 tons, a size which limited the numbers that anxious Irish traders could afford. There were only about sixty-seven Irish-owned ships of this size even as late as 1790. This probably explains Wolfe Tone's comment in his diary that year that Ireland should not follow England into war with Spain and risk attack because 'from the discouragement of Irish navigation [by England] our privateers are few'.

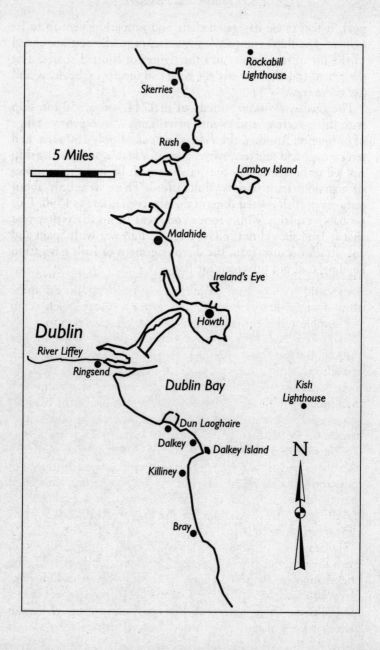

FIVE

To a Fair City

AFTER TOSSING UNCOMFORTABLY in the tide race off Wicklow Head, we started sailing almost due north. It looks like the open sea here, but effectively the hidden banks create a channel some four or five miles wide and twenty miles long until it reaches Dalkey Island, which marks the southern entrance to Dublin Bay. Buoys indicate the banks – the India, the Codling, the Kish – the origins of their names a tantalising mystery. At lowest tides the water tumbles over the banks, and if a boat runs on to them the tidal currents eat at the ground on the downstream side and form a hole into which a craft will tumble and eventually disappear, digging its own grave.

In the early years of the nineteenth century, a lightship patrolled the Kish Bank at the northernmost limit of these shoals, just seven miles from Dun Laoghaire. When ships approached the shoals in foggy weather, the lightship crew struck a gong in warning and then fired a gun to signal that they had safely cleared the bank. It seems a very hit and miss way of navigating through this watery maze.

Soon we could see the light tower, the Kish's modern marker. I have never been able to watch that seamark, so familiar to tens of thousands of cross-Channel passengers, without feeling astonished that the account of the greatest disaster to befall Irish people travelling in Irish waters during the First World War has been almost forgotten.

The tragedy happened on the morning of 10 October 1918, when the mail steamer *Leinster* was torpedoed shortly after leaving Dun Laoghaire harbour, a mile or so from the Kish lightship. Over 500 lives were lost. The Armistice in Europe was just a month away. The tragedy now lies at the furthest tip of human memory. Even at the time its details were blanketed by almost total press censorship, and there was little popular feeling for a misfortune that was seen as part of Britain's war. The bitter years that followed the struggle for Irish independence also led to a selective amnesia, indeed to a deliberate turning away from the reality of Ireland's participation in that war, though thousands of Irish men and women had fought voluntarily in the Allied forces and helped the general war effort by their work in factories and army and naval bases.

Much of that story was allowed fade into obscurity until recent decades. For rescuing this small part of Ireland's maritime past my gratitude goes to Roy Stokes and his book *Death in the Irish Sea*. I have found much detail in its pages.

By 1917, German U-boat attacks on Allied shipping had reached crisis levels. 'The Germans are building submarines faster than the English can sink them,' the US ambassador in London wrote. 'If this goes on long enough the Allies' game is up.' But in April 1917 America entered the war, and flotillas of US destroyers arrived in the naval base at Queenstown (Cobh, Co. Cork) to hunt U-boats and provide escorts to shipping in the Atlantic. The Americans demanded the return of the convoy system, which had not been used since the Anglo-American war in the early nineteenth century, and it proved an immediate success, a true turning point in the war. However, U-boat commanders changed their tactics as a result and pressed into the Irish Sea, where they could concentrate on slower cross-Channel shipping or waylay isolated vessels.

The Irish Sea Hunting Flotilla – one light cruiser, eleven British and seven US destroyers and submarine chasers – operated from Holyhead and Dun Laoghaire, then known as Kingstown and effectively a naval base. Ships like the *Leinster* were also armed to fight gun attacks from surfaced U-boats, though in the entire period of the war only one submarine was destroyed in the Irish Sea basin: in Caernarvon Bay in May 1918.

U-boats were more vulnerable in the actual approaches to the Irish Sea, where minefields were extensive and patrolling aggressive. Six were lost in the waters between Pembrokeshire and Wexford and in the North Channel between Antrim and Kintyre. Minefields were extensive in St George's Channel, though in the

North Channel the waters were too deep and the tides too strong for effective mine laying. Instead, some forty trawlers were used to maintain wire nets, each over a mile long and a hundred feet deep, which released phosphorous flares when a U-boat hit them, revealing the submarine's course. A hydrophone station was established on Antrim's Toe Head to detect U-boats passing under the nets, though they avoided detection by running their engines slowly and quietly and slipping into the Irish Sea on a fair fast tide.

The *Leinster* was the flagship of Ireland's fleet of four mail boats, each bearing the name of a province. Crossing on her was a social occasion when congenial people were entertained by a notable captain and his officers. It was a civilian ship, though it also did important war work, and as the numbers of troops crossing the Irish Sea increased, high ranking British and American officers regularly used the *Leinster*'s comfortable service. On 10 October 1918, 492 of its complement of 771 were troops.

The ship had several narrow escapes as conflict in the Irish Sea intensified. On 27 December 1917, a 'torpedo missed by yards'. On 15 March 1918 and again on the night of 21 April, the ship 'went full speed astern to avoid a submarine close alongside'. On 14 August a submarine was spotted 'on the port bow three miles away. Following another incident, Captain Birch told a colleague on the bridge: 'If this ship goes down, I go with it.'

That was on 9 October. The next day Commander Ramm of UB-123 sighted the *Leinster* at 0945, sailing directly ahead and without escort. His first torpedo missed the ship. The lookouts shouted out a warning of the second, but it was too late, and the stricken ship began to settle by the bow in a rough, cold sea. A third torpedo turned the postal sorting room into a steel tomb, killing all but one of twenty-two postal workers, and set off a horrific explosion in the boiler area which killed hundreds more below and blew scores of people off the decks. The *Leinster* now sank very quickly. Over 500 people died.

Later today we would see a memorial to the tragedy, erected belatedly on the seafront at Dun Laoghaire. The owner of the wreck, Desmond Brannigan, got divers to recover the *Leinster*'s starboard anchor in 1996, and the local authority, the harbour authority and ferry company Sealink combined to give the

Leinster a memorial near the ferry terminal where she could be remembered. The wreck itself lies in about 100 feet of murky water, her top row of portholes protruding from the silt.

'WIND'S FRESHENING,' Martin said, glancing astern.

A wind from behind, pushing you along, disguises its force and can steal up on you unawares. *Sarakiniko* was probably achieving five knots, so this breeze of perhaps ten knots blew as a gentle five-knot breeze on the back of one's head. But if we turned to beat into it at five knots, its apparent force would be trebled.

'It's gone a bit south too,' Joan said, 'more of a gybing course for us now. That boom could sweep across,' she added.

I took the hint and sat down. Opposite me Martin was concentrating on this exacting and least appealing point of sailing, watching aloft for the flutter which gives last-minute warning that the wind is about to catch the 'wrong' side of the mainsail and swing sail and boom violently across the boat. In very severe conditions, an involuntary gybe can smash rigging and even lead to dismasting. Today the only possible damage would be to the professional pride of our helmsman.

Joan and I sat back, watching the occasional east coast train entering and emerging from the tunnels beneath Bray Head, the Martello Tower a knob on distant Dalkey, and a white gleam at Killiney which must be Sorrento Terrace. We could see Howth too, like a long grey island in the distance.

Joan broke the silence. 'Should we delay pouring some pre-lunch beer?'

We looked startled. 'Let's stop living on the edge!' I cried. 'We can sail ten degrees off and easily fill the sail.' This we did and the beer cans hissed open. Presently, Martin glanced at the burgee, stiff at the masthead.

'Wind's still rising. Why not just drop the main and enjoy our lunch. We can run under the jib. It's being blanketed anyhow by the mainsail.'

We settled down under jib alone, and the chuckling sound of the water ran along the boat as the sandy beaches of Killiney drew past to port. Shoaling depths marked the approach to Dalkey Sound, which is effectively only about 200 yards wide. The following sea lifted into swell, smooth-backed billows on each side, urging us on past Dalkey's sloping lawns and the ancient stones of its medieval harbour. It is hard to grasp that Dalkey was once so important seven castles were built to guard it from pirates from the sea and freebooters from the hills. But the harbour was one of the principle shipping points for Dublin, the approaches to the Liffey river so notoriously silted up that ships of over 100 tons would not enter, preferring to discharge their cargoes by anchoring off Dalkey. No less than three tiny harbours nestle along a mile or so of this rocky coast – Colimore, Bullock and Sandycove. Bullock, just west of Dalkey, was also a fishing port of such importance that in the twelfth century Cistercian monks built Dalkey Castle to protect its fishermen from robbers.

Killiney and the heights of Howth define the arms of Dublin Bay. North of Howth, flatlands open as far as the estuary of the Boyne. No significant physical barrier protects this ancient region, which may have been, in history and prehistory, the most crowded corner of Ireland. Since perhaps 3000 BC, Newgrange has stood here, the most impressive of Ireland's prehistoric monuments. Not far off is royal Tara, where green mounds mark the site of the palaces of ancient kings. From earliest times, this has been the richest part of Ireland, a valuable conquest for any invader.

The Vikings set up their first permanent bases along this coastline, one at Annagassan in the south-east corner of Dundalk Bay on the coast of Co. Louth and a southerly one at the mouth of the Liffey. There were sixty Viking ships on the Boyne by 857 AD and a similar number on the Liffey, for by then voyages, whether for trade or booty, were organised on a large scale. Dublin was a vital base, and remained so. Strongbow himself hurried north to possess it within a month of landing at Waterford. At the other end of the region, near Dundalk, the Scottish invader Edward Bruce had himself crowned king of Ireland in a curious dream of pan-Celtic monarchy.

England's fifteenth-century government also maintained its most secure foothold in this region, stretching from Dundalk to Dublin, which came to be called the Pale. It was a critical base for a country which feared invasion through the back door. However, when they came, the sea-borne attacks were upon the south and west coasts, at Kinsale and Bantry, and at Killala in far Mayo. Why did France and Spain not use the Irish Sea to descend upon the very capital of Ireland?

The dangers of this open shore seem not to have been understood until the later years of the Napoleonic wars, when it was decided to build massive Martello towers – some twenty of them – to guard the coast. Their guns were never fired in anger, but the decision to erect them may have been influenced by a report issued to the Irish authorities by a Colonel Napier in 1794 or 1795. His warning was as persuasive as that which Erskine Childers would one day give, in his great novel *The Riddle of the Sands*, of a possible German invasion of the flat east coast of England around the Wash.

Napier said quite simply that a French force of around 3,000 men, sailing north from Brest or l'Orient, could enter the Irish Sea, land on the beaches near Dublin and capture the city within twenty-four hours.

A wind from the west round to the south lasting for three days would be enough to ensure their success. A great part of the British fleet was stationed in the North Sea to combat the French navy, which was in possession of parts of Holland and the Zuider Zee. A west wind, Napier pointed out, 'would waft over an armament from Brest and bring them under the Irish land and in smooth water, their track being a line with scarce an angle,' while 'that same wind would shut the British fleet into the North Sea'.

A glance at a sea chart bears this out. Each fleet would have to round Land's End, but for the French Dublin was a mere 150 miles from Brest, while the British fleet off Holland would have to sail 360 miles and, crucially, tack against south-westerlies in the English Channel, doubling the distance to Ireland.

Napier's report went further. Killiney, he said, was 'a firm sandy beach where at least 1,500 men, together with field pieces, might be landed all at once and at any time of tide, not even up to their knees in water. If the tide did serve, similar landings could be made at Dalkey, Dunleary or Bullock, or at Balscadden at the back of Howth.' He suggested that a landing each side of Dublin Bay should also be considered as this would be likely to split the Dublin garrison.

In all, he anticipated that the French could succeed with some 3,000 troops. The fleet, travelling north in 250–300 ton ships, would carry '500 artillery men and their guns, perhaps some hundred marksmen and six of the new French gunboats, each with a twenty-four pounder in the bow to support the main fleet. Forty or fifty horses would be needed to draw the guns to Dublin.' The essence of the French plan would be speed and surprise. 'Two day's bread in the haversacks and sixty rounds of ball ammunition is all that need clog the soldiers' intended rapid movement, and the invading force would not be without a sufficient number of Rush and American pilots. All would be over in about four hours from their landing.'

Could British warships have blockaded the French navy, preventing them sailing from Brest or l'Orient? British efforts to contain a breakout by French ships were not very successful in the 1790s, and the laxity of the blockade was glaringly revealed when, on a dark squally day in December 1796, the French put to sea to attempt a landing in Bantry Bay. About half the British Channel fleet was then in winter quarters at Spithead, and when the wind came east to urge the French into the Atlantic, it hampered the Royal Navy's efforts to clear from Spithead around the eastern corner of the Isle of Wight. The French Directory had provided republican revolutionary Wolfe Tone with 12,000 battle-hardened soldiers, three times the amount which Napier said could take Dublin, but they saw fighting only in the west, and the Pale remained untouched and intact.

And in the end, the Martello towers, when they did come to be built, may not have been effective against a lightly armed, fast-moving invading force. Walls of local stone eight feet thick may have made such a tower virtually bomb-proof, but its cannon, set on a traversing carriage peering above the parapet, had a range of only about a mile.

WE TURNED for Dun Laoghaire, entering the semi-circle of Dublin

Bay. Six miles to starboard, fields and suburban houses climbed the great nose of Howth, while the mile-long granite arm of Dun Laoghaire harbour lay to port. Its entrance was hidden from view, but then a superferry came out, looking like a white block of flats mounted on a catamaran and spuming ribbons of foam as it accelerated across the water. A haze lay over Dublin city, sheltered in the curve of the bay, but two pencil-like power station chimneys rising into the sky showed the general direction of the city's docks.

The bay reaches in a five-mile diameter between Dun Laoghaire and Howth Head, its radius extending some four miles in towards the security of Ringsend or the Liffey quays. It was a truly fearful place for early mariners, especially in thick weather or onshore winds. The mouth of the River Liffey lay further west than we know it now. 'It is difficult to realise,' wrote Professor MacLysaght, 'that all the large part of Dublin between O'Connell Bridge and Sandymount was, in the seventeenth century, covered by sea twice a day, with the exception of the neck at Ringsend.'

At low tide, over one-third of the bay became dry land (part of its north shore is today a golf course) while another one-third had no more than five to ten feet of water. Take a glance, as Stephen Dedalus did in Joyce's *Ulysses*, at 'the whitemanned seahorses champing brightwinged bridled' when the wind has east in it, or walk in fancy with him by 'the lacefringe of the tide' at Sandymount, 'splayed feet sinking in the silted sand', and one realises why as late as 1854 Dublin Bay was still described as 'proverbial for shipwrecks'.

In earlier times the Vikings had drawn their craft ashore, galleys that 'ran to beach in quest of prey, their blood-beaked prows riding low on a molten pewter surf'. Or they could sit out on 'the lager', a medieval term for mudbanks, offloading their cargoes laboriously at low tide. By the early thirteenth century, however, ships were larger and had deeper keels, but though King John in 1209 permitted the building of 'edifices' to improve landings at Merchants' Quay and Wood Quay, the perils of reaching the city's wharves remained. Dublin had to create a safe channel into the Liffey or accept that shipping must use safer havens, such as those little harbours around Dalkey. Eager to maintain control over shipping, the merchants of the city petitioned King Edward III to expand the market area they controlled – the staple – to take in other ports. When the King extended the staple by six leagues (eighteen miles), small ports such as Dalkey grew prosperous, while the city's merchants increased their jurisdiction and their income from dues and charges.

In the meantime, 'Dyvelyn,' declared a writer in 1571, 'is in many respects comfortable but less frequented of merchant strangers because of the bar haven.' The bar which hampered access into the Liffey quays was made of sand, not river-borne silt, with channels cut by the Liffey and its tributaries, the Dodder and the Tolka. Once over the bar, smaller vessels could crowd up the Liffey on the rising tide to the junction with the Poddle river by old Essex Bridge, but ships needing six or seven feet of water, said a critic in 1653, 'cannot go nearer than Rings-end'.

The name describes the spit – or 'rinn' – which separated the Dodder river from the tidal bay and once formed a landing place with shelter for shipping. Inside the spit, stretching back to where the railway runs now, was an expanse of shoaling water and sandy beaches, with an isolated group of cottages running along the tongue of dry land. Travellers disembarking at Ringsend in the seventeenth century found little or no accommodation in the village. Instead, they waited for the tide to drop and hired a horse-car to drive them across the strand to a point near Trinity College, close to the high tide line, and along modern Dame Street, then a rough road outside the city proper, bordered by the houses of prominent people. Ringsend itself seemed to lack appeal. One traveller, John Dunton, a London bookseller who landed there in 1698, records seeing the body of a German doctor hanging on a gibbet at the highest point of the spit. Evidently he had lured a Dutch officer to his lodgings and murdered him for the sake of his silver shoe buckles.

What could be done to improve the approaches to Ringsend? In 1717 the channel through Dublin Bay was improved by driving a line of massive tree trunks into the sands, and about forty years later this was widened into a roadway. An enterprising man named Pidgeon built a house at its seaward end. It later became a hotel – the Pidgeon House – and packet boats began to use it as a terminal. Over the years that great southern wall across the bay has been much extended. I cycled out there many years ago when I was a student in Dublin and found myself seemingly marooned in the centre of the bay, at least three and a half miles from the city docks, with Dun Laoghaire and the Hill of Howth to my right and left, but still miles away across the shallow waters.

The Grand Canal, started in 1790, soon reached right across Ireland to the Shannon, carrying passengers and cargo from the midland towns to the capital. It made its exit at Ringsend. Here the ground was relatively easy to excavate, and Ringsend housed the control terminus for the canal, a big lock alongside a thirty-five-acre dock. Today the last of it is just an expanse of stagnant water, but refurbishment is afoot, and no doubt it will help to further develop Ringsend's growing popularity as a place to live.

While Dublin was slowly developing its port facilities, just 130 miles away Liverpool was growing rapidly, boosted by the colonisation of north America and the developing trade with the West Indies. To compete with a rival which by the end of the eighteenth century was developing new docks, Dublin established a Ballast Office to take responsibility for clearing the port's channels. Departing ships were obliged to draw ballast for the homeward journey from the sandbanks in the bay, and over time millions of tons of sand and shingle were eventually spread behind the North and South Walls, defining the entrance to the city. The young French traveller, de la Tocnaye, wrote about 'the immense embankment constructed to prevent the accumulation of sand at the mouth of the Liffey' in 1796.

But neither Ringsend nor Howth could cope with a big rise in traffic. One-third of the vessels arriving at Irish ports at the start of the eighteenth century were colliers, and by the end of the century the proportion had risen to half – some 100 sailed into Dublin Bay in one week alone in 1772. Congestion was a serious problem, especially when the prevalent south-west winds held these unwieldy craft in their home ports – when a fair wind returned, they all tended to set sail for Dublin together. ''Tis frequent in time of war or upon the ordinary occasion of cross winds to have 200 sail of ships at a time go from this place to Dublin laden with coals,' Daniel Defoe noted in his *Tour Through Great Britain*.

Demand for coal, however, continued to soar as the city expanded, so the Coal Harbour was built at Dun Laoghaire to offload Welsh coal brought across on ships from Whitehaven and Wokington in the north-west of England, and carried into the city on Ireland's first railway line, which opened in 1834 and ran from Dun Laoghaire into Dublin. A roadhouse called the Purty (Pretty) Kitchen was also set up at the Coal Harbour – its hospitable doors are still open.

As Dun Laoghaire developed, the great pincer-like piers were built, each the best part of a mile long and together enclosing a sheltered 250-acre harbour. The packet boats, which had upped anchor from the Pidgeon House for Howth in 1813, moved south to Dun Laoghaire, now happy to be renamed Kingstown after the visit of King George IV in 1821. By the 1840s, Dun Laoghaire (or Kingstown) was Dublin's major port and the chief passenger terminal for Ireland.

FOR SMALL craft like ours, however, Dun Laoghaire continued to be an uncomfortable spot when the wind blew from the north-east. When gales and swell entered the harbour, my old pilot book advised, there were two things a yachtsman should do: first see that his mooring chain was firmly lashed down – for if the choppy water made it jump from its fairlead, it could saw the bow down to the waterline; and secondly, go ashore for the night.

All is changed now, and a new breakwater inside the harbour encloses small boats in a smart marina in front of the Royal Irish Yacht Club, that gem of Victorian grace. It was not yet in commission when we arrived, but the club welcomed us hospitably to its own pontoon, and we went ashore to a town which still displays the charm of another age, despite the development of malls, arcades and hamburger havens on the back of Ireland's booming economy.

The following day was set aside to introduce Martin to Dublin. One day was of course far too short to absorb the city's inner rhythms and hidden complexities, and I did not find it easy to map out the new Boomtown – the familiar streets decked out in glitzy chainstores; the gridlocked traffic and trendy apartment blocks replacing the city's old communities, while system-built 'executive' homes for the upwardly mobile spread throughout the city's sprawling suburbs. Dublin's distinctive sense of place seemed to have faded a little. We rejoiced that the squalor of poverty was passing, but the contrast between rich and poor seemed to be greater now, and in a sense Dublin seemed to be moving everywhere and nowhere. On these occasions, of course, one is making two parallel journeys: the journey of today and the journey through one's memories.

Martin turned from gazing out the window of the train speeding us back to Dun Laoghaire and tapped me on the knee.

'Your spiritual home may be in the middle of the Irish Sea.'

'That can be a rather lonely place,' I said, after a pause.

But I saw his point. I had the advantage, and the disadvantage, of being committed to three of the countries bounding this sea. Reared in Co. Waterford and married in Scotland, I have spent most of my adult life in England – not Anglo-Irish but Hiberno-British.

Martin may have identified an unconscious reason for my traversing the Irish Sea. Most people identify with a place of birth or a place of prolonged residence, but really we are attached to several networks: family, friends, a school, a church; to our workplaces and social clubs, to our communities. We order these multiple attachments into a hierarchy; how we choose to do this has a real bearing on the issue of our national identity.

One may have a French father and an English mother – why not be equally attached to France and England? The arrival of European passports symbolises a new leaning towards a 'European identity'. The gravitational pull of personal loyalties can wax and wane; the spread of possible allegiances can also alter. Multiple attachments increase especially when communities share a language, and in the countries surrounding the Irish Sea our intermingling is well advanced. Most Scots have little difficulty in being British-Scots. The Liverpool Irish have been around a long time.

Most people around the Irish Sea – and elsewhere – have tangled racial origins, though in Ireland the nationalism of the nineteenth and twentieth centuries established an image of an uncorrupted native Irishness, for which one qualified by having Gaelic descent, the Catholic faith and an attachment to the ideal of a unified island state. In fact, in medieval times – maybe running up to the seventeenth century – Ireland really seems to have been a patchwork of regional loyalties. And in earlier centuries, the Irish consciousness was perhaps of an archipelago which embraced parts of western Scotland. Personal bonds, in any case, ran along lines of caste solidarity rather than national identity.

Is it not the case that, for too long, there has been a denial of plurality and diversity, a depressing failure to accept all the layers of identity accumulated down through history? Travelling the coasts of the Irish Sea sharpens one's thinking about the nature of borders and communities. 'Where are you from?' people say. While at sea, at any rate, *Sarakiniko* was home; and in the world of sail, the question often simply asked what was one's last port of call. From a sailor's perspective, allegiance can be seen as an option, not an unalterable inheritance.

THESE SOBER reflections were dispersed by the fresh north-east wind that met us at the rail station exit. As we came down the ramp to the pontoon, it was beginning to rock slightly. Feet planted apart, we swayed along the undulating slats.

'Forecast bad?' I asked a man adjusting fenders by his yacht.

'Yes. Coming in tonight. Could be a northerly gale.'

I caught up with Joan and Martin and gave them the news. 'Let's get to Howth,' I said. 'It's not far but it puts us on our way, and we can make it by dusk.' The Gibralter-like headland of Howth was just five miles off, with the harbour just two or three miles beyond.

We stowed the shopping away and were soon bucking into a chill headwind, sea-spray fanning down the deck. Sutton lay to port. In darkness, without engine power and the modern buoys which define the Liffey entrance, one could understand how boats had so readily been driven onto the foaming shallows.

The ride grew more bumpy. As we elbowed through overfalls off the headland, it seemed to take an age to move the Baily light-house from our port bow to our stern. The harbour grew closer, a lively chop running between the piers. We twisted around buoys towards the marina pontoons and catwalks, the clink and jangle of steel rigging against alloy masts ringing out like bells in the rising wind. The marina was quite full, the boats like big plastic toys wedged into their slots. Coming up with a strong wind astern, we saw a space available beside a shark-nosed motor yacht with windows of smoked perspex, but as we turned, the wind, now on our beam, pressed us maliciously alongside. To defeat it one had to keep on power and speed and then at the last instant go hard astern to avoid the boat moored just ahead. And the wind did the rest now, pushing us sideways as the crew sprang ashore with bow and stern lines and just seconds to spare.

Joan looked at the distant yacht club and breathed, 'Showers and armchairs.' Martin and I insisted on pouring a slug of whiskey first.

We had arrived at an ancient place. Howth came under Dublin's jurisdiction when King Edward III extended the staple for six leagues and drew in the harbours of 'Houthe, Malahide, Rush and Skerry'. Small though they were, these were more than just fishing harbours. They were arteries of local life which traded far and wide, like many similar places scattered throughout the Irish Sea.

In Wales, for example, the great curve of Cardigan Bay held dozens of small harbours which were used to ferry agricultural goods, limestone, coal and timber for local industry. A mountainous terrain imposed three main roads on the country: from Chester on to Caernarfon, from Hereford to Brecon and Carmarthen, and, in the south, from Cardiff to Swansea and St David's. This geography heightened the importance of sea traffic along the coast, with scores of locally owned boats, rarely over forty tons, carrying farm produce to market towns, and cattle, wool, corn, butter and cheese to the big markets of Bristol, Chester and Liverpool.

South Wales and north Wales were to some extent segregated until the railways arrived. North Wales looked towards Chester, and subsequently Liverpool as that city expanded; these cities, in turn, were more familiar with Dublin than with any south Welsh town. In the south, Bristol was the focus for commercial and social life.

Similarly, in Ireland there were many landing points for local goods and heavy cargo. A simple pier might do for the unloading, even a beach at low tide. Our container-ship age can confuse perspectives – in earlier times, these small ports also traded with Europe. The *Calendar of State Papers, 1601-03* noted seventy such trading harbours and assessed their qualities. Ardglass in Co. Down was 'a crib for small boats'; Dundrum 'for small boats and barks'. Dundalk was 'a shoale bay', Malahide a 'bar haven'. With shipping putting in and out of so many coves and bays, the English authorities found it difficult to control the coast and complained that the Irish rebels, the Scots and the French traded together extensively. Scottish barques sailed into northern harbours 'with munitions, cloth, wine and aqua vitae, and some of the Scottish galleys trading with these places bring victuals and other necessaries to the rebels'. No doubt Queen Elizabeth had these difficulties in mind when in 1581 she extended the jurisdiction of Dublin's Court of Admiralty right down to Arklow.

The best natural harbour on the entire east coast of Ireland is Skerries, just thirteen miles north of where we sat now. Behind its small hooked promontory was shelter even in easterly and south-easterly gales: records indicate that no less than 1,100 vessels came in here to escape stressful weather in the decade 1756–66. It became a leading fishing port in the later eighteenth and early nineteenth century, but, above all, grew in the eighteenth century into a major centre of smuggling. Small harbours like Skerries and Rush were close to Dublin, its wealth and markets, yet sufficiently distant to avoid constant surveillance by the Revenue cutters. And crucially, of all the small sea communities around the city, they were nearest to the Isle of Man, an island which exploited its natural independence to dominate the supply of contraband throughout the Irish Sea.

That was where we were headed, first sailing north in the shelter of the Irish coast. Sadly, Martin had to leave us now. He would be replaced by Pat O'Donnell, a Tipperary farmer full of the vigour of the semi-retired and a veteran of small boat sailing on the River Shannon.

'Come tomorrow if you can, Pat; we're forecast a northerly gale.' As I replaced the telephone, I wondered if I might have chosen my words more carefully.

All next day a fresh wind kept rubbing our squeaking fenders against the pontoon, slapping the sides of the boat with angry wavelets. By 7 PM a full gale was blowing, ripping down along the coast between Malahide and the off-lying islands of Ireland's Eye and more distant Lambay. The marina became a true wind instrument, a marine orchestra, its strings those hundreds of halyards drumming on masts, the wind developing a strong, deep bass. Away on the long east pier, walkers clung to one another as they staggered along, enjoying the novelty of being blown about by the wind before returning home. At dusk I doubled our bow and stern lines. The seas rolling up from the north – an unusual point – were partly broken by Ireland's Eye and could not build up into true rollers, but the jagged wavelets were turning the water white.

The wind howled all night, rocking and rolling us into fitful sleep. At 7 AM, to escape the rasping of our creaking fenders, we staggered in the rain, weary and unrefreshed, to the blessed silence of the yacht club and the balm of hot showers. A woman with a mop and bucket offered me kindly advice: 'Watch you don't slip, dear, the floor's a bit damp.'

As I left the club past bar tables still cluttered with glasses and empty bottles, where many had found solace from the gale-torn evening, another figure appeared with towel and sponge bag. He had picked up the Irish forecast for coastal waters, which is generally more accurate than the BBC's brief verbal brush strokes, describing 10,000 square miles of sea area in five seconds lest a Test Match audience should grow impatient. Our wind, he declared, was to moderate and go north-west.

So we waited for the angry weather systems to settle their differences, for the isobars to drift apart and the wind to ease, and for Pat to arrive. He turned up late that blustery evening and immediately showed his practical bent by extracting two empty fertiliser sacks from his brother's car and pushing the heavy-duty plastic between our fenders and hull, silencing them for the night.

We had decided to sail to Carlingford Lough, boundary between the Republic and Northern Ireland, visiting the marina on the Republic's side and later going on to Northern Ireland. The morning wind blew almost from the north, light now, and as our course would be only ten degrees east of north, we knew we could do no more than keep the engine on and fill the jib to steady us.

We were biting into the first of thirty-eight miles by 0840, soon thrusting past the green slopes of twenty-five-hectare Ireland's Eye, the sprayhood lowered so that we could see the occasional pot-buoys in the chop. We looked for but could not spot the remains of what may be the earliest monastery in Ireland, said to have been founded on Ireland's Eye by St Nessan in the sixth century. Perhaps we were distracted by discomfort: it was quite unreasonably cold. Malahide drew past, marked already by a flutter of dinghies, then the sixty-foot tower near Donabate and, out to starboard and six miles from Howth, the surprisingly large mass of Lambay Island; arable fields climbing to woods, houses by its harbour.

The roughly rectangular island, a square mile in area, rises to about 400 feet. Neolithic man lived here, and the Romans, who called it Limnios, probably had a station there trading in gold and skins from the Ireland they never invaded. Modern evidence suggests that the Viking raid here in 795 AD was the first on any part of Ireland.

Archbishop Usher of Dublin (who in 1650 estimated the date of the world's creation at 4004 BC) had his palace built here, though it cannot have been a convenient place for attending to his pastoral duties. The island's isolation, however, made it an effective prison camp for the losers in the Battle of the Boyne.

The Talbot family, hereditary Lords Admiral of Malahide and the Seas Adjoining, acquired Lambay in the seventeenth century and sold it to the first Lord Revelstoke in 1903. Today Lambay is privately owned, and the modern house on the island is a reconstruction by the talented architect Lutyens, apparently the only example of his work in Ireland. The lovely gardens were designed by Gertrude Jekyll.

As we passed the north-west corner of the island, the Tayleur rock came into view. It was named after the *Tayleur*, one of the emigrant ships that left Liverpool for Melbourne in January 1854. Thick weather added to the gloom of short winter days, and as the ship tacked to and fro to get down the Irish Sea, a maladjusted compass brought her far off course and on to Lambay Island. She tried to go about, but it was too late: the *Tayleur* smashed among the rocks, and close on 300 people were drowned.

From here we could see at least five Martello towers running along the coast from Ireland's Eye to Skerries. To the east, three miles from the shore, the Rock of Bills (as it was known until the name Rockabill was adopted) pointed the course to the Isle of Man. Even before the Rockabill light came on in 1860, sight of this great seamark assured incoming vessels that they were directly on course for Skerries or Rush, or the more obscure inlets on this low, featureless coast. For us the mainland now gradually faded, for hereabouts a vessel on a passage north leaves the coast and the plains of royal Meath and begins to cut offshore.

SIX

Smugglers

DUBLIN GREW IN wealth as the eighteenth century advanced, becoming easily the second city in these islands. Liverpool, meanwhile, was the trading city for an expanding industrial population in Lancashire; the small Scottish ports adjoining the northern Irish Sea lay ready to supply Glasgow; Belfast was a growing market. No maritime region in Europe lay so richly open and ready to absorb smuggled goods, provided the point of supply and dispatch was conveniently located.

The Isle of Man might have been made for this. Surrounded by four rich hinterlands, their hills visible in clear weather, Manx harbours offered shelter to all ships on passage in the surrounding sea. It controlled its own taxes, and though English Revenue cutters could visit the island's ports, they could not interfere there. The island became a huge entrepôt for imported goods, its sea trade doubling in the ten years to 1751, then doubling again in the following decade.

An Irish report in 1725 described the Isle of Man as 'the great magazine of goods intended to be run and from whence they are – as opportunity offers – transported hither in small vessels'. An act of George I stated that 'great quantities of brandies, strong waters and spirits and also tobacco and other foods ... are secretly imported into this Kingdom in small ships or vessels or boats under the burden of 20 ton from the Isle of Man'.

English Customs officers, stationed in the Isle of Man from 1672, had little power. One frustrated officer in the 1730s noted seeing '30 sail of vessels loading brandy and other goods for Britain and Ireland', but the exporters could claim to be acting quite legally, and no Revenue officer could make an arrest until the goods were landed at their destination without paying local duties.

Hardly a secluded beach in Britain or Ireland is without a tale of cunning smugglers and their grateful, complacent customers; the ride-by-nights and the outflanked Revenue men. The statistics of this trade are largely guesswork, of course, but it has been suggested that in the eighteenth century one-third of goods like tea, brandy, spirits, wine and tobacco imported into Britain were smuggled. By the time the duty on tea was reduced in 1745, three-quarters of the brew for that nation of tea-drinkers was the smuggled article.

The Irish Parliament passed its own taxes and tariffs, but in reality its power was limited, subject to veto by Westminster. For understandable historical reasons, communities in Ireland generally lacked enthusiasm for the entire British mercantile system, and controls over such conventional necessities as tobacco and tea met with little favour. And the Irish Revenue service was beset by intimidation and corruption – an anker or two of brandy (an anker was eight gallons) could generate a great deal of goodwill in the service – while penalties against smuggling were not as severe as the draconian British code.

As incomes increased in the eighteenth century, smugglers found themselves tapping an expanding market. The Isle of Man became so popular that the French base at Nantes lost importance by comparison, though it would continue to get tea in from the East Indies through the port of L'Orient and stocks of brandy from Bordeaux and La Rochelle. By now, any inhabitant of the Isle of Man with a few pounds to spare could become a merchant, buy brandy and silks from France and rum from Jamaica, and fetch them into the island free of duty. He would use fast Manx clippers, handled by crews who knew every mile of the Irish Sea and ran their cargoes on to the quiet coasts of Ireland, southern Scotland, Lancashire, Cheshire and north Wales. The only tax on their activities was the 'Lord's due', a small imposition which was paid to the Atholl family, Lords of Man. Many a Manx family laid the basis of its prosperity and position in the days of 'the trade'. Cellars were specially constructed in houses in Peel, I was told a few years ago, and in Douglas, Castletown and Port St Mary.

In the end, a frustrated British government decided it must treat with the Atholl family and offered to buy the island's fiscal privileges for a compounded sum. The Duke of Atholl dallied over the offer for so long that the British Parliament passed an act giving Revenue cutters a right to stop and search at sea every boat arriving at the island. This measure was of doubtful legality, but might is often right, and it threw the Manx trading community into consternation. The Duke and Duchess finally bowed to British pressure and renounced all rights to the Lordship's revenues in exchange for a joint annuity of £2,000. The Revesting Act was passed in 1765, and smuggling was now virtually halted.

Merchants closed up shop and moved out. One set up a wine business in Ayr in Scotland, another tried his hand at smuggling from Guernsey. Guernsey, like Man, also had an anomalous constitutional position and was therefore a free port. Maurice O'Connell of Derrynane in Co. Kerry received a letter from his trading partner in 1771 advising him that there was 'no risk or difficulty' in shipping from Guernsey. 'All that is required is the master's oath not to land them in the British Dominions, and one guinea gets over that same.' The O'Connell family, like many other Irish merchants, were deeply involved in dubious imports. The trade did nothing to undermine their status, as Daniel O'Connell's political stature would show during his campaign for Catholic Emancipation in the nineteenth century.

Traditionally the people of Rush had close ties with the Isle of Man – there were said to be fifty Rush-owned vessels operating from the island in 1760 – and after 1765 it was well placed to take over a rich trade. Rush had several advantages. It was very close to Dublin, by far the best market for luxury goods. Its fishing fleet had benefited from subsidies provided by the Irish Parliament, with the result that they had well-found boats and crews familiar with the northern Irish Sea and the north and west coasts of Ireland. Boats from Skerries and Rush regularly sailed to the rich fishing grounds off islands like Inishbofin (where their crews earned a reputation as troublemakers who intimidated the local fishermen). Now voyaging through the North Channel in fast schooner-rigged wherries, the men of Rush could cloak a smuggling run to a nearby Scottish harbour by claiming that they were making for northern and western waters.

The Scottish market was particularly attractive to smugglers.

From the Isle of Man, contraband might be taken to Drummore, the most southerly village in Galloway near the notorious Race of Galloway. Later in our journey we would find ourselves there, a cold drizzle chilling our very bones, longing for a bottle of brandy. Goods might also cheer the inhabitants of Sandgreen, just below Gatehouse of Fleet, or be hidden on the Isle of Ardwall near by, a place honeycombed with caves. It was inhabited by the Higgins, who kept open house for 'the gentlemen' while an efficient train of pack-horses moved goods inland without delay. The Isle of Whithorn was a useful haven, and Manxman's Lake, an area of muddy flats under the woods near Kirkcudbright, probably got its name as an unloading point for smugglers.

Belfast was a ready market, and the contraband was carried inland to the growing industrial towns of the Lagan valley. There was no lack of secluded caves to hide goods on the shore, and many old houses also had their walls adapted to store contraband. In the coastal village of Annalong, the Church of Ireland rectory, of all places, had a long tunnel connecting it with a cave on the shore. The nearby Ballymartin has a dwelling named, significantly, 'The Hollow House'.

Smugglers answered to the market. When a general cut in the duty on tea, from 1s 9d to 4d per pound, failed to apply in Scotland, where the cup that cheered was still weighed down by heavy tax, the Edinburgh Customs Commissioners noted in December 1768 that nine vessels from Rush were expected to run cargoes soon to the Ayrshire or Galloway coasts. Sometimes the contraband would first be landed on the Irish coast, convenient for a quick run to Scotland, in coves around Portmuck, at Islandmagee near Larne or perhaps at Red Bay in Antrim. A Coastguard post was set up at Portmuck to combat 'the trade' – its cottages are still seen on a hill above the bay. The names of local smuggling families are remembered also. The McNeillys plied these waters in their ketch, the *Mary Stuart*. Magee, of Islandmagee, was a hugely successful smuggler, and after his death in Lisbon in 1724, his widow transferred his 'business' to Co. Kerry, where the family name lives on in the village of Portmagee, across the strait from Valentia Island.

Further down the east coast, Arthur Hughes of Greencastle near

Newry, Co. Down, was described by the head of the Irish Revenue service, Luke Mercer, as the greatest smuggler in the Kingdom. Hughes landed goods from anchorages off the coast, which were then taken inland on pack animals – surefooted mountain ponies known as 'shelties' – along routes like the Brandy Pad, which ran through the Mourne Mountains to the smugglers' hideaway of Hilltown.

Perhaps the most well-known smuggler in Rush was Jack Connor, nicknamed Jack the Bachelor. His nickname is a puzzle, as his epitaph in the old Kinnure church near Rush records that he was married and had five children. Born in Wexford in 1736, his family moved to Rush, and at the age of twelve Jack was taken on his first trip to the Isle of Man. It was the first of many visits there, and to ports all around the Irish Sea. Rush men smuggled cargoes into Scottish, Cornish and Welsh ports – to Aberystwyth, Cardigan and Newquay and many more secluded places, such as the valley mouth at Curntudu very close to Newquay.

Connor's career brought him prosperity and some standing; indeed, in later years he became the hero of a book used in Irish schools. I suppose it was inevitable that a smuggler should become a romantic character. It was a small step from smuggling Ireland's 'Wild Geese' to the Continent to join foreign armies, or bringing fugitive priests to and from Europe, to moving goods without paying duties. A man could easily be seen as risking his life in a cloak of patriotism and rebellion.

And they were tough, skilled seamen. The articulate and educated George O'Malley, writing in later years of his own smuggling, recorded that 'Irish smugglers generally used fast vessels skilfully handled, and the common Revenue cutter of those days had no chance against the beautiful Guernsey cutters and luggers that engaged in the Irish coast trade.'

Thus, in July 1767, the Irish Revenue heard that Jack and his brother Michael's two boats and a third vessel, 'a new famous cutter', were now at Gothenburg in Sweden 'loading with teas'. They were expected to arrive soon on the Co. Down coast between Annalong and Newcastle, 'determined to come in company and fight their way ... each with upwards of twenty men ... and do carry four guns on each of their decks, besides swivels and small arms'.

Revenue barges set out from Carlingford and from Dunleary and Malahide in the south, and assembled at Ardglass close to the entrance to the North Channel. They were prepared for battle. On the night of 6 August the tea ships – two wherries and a cutter – were spotted just after 2300 approaching from the north. The fighting began and went on until about 0400. One of the Revenue barges was boarded by the smugglers, who forced the crew to retreat to the cabin and then tried to scuttle the ship. However, the crew managed to save the boat by throwing ballast overboard, and it and another Revenue boat were towed into Carlingford. One Revenue man had been killed and three severely wounded in the fighting. And Jack Connor's own vessel did not successfully make Rush. It ran aground near Dundalk after a southward chase and was later bought at auction by the Revenue service.

The Connors fitted out a new generation of three-masted, fast cutters, doubling their tonnage at sea and greatly increasing their range, and in 1770 had their revenge by outgunning a Revenue vessel, the *Pelham*, in Beaumaris Bay in Anglesey. They forced her to run aground and then plundered her. But the end was near. Michael died in January 1772 off Red Bay, Co. Antrim, when several smugglers were killed in a bloody fight with a Revenue craft. He was buried near Glenarm, though the master of the Revenue ship later requested, unsuccessfully, that the body be taken up so that he, Captain Long, could obtain the reward on Michael's head.

Jack Connor was still at large and a powerful force in the Irish Sea. In April 1772, Sir Edward Newenham, Customs Collector for Dublin, suggested that he be given a pardon and allowed return to a peaceful life of fishing. He never did go back to sea, though. He died that June, aged just thirty-six.

IN JANUARY 1781, Dublin's *Freeman's Journal* complained that 'the swarms of privateers who hover around this island ... points out the absolute necessity for ... vessels of armed force to cruise between our harbours'. It would be several more years before such a force would be established on a standing basis, though, and in the meantime smugglers carried on their lucrative trade. 'Certain individuals,' the *Freeman's Journal* pointed out, 'not far from Bachelor's Walk or the Quays, etc, are part owners of these piratical vessels which are frequently manned by smugglers and fishermen, the inhabitants of Rush, Skerries and other small towns along the sea coasts of Fingale.' These men were 'Unnatural traitors to their country,' the *Journal* thundered, 'plundering harpies.'

But these were times of shifting loyalties. The merchant who had a share in smuggling might turn to legal trade in wartime, due to an increase in naval activity. A ship which privateered under British letters of marque might change its allegiance and its crew serve French or American privateers rather than return home and risk facing the press gang. On the sea, boats could change easily from legitimate trading or fishing to smuggling, privateering and piracy.

The strange career of Luke Ryan illustrates the ambiguities and conflicting loyalties of that time. The son of an Irish farmer from Kinnure, Co. Dublin, he was apprenticed to a boatbuilder in Rush but bought himself out of his apprenticeship and turned to smuggling, after acquiring a share in the 120-ton vessel, *Friendship*. He took out British letters of marque, which entitled him to privateer against the French and Americans, with the blessing of Dublin traders alarmed at the raids of the American privateer, John Paul Jones, in the Irish Sea. Ryan set sail at the end of February 1779. The *Freeman's Journal* reported that 'The little fishing village of Rush has already fitted out four vessels, one of them [the *Friendship*] now being at Rodgerson's Quay, ready to sail, being completely armed and manned, carrying fourteen carriage guns and sixty of as brave hands as any in Europe.'

They returned to Rush in April with a rich cargo of contraband which was sold at Fingal, but a row developed as to how the booty should be shared. Three of the crew deserted and revealed to the Inspector of Customs in Dublin that 'the cutter was intended to be taken to Dunkirk, to be repaired and fitted out as a privateer to be used against Great Britain and Ireland'. The Revenue acted promptly, and while Ryan and his crew were celebrating ashore, the *Friendship* was seized and moored at Poolbeg. Ryan's partner and the crew on board were arrested and imprisoned in the Black Dog prison at Ringsend, but under cover of darkness they broke out, rejoined the rest of Ryan's crew and, using armed wherries which had sailed in from Skerries, recaptured their ship and sailed back to Rush.

The *Friendship* then set sail for the sheltered anchorage of St Tudwall's Roads behind the Lleyn peninsula south of Holyhead, where Ryan put the nine captured Revenue officers ashore and gave each of them a guinea to help them get home. Now he sailed for Dunkirk to seek French letters of marque. American agents were buying and selling privateering ships at the cosmopolitan French port, and Ryan transferred his vessel to an American, John Torris, and took on a new captain, Stephen Marchant. The crew of seventy-two included most of the Irishmen who had fetched her from Rush, but the vessel was registered now at the port of Boston and all aboard were sworn in as citizens of the United States.

Over the next three months, the *Friendship* captured or held for ransom about thirty ships, and sailed into Rush at the end of that cruise with apparent impunity, for a Dublin newspaper noted that 'the same evening nine mariners from Rush went aboard'.

By March of 1780, she was under the command of Patrick Dowling of Rush. On 8 March, Dowling was in the Irish Sea, where he captured two of the important post-office packets serving Holyhead. Ryan, meanwhile, commissioned a larger cutter in Boulogne and asked the agent, Torris, to secure for him an American letter of marque. Torris wrote to Benjamin Franklin, who was then ambassador to the Court of Versailles, hoping that 'the brave Mr Ryan' could be given rank in the new American Navy. For good measure Ryan wrote too, letting Franklin know that 'the American cause I regard as my own'. Franklin contacted the Marine Intendant of Dunkirk, and Ryan subsequently received a commission for his new cutter, *Fearnot*. Soon the Lord Lieutenant would be issuing a warning in Dublin that Ryan was at sea 'and intends to cruise off the Irish coast'. Indeed he was, taking several prizes, but in April 1781 he was captured by two powerful British warships near the Firth of Forth. He had been raiding in *La Colagne*, a ship of thirty-two guns with a crew of 250, flying the French colours.

After Ryan's arrest, the French authorities claimed that he was a French subject, naturalised in October 1780 by King Louis XVI. The British replied that 'no new allegiance can extinguish the original one', and King George III declared the French demand 'totally inadmissible'. Ryan was conveyed to the Old Bailey in London to stand trial for piracy. His French and American crew were released in exchange for British prisoners, but Ryan and his Irish sailors were charged with high treason and the piratical taking of vessels.

Ryan gave his name as 'Luc Ryan' and insisted on speaking French, though his command of his 'mother tongue' was not impressive. His counsel claimed that his father served in 'Dillon's Irish brigade' and that Luke had been born in the village of Gravelin in northern France, but on his father's death was fetched as an infant to be reared in Ireland and later apprenticed to a shipwright there. However, witnesses were brought over from Rush, and two first cousins gave evidence that they knew him as a child. His fate was sealed when his ship's mate made a deal with the prosecution and gave evidence against him. At the end of a three-week trial, the jury found Ryan guilty of piracy and treason, and he was sentenced to be 'caged' at Wapping Execution Dock. After being partly strangled, he would be locked in a cage and lowered into the Thames, to be drowned by the rising tide. His body would then 'be hanged in chains in some conspicuous part of the coast of Essex or Kent'.

Politics now entered the scene. While Ryan was lodged in Newgate Gaol, the Cabinet asked George III for a ten-day adjournment of the sentence. The King agreed unwillingly. He saw no reason for mercy, and he detested his Prime Minister, Charles Fox, who wanted to end the French war and grant greater independence to Ireland. When Ryan was told of the adjournment on the morning of 14 May 1782, 'he and another convict were on their knees, with a Roman Catholic clergyman praying with them'.

The adjournment was extended. Ryan remained in custody. By now England and France were close to negotiating an armistice, and the French, and perhaps the Americans also, bargained for Ryan's life. The Anglo-French War finally came to an end on 14 February 1783. The following month Ryan was handed 'His Majesty's Free Pardon'.

Ryan, however, faced a claim for '£435 and upwards' from his American agent, John Torris, who pressed for repayment, despite pressure from the French naval authorities to forego the debt. As a result, Ryan was not actually freed until February 1784. He settled in Hampshire and took legal action against Torris, the French government, and his bank at Roscoff for money which he maintained was owed to him (some $70,000). He was declared bankrupt in 1788. The following year Ryan was arrested for failing to pay £200 to doctors who had inoculated him and his family against smallpox. A few months later, he died in prison of septicamia.

King Louis' letter confirming Ryan as a Dunkirk skipper – that is, a privateer – declared that he had captured some eighty English ships, not counting those he sank. It is not surprising that when England was again at war with France in 1793, the Dublin authorities at once took the precaution of 'sending a sea party of Horse' to Rush and Skerries 'to unrig the cutters in those harbours to prevent their sailing to the ports of the enemy from which (as was the case in the last war) they might, under the sanction of hostile commissions, commit piratical depredations on their country'.

SMUGGLING BECAME more centralised and sophisticated after 1815, when the Napoleonic wars ended at Waterloo. Ships carried genuine as well as fictitious Bills of Lading. L'Orient, which competed with Guernsey in supplying American tobacco to the trade, was particularly generous in providing convenient papers. They would certify, for example, that a vessel bound for Ireland was simply returning to its home port in ballast, without any significant cargo aboard.

Smuggling into Ireland was mainly in spirits, tea and tobacco. Wine was not smuggled in quantity. Onshore, the duty was high but not prohibitive, and smugglers found it an unattractive cargo – shipped in bulky hogsheads and demanding long credit to carry sufficiently large stocks. Spirits, mainly French, were popular – possibly one-third of the brandy consumed in Ireland was smuggled – and some silks and fine linens came in also, though the amount was exaggerated. Tea, with its high value in relation to its weight and bulk, was the smuggler's favourite, until the drastic fall in duties in the later eighteenth century.

Tobacco was big business. All Virginian, it bore a four shilling duty per pound, and cost from eight pence to a shilling a pound onshore. It was estimated that over three and a half million pounds of tobacco came into Ireland illegally in 1819 alone. Armed vessels, laden with 1,000 half-bales of tobacco each weighing sixty-five pounds, crewed by fifty to seventy men, would bring the cargo, often from Flushing in Holland. The group of smugglers, called 'a Company', sold the cargo through a local agent, who made out tickets for half a pound of tobacco and supplied known dealers and distributors. A great deal of tobacco went to bonded manufacturers of finished tobacco, who bought small individual quantities so as to avoid detection by tax inspectors. Any remaining tickets were openly put on sale in local shops.

Smugglers supplied the goods demanded. The Customs Records of the Scottish port of Campbeltown in October 1785 note that '68 stone of wool was attempted to be exported to Ireland by Irishmen in return for linen, raw skin and tea'. In 1818 a cask of gunpowder was declared in a boat's manifest as 'sugar candy', and in June of that year twenty-one black cattle are described as 'put ashore at Carrickfergus'. Late in the next year 'An extraordinary quantity of potatoes and number of ships [were] shipped to Ireland from Scotland and suspected that whisky will be bought [there] for smuggling in return.' The port had a long-running relationship with smugglers. In January 1771, Customs recorded that the *Freeman* from Dundalk had carried off Revenue officers and put them ashore 'at the back of Dover'.

Fortunes in 'the trade' improved further after the Napoleonic wars when there were fewer English naval vessels at sea. In 1819, however, smugglers found themselves facing a new opponent, the Preventive Water Guard. The Water Guard was taken in hand by Sir James Dobrain, who, following his success in England, was sent to reorganise the service along the coast of Co. Cork. He set up stations on the coast which maintained contact with cruisers at sea through a signalling system, including for example using rockets at night-time. Dobrain was so successful that smugglers on the southern Irish coast were obliged to switch to working further east. The Water Guard, in turn, was extended from Waterford along the 300 mile-long east coast running up to the Giant's Causeway in Antrim. Dobrain became Comptroller General based in Dublin.

In 1822 the Preventive Water Guard was renamed the Coastguard, and within two years a line of stations defended the coastlines. Each station was manned by eight or ten men, and a group of about a dozen stations was under the overall control of an Inspecting Commander. An armed guard patrolled at night, one lot of men using the station boat – usually a six-oar galley and sometimes a smaller gig – the others walking the shore. Coastguard staff were originally housed in temporary accommodation in the local community, but eventually most men lived in 'watch and boathouses' now 'separate and unconnected with the people of the country'. For wives it must indeed have been a lonely life. And for the Coastguard men, who were seen as representatives of the Crown, it was often a dangerous life in the Ireland of the 1850s and 1860s. After the Fenian riots of 1864, it was common to have buildings fitted with gun loops and wrought-iron shutters.

The Irish smuggler, Captain George O'Malley, gives us a vivid picture of his battles with the Coastguard. Waiting near the Isle of Man on a December night in 1823, 'with low canvas set, good lookouts and keeping clear of vessels until dawn ... That evening I made a dash for Lambay Island and got in close to the old fort or tower near Rush. I sent the longboat on shore with 200 half bales [of tobacco] and seven of a crew and the spotsman, J. Taylor. [The men had] seven loaded blunderbusses at their command and as many cutlasses hanging at their sides and twice the number of loaded pistols ready for a passage at arms with the Coastguards, if required.'

They landed without opposition and Taylor got into Rush unnoticed. He returned with fifty men to unload the cargo under the cover of dark. 'For the last time another party came to the beach and these began to unload in great silence without uttering a word and, just as one of the party was taking the last bale out, one of the crew's eyes met his cuff and saw the anchor button on his sleeve.

'"Coastguards, by Jingo," he said. "Come; launch our boat at once." Despite the tide having ebbed they got the boat afloat. The

Coastguards slapped away at them, but to no purpose, and so there were none hurt. There was no fire returned, which was my order given to my men; not to use their arms but when required and by no means to lose their liberty or risk their lives without resistance.'

They rowed back to the ship and were hoisted aboard, when they realised that Taylor had been left ashore. O'Malley sent the cutter back to the beach. They found a mob on the shore, belabouring the Coastguard officers. 'The twelve sailors,' he recorded, 'sang out to the mob who seemed to show no quarter to the poor Coastguards who were only doing their duty ... which was quite natural as we all work to support life.'

The land party had retaken the tobacco from the Revenue men, but O'Malley's men 'sang out by the powers of powder and ball that any man who would strike a Coastguard another blow, they would strike out his brains.' The smugglers took the tobacco from the 'beaten and battered Coastguard, the chief of whom I afterwards knew well and who was a civil and agreeable Englishman, well nigh being killed. Taylor and Mr Thomas Doyle, son of Captain Doyle of Rush, once known as one of the most celebrated smugglers on the Irish coast, returned on board. Mr Doyle was once agent of the Leinster coast.'

As they sailed away, the Coastguard stations along the coast sent up blue lights and rockets. O'Malley had time to admire the scene. 'The coast looked beautiful and they could best be seen by us as we were in the bay. I admired the blue lights and rockets passing in a double direction from where the first were set off, right and left as it were, making the darksome atmosphere look brilliantly grand and beautiful. Our sail was made to get out of the way – and that as quick as possible.'

But he was not out of the woods yet. The next day they had another chase. 'I must say there were eight or ten cutters assembled to run us down or seize us by hook or crook. We were continually hunted by them till at last they would not attempt another chase but dodged along the shore.'

When the moon returned, O'Malley felt he could not safely land now, 'owing to the many and constant lookouts by sea and land. Finally I made a rush again for the Isle of Man and took up my old station there till I got a strong wind to take me in a few hours once more into Lambay. I got close to the Rock of Bills and I landed 200 bales of tobacco and, after that, I put off to sea before I would be seen by the Coastguard, and the men were all taken and paid for their trouble. I got on different nights into the Bay, notwithstanding the vigilance by sea and land.'

The Coastguard service was transferred to the control of the Admiralty in 1856, and its job was redefined as coastal defence, to be a naval reserve in wartime and to protect the Revenue. As smuggling declined, so did the Coastguard's role in combatting illicit trade. The achievements of the service in also watching over and protecting seafarers should not be forgotten – on innumerable occasions it was a Coastguard man who spotted a ship in danger. The de-manning of all lighthouses and the risks of arms and drugs smuggling has made it more vital than ever that there be watchers on the coasts today.

SEVEN

Through the Mannin Mists

I N ONE OF those Howth pubs not yet targeting the tourist –
not a fishing net or plastic lobster in sight – a retired
trawlerman, rheumy and loquacious, warned us not to arrive
at the Hellyhunter Buoy at the entrance to Carlingford Lough
while an ebb tide was running out.

'Ye'll never make it the five miles up.'

I was about to ask who Hellyhunter was but Joan had moved his
attention to the Isle of Man, and with gathering enthusiasm he
began telling her of tidal ranges that would require her to mount
ladders that rose forty rungs from deck to quay.

Now we were sailing slowly, ambling these last miles to let that
tide run slack. A barrier of steep and rugged hills emerged from
the haze, in graduated shades of blue. These were the hills of the
Cooley peninsula, whose northern slopes run down to Carlingford
Lough. We could see a gap inland, away to the west, and beyond
that again the shape of Slieve Gullion.

Over there is the Gap of the North. The Dublin–Belfast road
runs through it, just as a road from the ancient capital of Tara did
2,000 years ago. The road led to Dunseverick on the north Antrim
coast and was used by tribes from Ireland – the Scotti – when
they set up a rulership in the early centuries of the Christian era
which extended from Ireland up to the Isle of Mull. Cross-
fertilisation of the Irish and Scots goes back a very long way.

Soon the ranks of the Mourne mountains appeared. I counted
twenty hilltops, arranged like splendid pyramids. Rising out of a
flat landscape, they make the finest seamark on the east coast of
Ireland. When Frank Cowper sailed this way a century ago, he
found 'the colouring, shape and abruptness' of the heights around
Carlingford 'as fine as anything I have seen in the Highlands'.

We had arrived a little early – the weakening tide was still rippling against us along the side of the big Hellyhunter Buoy. Engine on, we made towards the 100-feet-high Haulbowline lighthouse, which lies towards the Northern Ireland side of the entrance to Carlingford Lough. Here it is a mile wide and cluttered with reefs so we were glad of a secure seamark. In earlier years 'ships could lie in here defended of all winds if it were not for the difficulty and danger of the entrance,' Gerald Boate, Oliver Cromwell's Dutch physician, wrote in his *Natural History of Ireland* in 1645, 'the mouth being full of rocks, both blind ones and others, betwixt which the passages are very narrow, whereby it cometh that this harbour is very little frequented by great ships.'

The scale of the fjord within was a surprise. It was two miles up to the quay of Greenore, which looked across a mile of water to Northern Ireland's Greencastle on the opposite shore. Just across the notional mid-lough border, in the lee of an islet, a Royal Navy corvette lay snugly anchored. No life was visible on board, but large rubber launches were tethered to its side.

Cowper had described Greenore as 'busy and new with its steamboat quay and railway hotel'. A local man, Richard Hayward, recalled the bustling port of his youth, and the railway which ran down from Newry until its closure in 1951.

'Long before that the life went out of Greenore when the fine steamers were withdrawn which plied between the little port and Holyhead, a popular route for people who wished to reach London early in the morning. Nothing is more mournful now,' he wrote, 'than the deserted quays and works built in 1867 at great expense that stand in a desolation of weed-hung masonry and massive timbers.' His boyhood memory was of 'bustling, activity, rattling trucks, whirring cranes and sudden startling bursts of steam'. But things change again, or so it seemed as we passed close to a prosperous quayside and lively-looking village.

Greenore was the first purpose-built railway port in Ireland, the key to a new route from Belfast to Holyhead, opened by the London and North Western Railway (LNWR) in 1873. The Railway Age established a new era in Irish Sea crossings. Ships were concerned with tides, railways with timetables, and while the two did always not fit hand in glove, it was natural that they would develop together. As railway companies began to spread rapidly on land, they also ran their own ships and put money into dredging channels and building deep-water quays to berth them.

Holyhead was a special port for traffic across the Irish Sea, the first to offer fixed timetable services from England to Ireland. Indeed, the service from Holyhead was run by the Admiralty until 1848, after which the City of Dublin Steam Packet Company acquired the contract, and on terms generous enough to give a standard of speed and comfort probably unequalled in the world at the time – certainly better than anything in the English Channel. By mid-century several ports in north-west England had also begun to increase trade by improving their harbours and connecting them to the railways. The railway companies, for their part, saw profit in the Irish Sea. The Maryport and Carlisle Railway in Cumbria aimed to increase coal exports. Fleetwood, Morecambe, Barrow and Silloth – in the Solway Firth – developed to serve the Irish trade. Preston and Whitehaven expanded. Even more isolated ports realised that, with the advent of the railway, cargo and passengers could reach the coast more easily.

Late-nineteenth-century steam-power increased the web of communication. A daily service ran, for example, from Morecombe Harbour near the Lake District to Belfast, and twice a week to Derry. The watering place of Silloth, far up the Solway Firth, became linked to the Isle of Man and Dublin. Tidal problems remained – after all, the tidal maximum rise and fall at Morecombe is over twenty-eight feet – and this disrupted the routine of transportation, but by the later years of the century rail and sea had been irrevocably tied together. The benefits of fast communication spread outwards, helping fishing ports like Kilkeel to speed huge quantities of fish to the British urban markets in the herring boom of the 1870s and 1880s.

We were approaching the village of Carlingford. Pat had the binoculars focused on the ruins of the great castle built, in part, by King John in about 1210. Across the lough, in Northern Ireland, a stronghold of similar design and vintage stood above Greencastle.

'Carlingford marina is about a mile on from the village,' he called, 'just under a slope of trees.'

'I see bare trees – maybe masts.'

'Masts; not a doubt.'

'We must get around a long shoal between here and Carlingford,' I said. 'We go on and then come back around it.'

I throttled right down to allow a small trawler ahead of us pass by, but he responded by slowing down and turning towards us – a strange decision as he was working with a trawl cable extending from his stern. He increased his speed, heading at us, and I swung hurriedly away. It was the nautical equivalent of being jostled off the pavement. Perhaps it was just paranoia which made me think of our British ensign flying at our stern.

Soon, however, we were enfolded in the rural tranquillity of Carlingford's marina. 'We expected twenty boats up from Howth for the May Bank Holiday,' said the girl who waved us to a pontoon where a Labrador swung his tail in welcome, 'but only four or five made it in the bad northerly.'

The little marina had an informal atmosphere, and behind the village a tangle of early-summer fields and woods climbed along the country road to Newry and into the mountainside. Hills of dappled glory stood all around, a very heaven for anyone who likes to tramp in quiet, unspoilt countryside.

The whole of this Cooley peninsula, which stretches its flank along Carlingford Lough, is associated with the legendary hero Cúchulainn and the potent saga of the Cattle Raid of Cooley. People in these parts can still point to various features of the landscape and tell you of their connection with Cúchulainn's feats of courage and strength.

We had time next day to explore the village, the neat drying harbour and the twisting lanes that hint of the fortified town that once had charters from King Edward II, from Kings Henry IV and VII and from Elizabeth and King James I. A Royal Mint was established in Carlingford in 1467, and one of the town gates still straddles a narrow street, surmounted by a small chamber known as the Tholsel. There are plans to restore one of the decorated houses near the water which wealthy merchants built in the sixteenth century in a burst of civic pride.

Carlingford village woos the visitor but does not seem to have been thrown off balance by the demands of tourism. As we walked along the seafront, the Adventure Centre spilled a dozen wetsuit-clad French and Irish children on to the beach for water polo, with canoes replacing ponies. Dinghies were already working up the northern shore, looking like a cloud of white butterflies. It would be a challenging afternoon for the Dundalk Sailing Club, who had travelled from their base just ten miles away for an afternoon of sailing. Lunch would come first, a genial, extrovert man carrying food into a large marquee told us. He followed Pat's gaze as we watched a flight of sail-boarders spread their colourful wings in the breezy sunlight.

'It's a safe lough here for everyone,' he said. Was there a slight twist to his smile as he added, 'After all, we have that nice British warship to look after us.'

We set sail on the afternoon ebb, bound now for the fishing port of Ardglass, twenty miles north-east of the Hellyhunter Buoy and the Irish harbour nearest the Isle of Man. Ebbing currents and a full-bosomed jib hurried us along the coastal strip under the Mournes, where the fishing ports of Kilkeel and Annalong dominate the fisheries of the Irish Sea.

Everywhere, however, the trawler fleets decline, many boats decommissioned under the European Union's rationalisation schemes. Now that fishing in the Irish Sea is threatened with virtual closure, it is difficult to grasp that hunting and processing and selling King Herring once gave employment to thousands of men and women in harbours all along the coast. A survey in 1877 showed 876 fishing boats based in Howth; in 1912 Kilkeel dispatched 30,000 barrels of salted herring to Russia. Harvesting the Irish Sea was a free-for-all in the years of the great herring boom. Of the boats operating out of Howth only a minority – about one-quarter – were Irish owned and crewed. A quarter were Scottish, a quarter owned in the Isle of Man and a further quarter came from Cornwall. Traditionally a fisherman competes with other fishermen, but their common territory was the Irish Sea, and an industry working on this scale meant levels of social contact which spread from coast to coast. Fishermen's everyday migrations created a network of news, gossip and social interaction long before our age of instant communication. This contact is not so readily preserved today, in an era of fishing quotas and frontiers patrolled by radar and naval corvettes.

As we passed the harbour piers at Kilkeel, I recalled how we had come down this coast some few years ago, *Sarakiniko's* spluttering engine dying as the wind faded and darkness closed in. Harbour raises images of shelter, and the dock lights of Kilkeel lay only a mile off, but it was a nail-biting time for the tide was pulling us away as the mainsail drooped in the last breaths of wind. We edged in as Saturday night became Sunday morning. Nobody was about. We lay against a silent trawler in the empty millpond of the dock. On the gable of a fish shed near by, King William was painted victorious upon a prancing charger, white in the arc lights above the ritual graffiti and the Union Jack. At dawn the engine fired long enough to free us from the oily water and a sense of grit and menace. Outside, a lovely morning breeze swelled the sails. It was a year of particular violence, and we had felt it unlikely that an engineer would be available on the Sabbath for a Dublin-bound yacht.

It was curiously heartening later to come on a 'Journal of the Mourne Local Studies Group' and read the memoirs of Francie Cunningham, which gave a human face to the place. He was born here in 1918, one of six brothers and two sisters. 'A large family,' he wrote, 'but not unusual for those days. During the First World War my father served in oil tankers and I can remember him showing me his medals which he kept in a drawer in the bedroom.'

He records a family linked to the sea – brother Pat in the Royal Navy, serving on the aircraft carrier HMS *Furious*; another brother, Jim, who 'fished the herring'. And there was Thomas, 'the intellectual, who excelled in copperplate writing and worked in shipbuilding in Barrow-in-Furness and eventually in the fish factory in Kilkeel'. Another brother became a local fisheries officer, while Dermot went to New Zealand, where he built a successful fish exporting business. He pays tribute to his sisters, too, and to the aunt who took over care of the family after his mother's death, 'in days when there was no State help, no home help or family allowance. She carried on with her mammoth task without any thought of recompense ...'

Cunningham traces a vivid picture of life on these waters. 'When I was sixteen,' he writes, 'I worked with my father on Carlingford Lough, tending to the lighthouse and buoys. There were three lighthouse keepers who all resided in the cottages in

Greencastle. Their rota was ten days on and four off. Our job was to provide the lighthouse [Haulbowline] with provisions, including fresh water which came in wooden casks. Tuesdays and Fridays were the days designated to supply and relieve the keepers but it did not always work out, especially in the winter months, when the weather was foul.' He and his father maintained the buoys also, notably the Whistler and the Hellyhunter lights. 'The Hunter was a carbide buoy which operated on the same principle as the bicycle lamp, namely, water dripping on to the dry carbide and emitting a gas through the jet burner which was ignited.' They visited the light 'every so often' to change the spent fuel and put in a fresh charge.

Men from all around the coast had boyhoods like this, learning to work at sea under the tutelage of their fathers. When I read Francie Cunningham's memoir, I thought how his story enriched the Irish personality. Such accounts of people's real lives help re-focus our thinking about borders, communities and the allegiances we give to each.

The soft stern wind was beginning to fail us as Kilkeel drew astern. 'Still sixteen miles to Ardglass,' I said, 'let's have some engine.' We left the jib up though it flapped and snapped in the hesitant breeze. An outline in grey became discernible on the horizon – our first sight of the Isle of Man thirty-seven miles away. We crossed the ten-mile-wide mouth of Dundrum Bay as shafts of sunlight played like searchlights on the hills. Newcastle was in there, 'a favourite and pretty watering place with a dry harbour,' declared Cowper long ago, 'where, for those who are energetic, Slieve Donard is a perpetual playground.'

We had clipped on the automatic steering, its little two-foot arm attached at a right angle to the helm and moving every few moments to hold the approaching lighthouse of St John's Point just off our port bow. I touched a button and it obediently altered our course ten degrees to starboard to take us away from a reef-strewn promontory marked by a lighthouse painted in black-and-yellow bands like a wasp. It has a sectored light, so that if we were approaching it at night but had slipped further into shallow Dundrum Bay, the beam ahead would have been flashing red, a warning to turn at once to starboard into the deeper water offshore.

It made me think of the ship *Great Britain* from Liverpool, en route to New York on a night in September 1846. St John's Point lies on a line from Liverpool which passes close to the southern tip of the Isle of Man. The navigator on the *Great Britain* did not spot the island as they went past, and so much did he underestimate the speed of the great ship that when he saw St John's flash to starboard he assumed it was the Isle of Man. He ordered a turn to get around it, and ran the massive vessel on to the shelving sands of Dundrum Bay. Fortunately she was salvaged without much damage.

We opened Killough Bay now. 'Unattractive to any kind of craft and harbours none; very ancient and clogged with mud,' declared my 1982 *Irish Sea Pilot* by Dr Kemp, which I still keep on board for sentimental reasons. Convenient Ardglass, with a small marina now, was a little over a mile further on.

A local landowner developed Killough in the late eighteenth century, giving it 'a strong key where ships may now lie very safe ... a decent church and a barracks for two or three troops of horse'. Thus in 1744, Killough, with 'fifteen ships belonging to the port and about twenty fishing boats', was the export point for grain, especially barley, and potatoes, cattle, flax and kelp. Coal, as in so many places, was the main import, but the local countryside also bought in salt and tar, hardware, limestone and paper. The life of the small coastal skippers who plied their trade from here was described by R.H. Buchanan in a contribution to a maritime history conference for the Institute of Irish Studies in 1989:

'William Donnan's routine was to carry in up to seventy-five tons of coal, usually from Whitehaven eighty miles away in Cumbria. His would be a round trip of about three weeks, including the loading time. Occasionally he would carry other cargoes, such as oats to Glasgow or barley to Dundalk, but the high days of coastal trading had declined by [the mid-nineteenth] century and, by its end, a branch railway connected Killough to Belfast and coastal trade fell away.' Buchanan himself recalls seeing the last cargo of Whitehaven coal being discharged at the small quay in the 1930s.

Small-scale shipping on the Irish Sea brought personal links as well as trade. 'In my youth,' Buchanan says, 'several men and women in Killough were descendants of such marriages ... but those old connections, built on trade, disappeared with the small ships sailed by men like William Donnan.'

Five or six trawlers lay silent by the quay as we nosed in to the marina at nearby Ardglass. A port since medieval times, the ruins of the village castles (Ardglass has five or six) rose as black, rugged shapes above the streets. It was hard to believe that this was once one of the busiest fishing ports in Ulster. A census in 1830 gave it thirty-nine fully decked vessels and 100 half-decked, sixty-nine open sailboats and 300 rowing boats. Some 2,440 of the village population claimed to be fishermen. I had yellowing sepia photographs showing it all: the thicket of masts at the quay, nets and fish boxes and gangs of women who gutted the catch at astonishing speed. Even as late as the 1920s, Ardglass had fourteen canning firms and still sent twenty tons of fresh herring around Ulster every day, by rail, lorry and hawkers' carts.

The berthing master on night duty in the quiet marina office sympathised with us when we told him the discipline of the tides obliged us to leave again before breakfast – earnest calculations at the chart table had indicated that we must be off the Isle of Man by early afternoon, before the tide fell too far. Otherwise we would pitch and roll at a visitor's buoy off the beach at Peel, just clear of the breakers, waiting for a rising tide to bring us directly to the quays in the inner harbour. It is a remarkable harbour, built in the nineteenth century to hold over 600 fishing boats – I have found no statistic which more vividly illustrates the decline of an entire industry.

But though we could not tarry in Ardglass, neither could we leave without inspecting the impressive galleys of the Ardglass Viking Association on display in the marina car park.

'I expect they challenge the Isle of Man,' I said. 'Building longships is a strong tradition there.'

We walked around them, admiring the lovely curve of the gunwales tapering symmetrically to points at bow and stern, the slim ship's great sweeping high ends. These boats, the successors of the original Viking craft, were the common vessels of these waters right into the late sixteenth century. As well as being a working boat, the galley was a lethal weapon in the hands of men like the lords of the Scottish Isles, or Grace O'Malley, the sea raider of Co.

Mayo. Swift and deadly, they would chase and board cargo vessels or ships of war when they were becalmed. But when those ships acquired broadside guns which could smash the thin scantlings of a galley with roundshot, the age of the galley ended.

The vessels we were examining were probably the much smaller version of the galley, called birlins. They were parked on low-loaders, which provoked Pat's scorn. He felt that Ardglass youth should wear horned helmets, encase their nether limbs in cross-gartered hose, and set their prows on a course for that island which was Viking-ruled for 300 years. A few days later we saw all-girl crews pulling on their long oars past the beaches of the Isle of Man, looking ready to take on allcomers.

WE HAD planned to leave at 0800 for the thirty-three mile crossing to Peel, but when I looked out at 0600 on sunshine, smooth water and the whiskered face of a seal, I thought why not leave now? The crew were awake and took the suggestion very well. Before we cast off, Pat looked aloft and called to Joan: 'Shall I remove the Irish tricolour or is the skipper making some point?'

A yacht flies its host's national flag at the starboard crosstrees while it is visiting another country. Such had been the case since we arrived in the Republic's territorial waters off Arklow. It came down rather hastily now.

'Next we will need an Isle of Man flag,' Joan said. 'It's an independent country with its own parliament.'

'Are you saying it's a foreign country?'

'No, not quite – Queen Elizabeth is the present Lord of Man. And anyhow,' she added, 'we do fly a Scottish flag when we sail in Scotland. I think we should have one for the Isle of Man.'

'It's all a matter of courtesy,' I said, 'not strict law. But we may be able to buy one on the island.'

The Isle of Man flag – three legs extending from the centre of a circle – is extremely old, and, like the swastika which it resembles, was first used in Sicily, where it represented the island's triangular shape. It probably derives from a design representing the wheels of the sun, the seat of light and power – hence the circle. It may be that the Vikings came in contact with the design in Sicily and brought it to the Isle of Man. Later, some historians say, Alexander III, King of Scotland, adopted the symbol when he seized the Isle of Man from the Vikings in 1265.

These speculations lacked compelling interest at six in the morning, as Ardglass faded astern and we engined gently on, sprayhood lowered to make it easier to spot the occasional pot buoy. The Isle of Man, some thirty miles long and about eleven miles wide, had hidden itself since last evening. We knew it was prone to the Mannin Mists, sudden veils produced by the ancient sea god Manannan Mac Lir so as to confuse invaders. Peel is the only sheltered harbour on the Irish-facing side and lies close up to St Patrick's Isle, traditionally the birthplace of Manx Christianity. Now it is a place of grassy mounds and ancient ruins protected from the surf by towers and curtain walls, its eight acres connected to the mainland by a very short causeway.

Tradition claims that the first missionaries sent over by St Patrick landed here in about 450 AD. Its earliest Christian ruins are St Patrick's church and a round tower designed, as in Ireland, to act both as belfry and refuge.

The Vikings arrived here in the ninth century and made 'Mann and the Isles' a kingdom that extended throughout the Irish Sea and up to the Western Isles of Scotland. A forthright Norse ruler, Magnus Barefoot, arrived here in 1098 to stamp his authority on the new Viking territory and used St Patrick's Isle as a base for attacks on Ireland. The 'peel tower' he built gave its name to the settlement he established by the local river. Seven Viking burials have been uncovered on St Patrick's Isle: one of a lady equipped for the afterlife with a Scandinavian-type necklace, a cooking spit and a workbox filled with needles. She may have died in the second half of the tenth century.

Norse rule lasted until 1265. The Scots succeeded them, and then the Lancashire family, the Stanleys (later the Derbys), were installed in the Isle of Man by King Henry IV in 1405. Their links to the island lasted nearly 400 years. It was they who built the castle on the islet whose long ramparts create such a romantic skyline today. Close by, among the bobbing seapinks, is the ruined cathedral of St Germain, reminiscent of the church on Iona and named after one of the early Irish missionaries.

The sea remained flat, the swell suggesting a gentle breathing. Landscape emerged above scarves of haze, shadows indicating valleys and combes, hills ribbed by stone walls. Well before noon we turned a pier, passed an esplanade and curve of beach and puttered down the long scruffy harbour under St Patrick's Isle. Much of the quay space was lined by trawlers, several being gutted and welded, sanded and painted in the prospect of retirement as houseboats: a sign of the time. Where an iron ladder seemed convenient we edged in, the red flicker of our depth finder indicating ten feet of water. It was half an hour after high tide. The level would fall another sixteen feet, so in a few hours we should be sitting, sedately we hoped, on level sand.

Bikers in black leather roared along the far quayside occasionally or posed self-consciously for their girlfriends' cameras. The bikers are a traditional, if noisy, part of the scene – the Tourist Trophy motorcycle race for which the island is famous has been a part of life here since 1907.

The drizzle which was approaching waited until we had finished a cockpit lunch of tomato soup, blue cheese and beer, and then Joan, quailing at the height of the ladder, stood up and asked for a volunteer to climb it close behind her.

A yachtsman's first step ashore usually leads him on a pilgrimage in search of food and fuel, a launderette and a telephone. Here, I told the crew, the priority was to meet a Manx cat. We found one within half an hour, stretched lazily in a glimmer of sunshine.

When it stood up we could see a short, deep body and rather long back legs. Perhaps its head was bigger and more rounded than one might expect. The eyes also seemed bigger, and it walked away in such a very stilted fashion that I recalled reading that people once believed a Manx to be a cross between a cat and a hare; they can even have a hopping gait. Promiscuous living led, of course, to tailed and half-tailed cats, though a 'cattery' in Douglas tries to cultivate pure-bred ambassadors for the island. The resulting litters will contain kittens with normal tails, some with short tails (called 'the stumpies') and some without any tails at all: the rumpies. And, though we met four or five rumpies, we had no chance to observe if they really do fight by springing over an opponent to spar with all four claws. My crew refused to check this, or to try to find out if a rumpie has a hollow at the end of its spine where a tail would normally begin.

As to the Manx cat's origin, opinions differ. One is that, as Noah finished loading the Ark, two cats who were playing carelessly outside sprang for the boat just in time – but lost their tails as the door was slammed shut behind them. Few believe that they resulted from a liaison with a rabbit or a hare: the general opinion is that they are a mutation of the common short-haired British cat which arrived two or three hundred years ago. We found few Manx people who would agree that the cats are also found in several parts of Asia and could have arrived on the island as sailors' pets.

After these encounters I chanced upon a shop window displaying a notice for the Cat Protection Trust. It was set up to offer veterinary care and 'life in good comfortable surroundings' to any Manx cat who needed it 'because of appearance, handicap, medical or social problems, or age or timidity'.

The Isle of Man's has greatly changed since the days of mass-market bucket-and-spade holidays before the Second World War, but I felt it had changed reassuringly less than most of Britain in those years. Peel seemed a very small town where past and present dovetailed perfectly. Though it taps into the market for nostalgia, the narrow streets run casually up from the harbour in unforced style, shops blend with local dwellings in pastel-shaded terraces, cars give precedence amicably to pedestrians, washing flaps from clothes-lines stretched across old alleys, and in a bookshop we saw four elderly ladies chatting at a table, each working on her embroidery as they tended the store. The harbourmaster was so willing to beguile us with chat that we almost forgot to ask about fresh water and showers.

The backdrop to the upper end of the harbour is a huge state-of-the-art exhibition complex, the House of Manannan, gallery after gallery presenting tableaux and audio-visual images in a brilliant exposition of the island's history. At the very top of the exhibition centre, windows look over St Patrick's Isle while pictures scroll across the wall to show how it developed. A plaque records the centre's formal opening in July 1997 by Mary Robinson, President of Ireland, as 'a symbol of the cultural links between two Celtic nations'.

At *Sarakiniko*'s stern, a rusty trawler was undergoing a cultural transformation of a different kind. It looked like a wreck awaiting the builder's hammer, but its owner, who was busy removing the boat's wheelhouse, stopped to explain that last year it had been fetched from Iceland and he had bought it for £3,000.

'It will be cheaper than a house up in the town,' he said. 'I'll have it ready in two years and perfect in three. Like a look round?' Pat and I stumbled in near darkness through a very fishy hold, while our host, gripped by his happy commitment, explained the layout for a galley, cabins and living quarters. To our surprise, we found that we almost envied him.

We took a bus the ten miles across to the east side of the island to the capital, Douglas. Hamlets ran into each other along the main road. Villages and landscape had a diminutive quality: little stone houses roofed in slate, neat gardens and, just off the road, wooded dells filled with cow parsley, wild garlic and lush grass. Fields marked by winding hedgerows criss-crossed with gorse reminded one of parts of rural Ireland, but with fewer of the unfortunate Irish bungalows. Sometimes a Mercedes went by, far too big for the narrow roads. When we glimpsed a new BMW parked on a bright new drive beside a Spanish-style villa, palms peering over a high wall, electronic eyes guarding heavy gates, Pat pointed: 'Tax Exile!' I expect he was right. In Douglas we passed Athol Street, the island's Wall Street or the City. The banks here trawl for rich immigrants, exploiting tax differentials between the Isle of Man and the mainland, an exercise worth far more than the island smugglers ever made from the differences in duty on brandy or tea.

The 'Roadracing Capital of the World' was having a sad summer: the Isle of Man TT had been cancelled due to the foot-and-mouth scare. The races can attract some 40,000 visitors and improve the economy by around £16 million, but most regulars had cancelled their bookings. Substitute shows were being arranged for those who came, but fireworks, the Red Arrows and even Miss Wet T-shirt competitions would be decidedly second best to the thrills of the racetrack.

However, horse-drawn trams still went clip-clopping along the Douglas seafront, and the electric railway, built in Victorian times, trundled past. Going south from Douglas is a steam-driven train with a locomotive which is every child's conception of Thomas the Tank Engine. Who could resist this dignified thing, its great solid parts hissing and rumbling and smelling of oil, its gleaming brass polished with years of fierce devotion? Under a cloud of steam and smoke, it took us to the old capital of Castletown, where the curator of the town's Maritime Museum, Mr Ronan, showed us not only ancient net-making and ships' biscuit-making machines, large and cumbersome as grand pianos, but the schooner *Peggy*, built by Captain George Quayle as one of his three trading craft. 'It was walled up in its original boathouse,' he said, 'and not rediscovered until 1935.' The clinker-built craft was only twenty-five feet five inches overall, but with its two-masted schooner rig, it could carry a large sail area, especially as it had drop keels. It had also carried eight guns to protect it against the privateers of the Irish Sea.

'And its guns?' I asked.

'Come upstairs.'

Here were six brass guns, each some fifteen inches long, and a bow and stern chaser a few inches longer. Presumably they clipped along the gunwale like rowlocks.

'The *Peggy* traded all around the coast,' our guide told us, 'and in 1796, when she was in a harbour in Cumbria, Captain George even trailed her over the hills to Lake Windermere for a regatta.'

After Britain got control of the revenue laws in 1765, the island's prosperity declined, but a new source of income came on board the steam-driven ships crossing from Whitehaven and Liverpool – visitors from the industrial areas of Lancashire. In 1819 a weekly steamer service was set up between Douglas and Whitehaven, forty miles away in Cumbria. It was the first regular service to the island; up until then a visitor had to arrange his own passage with the skipper of a boat. At around the same time, a steamer service linked Greenock in Scotland with Douglas and Liverpool. By mid-century the visitors were flooding in: 25,000 a year in the 1830s, 90,000 in 1875, and Douglas began to glow in Victorian splendour as hotels, boarding houses, theatres and ballrooms spread along the front. The boom continued. In 1913 the island accommodated 634,000 visitors; after World War II around 600,000 were still arriving each year. But a slow decline set in when blue-collar British workers turned instead to the charms of Mallorca and Miami.

Beside the grand sweep of pastel-painted hotels, we found 'Billy' harnessed to the municipal tram, and joined four leather-clad and almost middle-aged bikers who were already aboard. Our companions on Billy's tram had left their 900cc Kawasakis, with 'I Love Satan' painted in flames on their tanks, in front of the grand old Balmoral Hotel. Perhaps it was just as well – they had come to ride the TT circuit on 'Mad Sunday', when there is no speed limit on the island's open roads. In the three days we spent here, three bikers were killed in separate accidents on the narrow highways.

Billy trotted sedately, hauling the tram along the three-foot-gauge rail, and was eventually tailed by a dozen patient motorists. Billy was no slouch, but he knew when a refresher of hay or oats was due and stopped altogether when he saw a companion waiting to take over. Given that he spends the winter grazing in the fields, Billy's life working Europe's only horse tramway seemed quite tolerable, especially on a morning when his load was just three yachties and four leathery bikers.

IT WAS time to get on around the island's south-west corner to the harbour of Port St Mary, and then, after a brief stay in Ramsey, up the north-east coast to aim at southern Scotland.

But between Peel and Port St Mary lies Calf Sound, where islets and reefs cut the safe passage to the width of a city street. At one side are mainland cliffs, at the other a craggy islet, the Calf of Man. The sound lying between them has been described as a chute through which one half of the Irish Sea does its damnedest to fill up the other.

The alternative meant sailing well outside Calf Island to avoid the Chicken Rock and the tidal races and heavy overfalls which surround it. Going through Calf Sound, however, saves at least eight miles on the run to Port St Mary. I studied the pilot book, which declared: 'this stretch of water appears inoffensive on the charts, but this belies the fact that it has been the scene of innumerable shipwrecks and much loss of life. It has a fierce reputation with Manxmen, land-based and seafarer alike, as the most dangerous piece of water in the Irish Sea.

'The chart shows a spring tidal race of 3.5 knots (up to 8 knots if the locals are to be believed), and not much less at neaps, with no slack to speak of. This, along with the confined space in the sound, leads either to very short, steep, foamy seas with a westerly wind of Force 4 or above blowing against the tide, or to large, towering toppling seas running with the tide, with rocks and crags all round.

'After this horror story,' the author goes on, 'it won't be surprising that most skippers elect to take the longer route around Chicken Rock, though this isn't always a particularly calm alternative.

'Calf Sound is a viable route, provided that the conditions are absolutely right. But the more conditions deviate from this proviso, the more uncomfortable the passage will become, until it becomes impossible.'

At any rate, declared the author, if you were heading south the sound was best attempted between low water and two hours after. Our burgee showed the wind favourably in the north-east; the forecast was for breezes of Force 4 to 5, occasionally 6, in the North Irish Sea. Pat climbed ashore to bin our rubbish and reported a heaving, uneasy sea but no strong wind outside the harbour. I checked that low water down at Port St Mary had been at seven this morning. If we left right now, just after 0900, we could make the ten miles to the sound in about two hours. The tide would certainly have started against us in the narrows by then, but that also meant we could turn around and funk it, 'Fall back and Chicken out round the Rock,' as someone said.

The cliffs of St Patrick's Isle were desolate as we turned south into the drizzle, the jib snatching and filling, *Sarakiniko* rolling uncomfortably.

'As usual, I forgot to take my seasick pills,' Joan said disconsolately.

'It's just backwash from the cliffs,' Pat comforted her. 'It will soon settle down.'

Short of inspiration but feeling some duty to cheer the day, I pointed up to Contrary Head. 'It's called that because the tides flooding into the Irish Sea from north and south meet here. So there's very little actual flow ...' I could see this was not absorbing the crew's interest, so I added, pointing at the tower on the summit called Corin's Folly, 'He was a staunch Freechurchman. He wanted to assert the right to be buried in unconsecrated ground, so he had his wife's and children's remains transferred here from a local churchyard. He joined them here himself later. It made a fine landmark for the fishing fleet,' I concluded rather lamely.

The wind picked up; the morning wore on. Calf Island emerged from the haze; Joan made mugs of coffee. The sun lit up the sand below a row of Edwardian terraces in the little resort of Port Erin, a pretty name. But the salts on *Sarakiniko* had their eyes focused on the watery serrations ahead, the tops of standing waves in the sound, perhaps a dozen of them, seven or eight feet high and occupying half the channel. Easier water seemed to lie to one side, but whirlpool eddies were dragging at the tiller, which felt as if it were turning in air one moment, in glue the next. We revved up the engine and, keeping as close as we dared, passed within a few feet of sluicing, sloshing rocks, their white foam reaching out to our topsides. In a few moments it was all over; *Sarakiniko* was shielded from the north-west wind and in water like a ruffled lake. Giddy with exhilaration, we ran the last four miles to Port St Mary, where the pier crooked its arm around us protectively.

As I folded our chart away, I noticed that if you pencilled a square on it, with the horizontals running east and west and each side representing some sixty miles, the four corners lay very close to Howth, Carlingford, Peel and Port St Mary. A day's sail from Dublin, Port St Mary has always been popular with mariners from that side of the Irish Sea, though until recently a line of trawlers would be likely to crowd its pier and a yacht might fret for space. The sad decline of fishing, however, means that a hundred yards of the root end of the pier has now been reserved for yachts and an excavated pool provides water at any state of tide for seven or eight craft along this reach of wall.

The Isle of Man is widening its appeal for the leisure sailor. Douglas boasts a marina, and there are rumours that Ramsey is also considering a lock which would provide a walk-ashore amenity for the fin-keeler. Cruising vessels may then be tempted, not only to Ramsey, but onward to the south coast of Scotland and the Lakeland hills of Cumbria just on the horizon.

We moored alongside an ancient wooden yacht, where two elderly men dressed in old trousers and floppy sunhats were having tea in the cockpit. We fell into their good company and later wandered uphill through terraces of net-curtained cottages built of local limestone, rising irregularly above the harbour. It was a peaceful weekday afternoon in the village; the butcher put a 'closed' sign on the door once Joan had bought the last three lamb chops. We walked on, politely skirting an occasional dog resting on the pavements and bidding good-day to a woman and her two teenage children who were painting the park railings. We liked Port St Mary.

Next morning we set a course east along the island's south shore and then, with that delightful combination of a tide building in our favour and a freshening wind blowing in relatively smooth water as it came off the coast, we turned north-east for Ramsey.

One could just see the entrance to Derbyhaven, once a snug anchorage favoured by sailing ships unless the wind came north-east. The Derby family, who lived here, introduced horse-racing to the Isle of Man, and in a sense the origins of the Epsom Derby in fact lie here.

We were sailing so fast that Douglas Bay opened unexpectedly. 'Just one hour and three-quarters for the fifteen miles here to Douglas Head,' I called from the navigation table. I went up to the cockpit to gaze at the building that crowns the headland, Fort St Anne, built as a residence by the notorious Dublin playboy of the late eighteenth century, Buck Whaley, probably to avoid some local difficulties in Ireland. His rich wife's fortune kept him in style, but apparently her fortune depended on her living on Irish soil. It is said that Whaley sent for a schooner-full of Irish earth and put it into the foundations here to make a safe base for her income.

Fort St Anne was later the home of the more worthy Sir William Hillary, who founded the Royal National Lifeboat Institute (RNLI) in 1824. (An earlier body had the dismal name of the Liverpool Institute for the Recovery of Drowned Persons.) In a few moments we could see, close to the harbour piers, the once-dreaded Conniston Reef on which many ships were lost as they tried to run into the harbour entrance in north-east gales. Hillary set a solid building on the wave-washed rocks to act as a refuge for desperate mariners scrambling on to the reefs; here they could shelter until they might be rescued. He was a brave man, who put out in violent gales with his boat crew to save lives, but he died in penury after a bank failure ruined him. The refuge on Conniston Reef is his memorial and flies the RNLI flag.

It was now eleven miles to Maughold Head, where we would turn north-west for a three-mile beat into Ramsey. The mountains of the Lake District grew larger on the horizon. They were perhaps thirty-five miles away, sitting behind a coast running from the vast sands of Morecambe Bay north to the 450-foot cliffs of St Bee's Head and north again to the Solway shallows. The English coast of the Irish Sea is relatively short, not much over a hundred miles from the Solway Firth down to Liverpool and the River Dee.

The splendid tide was slackening as we bounced in the race off Maughold Head and turned into a chilly headwind. We punched hard against it, engine thudding, squinting through the spray to identify the harbour at Ramsey. The piers can be difficult to identify from a boat beset by rain and spume. One is running into fast-shoaling water at either side of the pierheads, where sandy beaches dry out for about 500 yards at low water.

A squat Victorian tower a half-mile south makes a good seamark against the sky, though it was not built for this purpose. In 1847, Queen Victoria and her consort, Prince Albert, were returning from Scotland in bad weather and the Royal Yacht turned into Ramsey Bay for shelter. The Queen was seasick and stayed aboard while Prince Albert ventured ashore, where he was met by an unsuspecting barber who suggested they take a walk to the local hilltop. The Prince joined his new companion, while the island dignitaries, who had half-expected a Royal visit, were assembled at Douglas. When they heard of the unscheduled hike they turned pell mell for Ramsey but arrived just in time to see the Royal Yacht disappearing out to sea. Worse again for this local rivalry, Ramsey decided to build the Albert Tower to commemorate the visit.

We turned a corner and confronted three coasters which seemed to occupy most of the quay space, but a solitary yacht lay to a ladder and we edged alongside it. A retired Coastguard man on a nearby boat welcomed me with a sweeping gesture to the *Queen of the North* and then declared that this was the most dangerous harbour in the Isle of Man when the seas came in big from the east. A din of rivetting vied with the clatter of the radio on the nearest coaster, but we enjoyed the energy and commercial activity of Ramsey, and when the tide ebbed *Sarakiniko* sat on the sand like a contented seagull.

She floated by 1130 next morning, and we departed for Scotland. Six miles up a featureless sandy coast, the Isle of Man tapers at last to the Point of Ayre; we would pass this close-to, keeping inside some formidable banks which lie in echelon, four to six miles long and three or four miles apart, the northernmost reaching almost halfway to St Bee's Head in England. At low water the depths drop at times to six feet, setting up a deadly chaos of foaming seas in bad weather. But in today's light wind, Joan's extraction of a piping-hot quiche from the swinging oven was not even delayed by some rock and roll from the nearby eddies.

The wind freshened but the sea grew more regular as the Point of Ayre fell astern. *Sarakiniko* pounded occasionally, one of her incurable habits, and we set a course for Kirkcudbright.

EIGHT

Scotland's Forgotten Hero?

KIRKCUDBRIGHT BAY lay twenty miles ahead. It is one of several bays along the Galloway coast, where Scotland sets a northern boundary to the Irish Sea. To the west, beyond the Mull of Galloway, is the North Channel and Belfast Lough, to the east the Solway Firth. Across these northern waters were enacted, in 1778, some of the remarkable adventures of John Paul Jones, a man who was born on this coast and became known as the Father of the American Navy. To the Americans he was a hero; to the English a traitor. And to the Scots? In the Isle of Man I had picked up a handbill advertising a new musical in Edinburgh devoted to this unique and complex man: 'Scotland's Forgotten Hero, Forgotten no Longer.'

The original thirteen plantations along the east coast of America had a population of some thirteen million by the middle of the eighteenth century. They were relatively prosperous communities, proud of their independence, and gradually obliged their governors, appointed by the British Crown, to leave real power in the hands of their own assemblies. They had defended themselves against French Canada in the Seven Years War – the French and Indian War, they called it – with the aid of troops and money supplied from London, and when they were asked to contribute to the costs of the war by paying a stamp duty and other measures, they insisted that there should be 'no taxation without representation'.

The Americans would not accept that they should be exploited according to the conventional mercantilist practice of the day, i.e. in the interest of the mother country. A colony, in that view, was an investment expected to yield prompt returns on capital. Britain insisted that this principle must be maintained, that a colony was therefore obliged to pay tax, and so, by a majority of one, Lord North's Cabinet decided to retain a single tax, that on tea. For a trifling sum of about £16,000 in revenue, Britain was to lose America.

Orders were given to the East India Company to ship a cargo of tea to Boston, where the company would sell it direct to consumers. The Americans protested and, disguised as Indians, boarded the ship and threw tea chests and British taxes into Boston Harbour. Military hostilities with Britain began on 17 June 1775.

Despite George Washington's genius, with no trained regiments, no warships and no financial credit the Americans would probably have been defeated had not France, cheered by the prospect of gaining revenge for their defeat in Canada, entered the war. The whole nature of the dispute was then altered. French fleets ruled the seas and allowed America's ships of war to range as far as Britain and Ireland. They had the use of French bases for repairs, recruitment and fitting out, and ports where prize crews could return with captured vessels. Suddenly the Americans were all too close to Britain, and fears grew of an invasion force crossing the Channel. Thus John Paul Jones' brief invasion of the important port of Whitehaven had a significance far greater than the physical damage involved. His landing immediately afterwards at Kirkcudbright emphasised Britain's disarray. The Royal Navy was reviled, the militia called out, guards mounted on public buildings in the ports, and overworked adjectives about 'defenceless coasts' and 'inexcusably lax government' filled the daily broadsheets.

Jones was an adopted name. John's father was William Paul, a gardener on the Arbigland estate, not far from the village of Kirkbean. The boy's parents decided that he should make a career at sea, and in 1761 he was apprenticed for seven years to a ship's master in Whitehaven to serve in a 179-ton vessel trading with the West Indies, bringing cargoes of rum and sugar back to Whitehaven. By the age of twenty-one John Paul was the master of a merchant ship and had an intimate knowledge of the Solway and Whitehaven not only as a long-distance trader, but also as an occasional smuggler between the Isle of Man and Solway's coves and harbours.

A few years later, while master of a merchantman in Tobago and under imminent threat from a belaying pin, he killed a mutinous seaman. A court would probably have acquitted him, but he fled to America, where there was no system for the extradition of wanted men. He arrived in America in 1775 and put his skills at the service of the soon-to-be rebel navy. The Colony of Massachusetts and others were already issuing letters of marque authorising merchantmen to make prizes of British shipping. In British eyes they were planning piracy.

On 16 June 1777, John Paul Jones, as he was now known, was appointed commander of the 22-gun frigate *Ranger* by resolution of Congress. He crossed the Atlantic to Brest, and in April of the following year began a fateful two weeks' cruise, recording his adventures in the ship's log and in letters which give, not only the detail of daily commerce on the Irish Sea, but a portrait of violence redeemed by moments of great humanity.

Four days out from Brest he sighted a ship bound for Wexford with a cargo of flax seed from Ostend. Totally out-gunned, the ship surrendered and master and crew were made prisoners, but the cargo was not particularly valuable to Jones, who had his eye on brighter prospects. Putting a prize crew on this vessel and dispatching it to France would deplete his command, so he scuttled it instead.

He sailed on north and off Wicklow challenged the 150-ton *Lord Chatham,* bound to its home port, Dublin, with 100 hogsheads of best English porter on board. Ship and cargo were promptly dispatched to a prize court in Brest. Jones raided another ship, en route from London to Dublin, which happened to be carrying a bundle of letters from the late Dr Samuel Johnson to an Irish clergyman, Dr William Maxwell. When James Boswell was writing the great *Life of Dr Johnson*, he was deeply saddened to be told of this loss.

Owing to persistent smuggling between the Isle of Man and the Galloway peninsula, it was not unusual for the English Revenue cutter *Huzzar* to patrol off the Point of Aire. At 1000 on 18 April, this fast fore- and aft-rigged vessel challenged *Ranger* and overhauled her as she stood away for the Scottish coast. As the ships came close-to, Jones resorted to bluff: he asked the cutter if she could supply him with a pilot. This request was refused; instead he was asked for his particulars.

'*Molly*, of Glasgow,' he replied.

'Where are you from and where now bound?'

Jones dropped his speaking trumpet and shouted, 'Open all ports!' A tier of guns ran out.

The Revenue cutter manoeuvred half astern of the *Ranger* and off that ship's quarter so that *Ranger*'s guns could not bear effectively. Jones' crew fell to using small-arms fire and then a broadside which damaged the stern of the cutter and put two holes in its mainsail. The *Huzzar* bore away and, with its more efficient rig, succeeded in escaping.

Next day John Paul Jones boarded a Scottish coasting schooner off the Mull of Galloway. The crew were taken prisoner and the vessel scuttled. Jones learned that a whole fleet of merchantmen was assembled at Loch Ryan in the North Channel, but the *Ranger* met a headwind and was unable to sail north at once. Later they did so and attempted to capture an armed cutter near the great sea pyramid of Ailsa Craig in the Clyde approaches. Turning south down the North Channel, *Ranger* encountered a sloop from Dublin and sank her 'to prevent intelligence'. The following day, off Carrickfergus, the crew of an Irish fishing boat told Jones that an English warship, HMS *Drake*, was at anchor in Belfast Lough.

Here was an opportunity to sail in by night and cut her out, but Jones found his crew opposed to the plan. Several, including some of his officers, saw their sea service as an opportunity to earn prize money. Despite the string of boats they had captured, the cruise in the Irish Sea had so far offered little, and now they were being asked to face a dangerous sea battle. Jones eventually won them over with a plan which seemed ingeniously simple. After dark, *Ranger* would present herself as a blundering merchantman and sail into the Lough, crossing HMS *Drake*'s bows as if attempting to anchor just up to windward, and then sweep the warship's decks with gunfire and grapple and board her.

The plan was clever but it miscarried. A crewman, taking Dutch courage from a bottle of whiskey, allowed the anchor to snag, and the *Ranger* came to a halt fifty yards astern of the *Drake* – which still believed this was a merchantman commanded by a fool. Jones cut his own cable and sheered off, intending to try his ruse on the following night again, but a gale blew up and his ship was forced to run for shelter 'on the south shore of Scotland'. The crew, in the words of the surgeon, Mr Green, 'was now very much fatigued'. The weather did not help. Next day, 22 April, was exceptionally cold. Snow covered the distant land. 'The three Kingdoms,' Mr Green wrote of Scotland, Ireland and the Isle of Man, 'as far as the eye can see, are covered in snow.'

Jones' aim on leaving Brest was to raid an English harbour. It may be that he had learned through the French secret service of orders dispatched to the Royal Navy to attack 'ports along the coasts from New York to Nova Scotia' if the English forces on the American mainland could not bring George Washington to a decisive land battle. Now Jones decided to revert to the original plan and made Whitehaven harbour on the coast of Cumbria his target. It was an important port, likely to have several hundred fishing and trading vessels in its drying-out harbour. It lay where the Solway Firth begins to form into a funnel-shaped gulf, close to John Paul's homeland. He would be now in familiar waters, beyond the treacherous Solway sands which are covered and uncovered twice daily by twenty and twenty-five foot tides. They sweep in, turning tortuous channels into rushing rivers. Sir Walter Scott evokes the place in his novel, *Young Lochinvar*, where 'Love swells like the Solway and ebbs like its tide.'

Jones must have found the prospect of attacking Whitehaven intoxicating. No enemy had dared invade the British coast within memory. A successful raid would be a resounding humiliation for the British Navy. In ports around the Irish Sea, John Paul Jones' exploits were already regarded with a mixture of admiration and fear. He would boldly water his ship at Caldy Island in the Bristol Channel and was said to have landed at Tenby town 'dressed all in black, with a whip'. He was the man who bombarded Aberaeron in Cardigan Bay and extracted a ransom of 500 guineas from the town. Welsh sailors sang songs about his ship:

'Mounting forty-four guns from New England she came
'With a noted commander, Paul Jones was his name.'

But his crew, many of them Scottish, were uneasy. The surgeon, Mr Green, opposed an attack. 'Nothing,' he wrote later, 'would be gained by attacking poor people's property; little coasters, fishers and colliers waiting in there for the summer's work.' And the Irish Sea was closely patrolled: after the raid they would have great difficulty in escaping from its confined waters. The ship came close to mutiny when a crewman rushed at Jones, but he put a pistol to the man's head and forced his will on the others.

The *Ranger* drifted slowly across the Solway Firth in the fading night breeze. By midnight they were still several miles from Whitehaven, so they anchored ship and forty officers and men set out to row into the port in two longboats. It took them three hours to reach the harbour. Still aggrieved with their captain and careless of the consequences, one of the boat crews found a tavern and, as a report put it, 'made free with the liquor'. Jones' party landed to more effect. They scaled the pier and spiked the batteries of guns, but their attack had barely started when a barefoot seaman went running through the sleeping streets, banging on every door and crying, 'Pirates! Pirates!' He was David Freeman, alias Smith, an Irishman who had enlisted at Portsmouth in America simply as a way of getting home.

Time was running out. The invaders had come with 'combustible candles' – canvas dipped in brimstone – to burn the boats in the harbour. John Paul Jones had estimated that there were about 150 ships of at least 200 tons aground on the north side and seventy to 100 vessels lying on the south. But the flint and tinder had been mislaid. Jones got a crewman to hurry for embers to a nearby house, lit a combustible candle and set a collier alight, throwing in a barrel of tar to help the blaze. A few more vessels were also set on fire, but it was now near 0500, 'the sun a full hour above the horizon and, as sleep no longer ruled the world, it was time to retire'.

The *Ranger's* crew made back to sea and rejoined their ship, which had managed to sail close-in on the morning breeze. The foray had been without bloodshed, but neither had it brought success: the early morning rain was already quenching the fires. And Jones was now in even greater danger, from a disappointed crew who had won no prize money of any consequence, and from the Royal Navy.

However, this very morning Jones took his ship across the Solway Firth to the estuary that runs up to the village of Kirkcudbright. He planned to kidnap the 4th Earl of Selkirk at his home in Selkirk Castle on St Mary's Isle, a promontory about three miles up the twisting channel to the village. The purpose of the operation was apparently to put pressure on the British government to authorise the exchange of naval prisoners as was already being done in the case of soldiers. Jones' log shows that this was something about which he felt very strongly.

ISLANDS CLOSE to the shore can be difficult to distinguish from the mainland. Little Ross Island on the estuary below Kirkcudbright today has a lighthouse, 150 feet above the sea, the keeper's dwellings no longer inhabited but visible from far off. As we closed on it, the tide was running out, and it was too late to reach up the channels to Kirkcudbright. We passed close to the island, gazing at the remains of an ancient church and a walled graveyard that seemed to have lain untouched for centuries. Lonely shores spread out on either side of the estuary, and we had to decide quickly where we should anchor. I opened the pilot book.

'It suggests we could anchor here behind the island.'

'We could get swell,' Joan said.

'Yes, I agree. There's an inlet called Ross Bay about a half-mile further up.' I handed her the book. 'The entire inlet dries out to sand at low tide. I'm sure we can still get in but we'd better hurry up.'

I turned inshore. When the echo sounder showed seven feet below our keels, Pat unclipped the anchor and lowered it into water so clear he could see the chain drawing tight on the sand as I went astern to dig its flukes in. We stood for a while lining up points ashore as a check on our position in case the anchor should start to drag, but all seemed secure. Soon acres of hard-ribbed sand lay all around us as the sea withdrew, and oystercatchers, squabbling and shrieking, scurried to and fro in the shallows. They have to move fast to get a swift strike at a worm before it burrows into the sand for shelter. Some probed more deeply, trying to haul up a mussel. There seemed to be two schools of thought among the oystercatchers on what to do with it then. If a bird has a very sharp beak, it can be inserted between the halves of the shell to cut the muscle. Alternatively, the beak can be used as a hammer, which is possibly easier, but the beak will lose its edge as a result. The question of correct technique made for noisy debate as these spindly soldiers of the foreshore set about harvesting the tide.

Later we walked across the wet plain to rocks corrugated with a million mussels. Tomorrow's lunch was assured. Pat's farming instincts broke through and brought him ashore again towards dusk to look at the black Galloway cattle we had seen chomping in the fields. He went no further than the public road as the foot-and-mouth restrictions were in force and Cumbria, not many sea miles from here, was a centre of the grim disease. We had not spotted any Scots at all, but knew the locals might be understandably anxious at the sight of crews coming ashore from a visiting yacht.

When the tide began to return, I went up to the cockpit, from where I could see Whitehaven and Workington stretched along the horizon in strings of light. Shore-lights make the sea seem so much smaller at night. Belatedly I sorted our bundle of flags and set about hoisting the Scottish lion to our spreaders.

Joan called up: 'Is Pat not coming back?'

I couldn't quite see the shore. The ripples of the tideline, tiny wavelets gleaming in the last of the western light, were advancing fast towards our stern. Finally I saw a figure splashing across the water. Pat hauled himself aboard.

'Another five minutes and I'd have water in these boots!'

The water began slapping at the keel, quietening as the level climbed to the hull, and as we muttered in comfortable agreement that sleeping-bags really could be made with zips that do not catch the lining, *Sarakiniko* began to bump on the hard sand. In ten minutes more she was riding to the gentlest, sleep-inducing swell. If we bumped when we touched the seabed again in the small hours of Sunday morning, no one noticed.

Next morning we passed by St Mary's Isle as we followed a cautious route between buoys to the long pontoon recently installed near the old trawler quay of Kirkcubright. Peace was dropping slow, and the village, which in Ireland would be called a small town, seemed to doze in the Sunday afternoon calm.

OFF Little Ross Island on that morning in April 1778, John Paul Jones launched one of the ship's boats and took command of two officers and twelve men. They splashed ashore at St Mary's Isle and entered the grounds of the Selkirk estate. They confronted the head gardener, telling him they were a press gang from 'His Majesty's Navy'. The gardener stood firm, but his under-gardeners took to their heels to speed the dire news in Kirkcudbright village that 'the press' was on its way. The head gardener, meanwhile, gave Jones the unwelcome news that the Earl of Selkirk was not at home – he was taking the waters at Buxton spa in England.

Jones was inclined to call off the raid, but his two officers, supported by the men, talked of friends' houses in New England which, they said, had been burned by British soldiers, and insisted it was time for revenge and plunder. Jones conceded that portable valuables like silver might be taken from the house but ordered that the dwelling must not be searched and that nobody in the household should be molested. He returned to the ship's boat while his two officers approached Selkirk Castle.

The house was occupied by the Countess, her seven-year-old son and daughters, a governess and four guests. They had just concluded a late breakfast when the Countess, as she later deposed, saw 'horrid-looking wretches' approaching through the grounds. Believing that they were pirates, the children were dispatched to the top floor and the Countess, the governess and the butler, Daniel, faced the two officers. They explained that they were off the American ship *Ranger* under Commander Paul Jones and had orders to take the family silver.

Lady Helen had little choice. Later she gave her impression of the two officers – the senior one, Cullan, had a 'vile blackguard's look' – though he remained civil, while the other, Lieutenant Wallingford, she rather took to. He was 'a civil young man in a green uniform, an anchor on his buttons which were white'. This was in fact the uniform of the American Marine Corps. 'He seemed naturally well bred and not to like his employment,' Lady Helen noted.

'I asked a thousand questions of them,' she wrote to a cousin. 'They behaved with great civility,' and accepted her offer of a glass of wine. When the butler was found trying to hide some of the household silver in a maid's apron, his mistress told him to desist. He had hidden the teapot used at breakfast and was ordered to produce it.

The raid over, the seamen in the grounds outside formed up and the party marched to the boat and made way. In the meantime, a servant who had escaped the cordon around the castle raised the alarm in the village, and local men dragged a cannon to the seaward edge of the promontory and began to fire out to sea; afterwards they realised they had been aiming at a rock. But the hunt was up for the *Ranger*, the first ship which had dared to raid an English port since the Dutch burned Sheerness in 1667.

Learning that John Paul Jones had been a local lad, Lady Helen wrote to her neighbour, Mrs Craik, to let her know that this man, 'a great villain', was 'born in your grounds and the son of a gardener of yours'. Perhaps Mrs Craik saw this as a touch of criticism.

Within a month the Countess was opening a letter from Jones, inscribed '*Ranger*, Brest, 8th May, 1778'. He wished to explain that his visit to her house had been intended 'to make your husband the happy Instrument of alleviating the horrors of hopeless captivity when the brave are overpowered and made Prisoners of War'. He had returned to his boat that morning, he said, but his officers had observed that in America 'no delicacy was shown by the English, who took away all sorts of moveable property, setting fire, not only to towns and to the houses of the rich without distinction, but not even sparing the wretched hamlets and milch cows of the poor ... I had,' he went on, 'but a moment to think how I might gratify them [the officers] and at the same time do your Ladyship the least injury, so I ordered that no seamen enter the house or damage anything and all to come away without searching.' He had, he thought, been obeyed, and now that 'I have gratified my men,' he wrote, 'I will gratify my own feelings by restoring [the silver] to you.'

After leaving Kirkcudbright Bay, Jones had decided to clear north around Ireland. He anticipated heavy naval activity in the Irish Sea, with avenging warships sailing from Glasgow, Liverpool and indeed Waterford. At dawn on 24 April, he saw HMS *Drake* coming out of Belfast Lough to begin checking on shipping. When the *Drake* sent a boat to establish the identity of this newcomer, Jones promptly took the *Drake*'s officer prisoner.

HMS *Drake* now came on, making its way towards the mouth of the Lough. This suited Jones, who wanted sea room for battle; in the strong wind and with a tide flooding down from the north, the British ship risked being set on to the Mewstone reefs off the Lough's southern exit. She managed to get clear without tacking and hoisted her English colours. The *Ranger* ran up the American colours.

'What ship is that?' HMS *Drake* signalled.

'The American Continental ship *Ranger*,' Jones replied. 'We have awaited you.'

Several yachts and small boats had also made for the area in anticipation of witnessing a battle.

'It was now near sunset and the *Ranger* was astern of them,' Jones recorded, 'so I ordered the helm up and got the *Ranger* across the *Drake*'s bows at right angles to her keel.' The *Ranger* fired a broadside of grapeshot which caused havoc on the British ship's decks, killing her commander and mortally wounding the first lieutenant. For the *Ranger* it was vital that HMS *Drake*, with her far larger crew, should not get alongside. The American ship concentrated its gunshot on the *Drake*'s sails and men, hoping to capture the hull as a prize. Nearly one-third of *Drake*'s complement were wounded in the gunfire, two other men were killed, and after just over an hour of battle her third in command cried 'Quarters'. Jones sent a boarding party across in the gig which had been captured earlier. They found the decks running with blood and rum – the British had brought a keg of rum on deck, prematurely confident of victory.

On *Ranger* the pleasant young Lieutenant of Marines, Sam Wallingford, who had impressed Lady Helen just the morning before, lay dead, along with two seamen. There were five others wounded.

The captured *Drake* was taken in tow and some 133 crew made prisoners. It was a very public humiliation for the Royal Navy. Off Donaghadee the ships were seen moving north between the Copeland Islands and the mainland and next day were noticed off Ballywater, some fifteen miles to the south. *Ranger* cast off her tow long enough to take a brig from Norway bound for Whitehaven;

then, as the wind had now become southerly, Jones decided to sail north.

He still had on board the Irish fishermen whom he had detained off Carrickfergus the week before. 'It was time to release the honest Irishmen,' he recorded. 'I gave them money to purchase everything new which they had lost and also a good boat to transport themselves ashore and sent with them two infirm men on whom I had bestowed the last guinea in my possession, to defray their travelling expenses to their proper home in Dublin ... The grateful Irishmen were enraptured and expressed their joy in three huzzas as they passed the *Ranger*'s quarter.' One may assume that they had a great deal more than fishing tales to tell when they got home.

Ranger now lay in calm weather between Torr Head on the north-east corner of Ireland and the coast of Kintyre, while the crews repaired the *Drake* and made her ready to sail for France. On 8 May the ship entered Brest, the English colours inverted beneath the American flag.

John Paul Jones' raid on an English port and his capture of a British warship almost within sight of Carrickfergus had a deep influence on Irish opinion. Irish Protestants believed England was now unable to protect Ireland from the threat of French invasion. And they had a point: when the Mayor of Belfast asked the Lord Lieutenant for reinforcements, he was informed that the authorities could spare only half a troop of dismounted horsemen and half a company of invalids. In the view of many Protestants, they needed to increase the ranks of the Irish Volunteers and secure an independent Dublin government.

But what of the Earl of Selkirk, whose abduction was the whole point of the descent on Kirkcudbright? He, like many in England, had some sympathy with the American cause. Within a few weeks he replied to the letter Jones sent to his wife, addressing his missive to 'Capitaine du Vaisseau Americain Le *Ranger* à Brest'.

'I have no interest whatever with the King,' he wrote, 'and am scarce known to him, having been in London maybe six months in all in the last twenty-five years.' He and his family, he went on, had been 'very friendly to the Constitutionalists and the Just Liberties of America', though he added that there was a general view in England that 'the unusual and cruel practices' had been first developed by the Americans. Acknowledging that the officers and men of the *Ranger* had 'behaved as well as could be expected in every respect,' he told Jones that 'we are sorry to hear that your young officer in green uniform was killed in your engagement with the *Drake*.'

And he went on: 'If you are unwilling to keep your share of the silver as Captain [fifteen per cent of its sale proceeds as awarded by a prize court] I would wish that part to be given to the private men who were on the party as an encouragement for their good behaviour. You, sir, are entitled to what is more honourable, viz. the praise for having your men under good discipline, which I take care on all occasions to make known. Your Obedient Servant.'

Officialdom took a hand at this point. The Post Office returned the Earl's restrained and dignified letter, stating that it would be inappropriate in time of war to deliver any communication to Jones. He never received it, and, as far as we know, did not return again to Scotland.

Jones had the silver examined in Brest under prize court procedures and was told there was no ready sale for 'old-fashioned English silver'. He therefore had it valued as bullion at $600. Excluding his fifteen per cent, he paid the crew $510 from his own pocket, and arranged for the French authorities to convey the Selkirk silver to London on a neutral ship. John Paul Jones had kept his word.

He was a man of honour. In his earlier letter to the Countess, he explained that he had arranged burial of the *Drake*'s men 'with the honours due to the memory of the brave ... I have drawn my sword ... for the Rights of Men, yet I am not in arms as an American nor in pursuit of riches, having no wife or family and having lived long enough to know that riches cannot ensure happiness'.

I SAT in the Kirkcudbright harbourmaster's office listening to Robert Thompson's reminiscences. They ran back to the 1950s.

'Around about then we had a murder on Little Ross Island.'

'Surely no one lived there except the lighthouse men?' I exclaimed.

'Yes, two of them; one killed the other. I had a sailing dinghy in those days, and I and another boy – he later became a bank manager here – had planned a sail down to the island, but I mistimed the tide and couldn't get my own dinghy off the mud that morning. So he went alone, and it was he who found the keeper lying shot.'

'And the suspect?'

'A day or two later he was stopped at a police check near Selby in Yorkshire; and I think it was simply a routine check. The case got a lot of publicity because, as I recall, it was the last death sentence by a Scottish court. The law was changed soon afterwards. But the prisoner didn't hang. He committed suicide in prison.'

Robert pointed to a pleasant landscape painting on the wall behind me. 'Everyone knows everyone else in Kirkcudbright,' he said. 'The bank manager's son did that for me.'

'But you have no memorial to John Paul Jones.'

He laughed. 'I think we have: the Paul Jones Sea Cadets. Some naval people thought that name was pushing it a bit far, but persistence won out. That reminds me – years ago, I had an auxiliary naval service job on the English east coast. There was a US naval presence there, too. Our lot were technically civilians so we couldn't use the privileges of the American PX canteen and shops. Then the lieutenant in charge heard that I came from Paul Jones country – well, perhaps I told him – and it was "Open Sesame" at the PX right away.'

'Can we visit Selkirk Castle down in the woods?'

'No, no. It's gone, burned down years ago. You could walk down the old drive and see the remains of the gardens, but there are probably foot-and-mouth restrictions just now.'

We had another small disappointment when we did not find the Countess's teapot in the town's Stewartry Museum. My guidebook was out of date; the Selkirk breakfast teapot is elsewhere now, reclaimed by the family's descendants.

'The tea-leaves are supposed to be still inside it,' I said to the lady at the desk. 'Is that true?'

'I do believe they are,' she said, laughing.

WHEN JONES arrived back in Brest, he was given command of his next ship, the *Bonhomme Richard*, a former French East Indiaman paid for by King Louis XVI and fitted out as a man-of-war. The following year, 1779, he was made Commander in Chief of the American Squadron in Europe, at the age of thirty-two. He sailed from Brest that August, and later in the month almost wrecked his new 44-gun flagship on the Skellig Rocks off the Co. Kerry coast.

'At 8 PM Mizen Head lay astern,' he wrote, 'and, with a fine breeze, the Squadron stood north-west along the iron-bound coast of Kerry. By noon we were five miles SSW of Great Skellig.'

At that point the wind died. To avoid being set down on the rocks, Jones ordered his largest rowing boat to be launched to tow the ship clear. This was done, but the oarsmen were mostly Irishmen who had been pressed into service, and when they realised that the flat calm was persisting they cut loose from the tow rope and rowed joyfully for Valentia and home.

It seems very likely that it was at this time that, as a child, Daniel O'Connell (the Liberator) was carried to a beach at Derrynane to be shown a ship at anchor there, under the command of the famous seaman, John Paul Jones.

Jones was supported on the cruise around Scotland to the North Sea by three French ships, but they proved to be unreliable allies. Two sheered off when British warships were sighted off Flamborough Head, Yorkshire. Jones was greatly out-gunned by a Royal Navy frigate of fifty guns, but after fierce fighting and with his ship about to sink, he laid alongside the vessel, causing its captain to surrender, and at once made it his new flagship. The battle, one of the bloodiest ever fought on the British coasts, was watched by the local population, who gathered on the headland under the light of a huge harvest moon.

Three years later, one of Jones' ships, the *Alliance*, came under the command of John Barry. Barry was born in Co. Wexford in 1745 and emigrated with his family to Philadelphia at the age of fifteen. He prospered as a captain of merchant ships and eventually offered his services, and his ship, to Congress. He arranged the fitting out of many vessels for the fledgling American Navy and in 1782, three years after the Battle of Flamborough Head, captured a fleet of British trading vessels bearing cargoes from Jamaica to London. When the prizes were sold in France, they enriched the American Treasury with the equivalent of £650,000 in gold.

John Paul Jones, Commodore of the United States Navy, died in 1792. Barry, whose fighting career was shortened by a severe shoulder wound, succeeded him in 1794. A statue of Barry, Father of the American Navy, stands on the quay at Wexford, his cloak billowing as he strides through the wind. In Kirkcudbright we could find no monument to his predecessor, who is also cited as the father of the American Navy.

Jones was buried in a lead coffin in the St Louis Cemetery, a plot outside the walls of Paris reserved for Protestant foreigners. He was largely forgotten by the American government. Then, in the 1890s, the American ambassador to France spent several years investigating the St Louis Cemetery, digging shafts and tunnels under the modern buildings which now covered the old burial ground. He found five lead coffins. Three had nameplates. Of the others, one held a body which had been preserved in alcohol and packed in straw. It was known that on his death friends had hoped to transfer Jones' body to America. On the head was a small cap with the letter 'J' inscribed upon it. An earlobe was found to have a curious, distinctive shape similar to that shown on a bust of the naval hero.

In 1905 President Roosevelt dispatched four cruisers to France to bring John Paul Jones' body home. Seven warships joined them for the final voyage to Annapolis, where Jones was buried in the crypt of the Naval Academy Chapel. An imposing sarcophagus stands there, inscribed in honour of the man 'who gave to our Navy its early traditions of heroism and victory'.

NINE

Scottish Shores

P AT HAD TO leave us now. While he returned to his farm in
Ireland, my daughter, Patricia, and her fourteen-year-old
son, Patrick, arrived on a short break from their Scottish
farm. The long-term shipping forecast suggested fine weather for
a voyage along the coast of Galloway and past the notorious tide
race of the Mull to the North Channel and Portpatrick. That
would place *Sarakiniko* at – indeed, beyond – the northern limit
of the Irish Sea. And it would mean a return voyage of over 200
miles to her home port at Milford Haven.

We ambled around Kirkcudbright's terraces, old Scottish houses
mingling with Georgian styles, and noticed, as we had at
Carlingford, the narrow closes which reveal a town's medieval core.
The light everywhere had a quality which intensified colour and
contrast, and since the 1880s artists and craftsmen have formed a
colony here. The tradition lives on in the art centres and galleries of
this small town, which seems to have everything you would want
in a community: bookshops, delightful tea-rooms, family butchers
selling delicious Scottish mutton pies, old-fashioned shopfronts
respectful of their surroundings, with plaques placed thoughtfully
on several buildings to let you know who had once lived there.

'In Kirkcudbright one either fishes or paints,' Dorothy L.
Sawyers writes in the opening of her novel *Five Red Herrings*, the
Lord Peter Wimsey whodunit set in the town's artistic community
in the 1920s. The French tourist at the Information Centre
seemed puzzled by another small mystery; his lips moved in silent
prayer as he read a poster advising visitors that the third syllable of
the town's name should be pronounced as his native cheese, 'brie'.

'That's not wholly accurate,' my Scottish wife and half-Scottish
daughter advised me. 'You should pronounce it Kirk-coo-brie.'

Was this place originally a fishing hamlet around the kirk of St

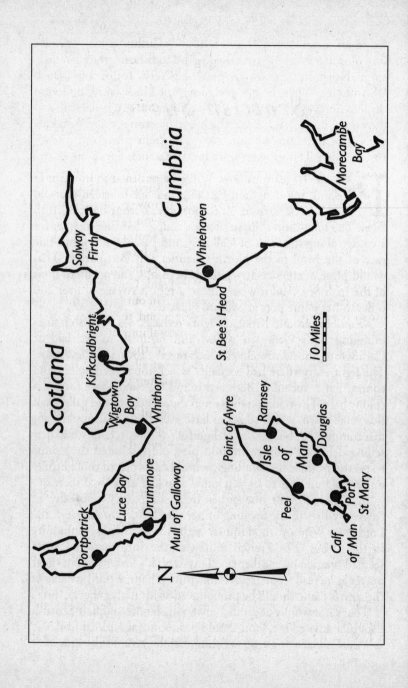

Cuthbert? Learned people have said so. St Cuthbert had a hermit's love of isolation and is associated with Lindisfarne, the island out from Northumbria which was the very fount of British Christianity. When he became Bishop of Lindisfarne, he found the loneliness of the nearby Farne Islands more congenial still, and died there in 687 AD. Eider duck are sometimes called 'Cuddy's duck' in the islands because he made them protected birds – Britain's first. Unfortunately, we found no such appealing stories about him in Kirkcudbright.

Our aim was to cross two great bays, Wigtown Bay and Luce Bay, before confronting the long, narrow peninsula which terminates in the Mull of Galloway. It is no place for cruising yachts in hard southerly or south-westerly weather, for the ebbing tides create tumbling rollers as they withdraw from the inner sections of these bays and a harbour of refuge becomes a quagmire of sand. Of the major inlet, Luce Bay, Frank Cowper wrote long ago: 'a dangerous place wherein to be caught out if it should come on to blow hard from the Southwest round to Southeast, as a heavy sea soon gets up and there is a natural indraft at most times into the bay [and] in all this wide extent there is not one safe harbour where a vessel may take shelter at all stages of the tide. Southerly winds blow for at least three-quarters of the year and the bay is at its worst then.'

To our east lay the Solway Firth, miles of shallows not to be explored without local knowledge. My up-to-date chart marked only a few channels through the shallows, their entrances set between barriers such as Two Foot Bank and Three Fathom Bank. At low tides the seabed can be exposed for as much as four and five miles from the shore, and the river-like channels running through the mud are liable to be altered by every winter storm.

To have such a marine landscape on the Anglo-Scottish frontier suited local smugglers perfectly. The age of cattle raiding had passed away by the time of the Act of Union with Scotland in 1707, but the absence of a customs union perpetuated conflict across the Solway Firth. Custom House letter books show the extent of such smuggling from the early eighteenth century right up to the early twentieth.

In 1746 the London authorities asked the Collector of Duties at the English town of Whitehaven 'if the sloop commanded by Captain Robinson' was fit for guarding these shoal waters. 'It appears,' he replied, 'that the sloop is rather too large, especially in the narrow channel up towards Silloth and Bowness, where there are many sands and banks over which the smuggling boats from the Isleman [Isle of Man] can pass at the lowest tides and the sloop only at or near the highest.'

The twisting coastline, the letter went on, extended for over a hundred miles between Scotland and England, and however well the Customs sloop was sailed, 'while he is cruising in one part frauds will be committed on the other. The smuggling trade on this coast is altogether carried on by open boats, sharp built, very light, carrying about thirty ankers [casks] of brandy or rum. They row or sail well and generally five or six Manxmen or Scotsmen are in each. On the 10th, we saw six or seven of them passing Whitehaven in a fleet steering north. And the riding officer at Flimby acquaints me he counted thirteen that evening together steering up for the Scottish Border where they generally land without much opposition.' The contraband, the letter concluded, would then be fetched on horseback 'in the night, into England under a strong guard, well armed', and sold in the northern English counties.

The poet Robert Burns ran a small farm in this region and supplemented the meagre income it gave him by patrolling the coast as an Excise officer. In an autobiographical entry in his collected poems, he wrote that in 1778, when he was nineteen, he spent the summer 'on a smuggling coast ... and made great progress in the knowledge of mankind'. The smuggling trade was very successful then, he remarked, and 'it sometimes happened to me to fall in with those who carried it on. Scenes of swaggering, riot and roaring dissipation were till this time new to me ... I learnt to fill my glass and to mix without fear in drunken squabble.'

He wrote the 'Selkirk Grace' in Kircudbright, possibly in what is now the Selkirk Arms Hotel. But did he stay at the inn or as guest of the grand folk at St Mary's Isle – or both? His *Poetical Works*, published in 1893, declares that on a visit to the Selkirk mansion the Earl asked him to say grace, and the poet declaimed:

'Some ha'e meat and canna eat

And some wad eat that want it;

> But we ha'e meat and we can eat
> And sae the Lord be thankit.'

Burns suffered poor health, not helped by riding a few hundred miles a week on the look-out for smugglers. Shortly before he died, aged thirty-seven, he referred to himself as 'a pigeon not worth the plucking'. However frail his body, his work – some 1,000 poems – suggests a remarkable spirit.

I DECIDED to pamper *Sarakiniko*'s engine and change the oil. We were at its mercy in calm weather, and though it had not let us down – apart from that inconsiderate jest off Pembrokeshire – I wondered how long it would sustain such faithfulness. I nursed a nagging mistrust of boat engines and suspected it still hankered after a little tease.

The job requires removing the companionway steps and two wooden compartment covers, and then probing the darkness with a small torch set in your mouth to find and extract the dipstick down at the ultimate reach of your fingertips. Use some tissue to clean it; put it back after finding the tiny, invisible hole it slots in to. That achieved, you pull it out again, check the oil level and insert once more. If needed, put oil from a can into the special jug with a pouring spout and lie across the engine, in some pain, to get at the tightly-screwed-down filling point. Do not drop the torch from your mouth, as it will disappear into the bilge. Finally, heat some water to wash and comment pleasantly when one of the crew calls: 'Don't get oil in the galley sink. Use a bucket.'

My equilibrium restored, I could not resist upsetting that of my crew. 'High tide at 0400 tomorrow.'

'We're not going to ...' Joan and Patricia left the appalling prospect trail away.

I thought I might relent. 'Perhaps we can leave at seven, with the ebb half run out. Though we will have to keep a close eye on the echo sounder.'

I went off to the local library, pausing on the way to watch a cluster of ladies bent to the rituals of bowls. Grey skirts enclosing ample hips, sensible stockings, flat shoes to protect the velvety turf, they would amble nimbly up to the line and deliver their balls with a quick twist of the wrist. A ball curved towards the jack and hit it, the next landed among flowers, another drifted to a stop, but the players' serene faces made them look the happiest people in all Kirkcudbright.

I found a quiet corner of the library and was soon absorbed in an account of local trade, recorded in the *Dumfries and Galloway Historical Society Journal* for 1958. The region imported wool, leather, butter and young horses from Ireland in the seventeenth century. The countryside was helped, too, by provisions urgently dispatched from English and Irish harbours in times of famine – one in the 1690s, and several more breaking out in Scotland until the nineteenth century, their memory overshadowed perhaps by history's preoccupation with Ireland's major disaster. I found churlish words from Daniel Defoe, who was here in 1724: 'A harbour without ships, a port without trade, a people without business and, that which is worse than all, they do not seem to desire business, much less do they understand it.'

So much for Defoe. An hour among the records suggested that, as the century closed, the citizens he found to be 'sober, grave, religious ... with no notions of acquiring wealth by trade' were turning more and more to trade and commerce. The region, of course, depended on the sea to link it to the wider world. About twenty-four ships operated out of here in 1794, forty-two by 1820 and fifty-four in 1840.

It was essentially a coastal trade, with Liverpool as its focus; such transatlantic trade as existed on this coast was seen as the monopoly of English merchants. In 1811, however, local people set up the Kirkcudbright Shipping Company 'to import foreign goods and timber in vessels belonging to the district, the profits upon which, to the extent of many thousands of pounds annually, are pocketed by merchants in England'.

Capital was raised by the sale of £100 shares, which were bought by local people and trade associations – the Shoemakers, Tailors, Clothiers and Weavers societies. Together they bought a three-masted ship, the *Britannia*, weighing 175 tons, some eighty feet long and armed with twelve guns. It had probably been a privateer, and would now be crewed by twelve men and a few boys.

The new venture faced huge difficulties: trade was in recession, and the war with America raised overheads. Profit depended on working the ship to the maximum, and the company aimed to mesh two long-haul voyages each year with coasting work in the Irish Sea or nearby ports in Europe. *Britannia* made a speedy first voyage to Nova Scotia in the summer of 1811. The winter saw her working a triangular route: Whitehaven coal to Ireland, cargo from there to Liverpool, further cargoes to Lancaster or Whitehaven. A second voyage to America was abandoned 500 miles out because the captain claimed it was dangerous to continue in heavy weather. He was dismissed, but the charterer and local importers were discouraged. Importing American timber was a lucrative trade in Maryport and Workington, just across the Solway, and dominated by English shippers.

Britannia was forced into tramp type operating. As the general trade depression deepened, offers of cargo to Lisbon and Brazil were secured but without any guarantee of a cargo home. Ships in West Indian trade were cutting rates in an attempt to get cargoes like rum or sugar and avoid returning to Britain in ballast. Even in the Irish Sea coasting trade, the company's agency system meant communications were poor. Letters to Ireland ordering the ship to Liverpool with or without a freight reached the captain only after he had returned to Whitehaven and reloaded with coal. A charter for flour from Waterford to Jamaica was lost when the captain, under earlier orders, took grain from Waterford to Liverpool instead.

Some voyages were successful. The *Britannia* brought a cargo of salt from Liverpool to Newfoundland and returned with timber; more work came from Scottish plantation owners in the West Indies. But the ship was out of commission through accidents as well as lack of trade, and five years after the company was launched, its bad luck came to a climax when *Britannia* hit a rock outside Gothenburg and sank, apparently while the skipper was drunk.

The Kirkcudbright venture was undercapitalised, and as a result the business was for ever chasing its own tail. The ship's owners were continually forced to accept heavy discounts on bills due because of their constant need for cash. An efficient captain – to deal with agents, arrange charters and handle freight, as well as navigating the ship safely – was vital, but the Kircudbright's captain does not seem to have been effective. In the Irish Sea, coastal shipping was the seed from which larger shipping companies could grow, but circumstances had to be right. Galloway's economy prospered from progress in agriculture and the growing demand for food in industrial areas, especially across the Solway Firth in Cumbria, but coasting trade catered for this. The local economy had neither the population nor the industry to provide a base to challenge the major shipping interests. War and recession, of course, did not help.

ANOTHER EVENING at the Selkirk Arms resulted in my forgetting the code to the pontoon's security gate. The women of the family achieved the correct combination, though not before Patrick and I had risked sensitive injury as we pitted ourselves against the metal spikes projecting from the gate. We were in our sleeping bags before midnight all the same, but fishermen work unsocial hours and a trawler thudded past at high water – 0400. By 0730 we had our own fenders and lines in and were heading out for the winding channel at a careful four knots.

We intended to inflict ourselves on Garleston, the harbour in Wigtown Bay some fourteen miles away, and though the fast ebb took us swiftly into deep water off Little Ross Island, I found myself reopening the Cruising Guide as the morning forecast spoke of strengthening south-east winds. At sea, the forecast is never the dull bit before the news.

We were motoring at present over a gun-metal sea, the wind so light that it mostly failed to fill the jib. Patrick had his first lesson in rolling it up, hauling on the reef line that extends along the side-deck to the spool by the bow at the base of the stay. As the spoolful of line empties, so the balloon of sail comes in and wraps itself around the revolving stay. 'It's simple!' he announced. Indeed it is, until you get salt-water corrosion and the ball-bearings seize up.

To arrive off Garleston more than halfway towards low water would be cutting things a little fine. Mistiming things at this point, my Cruising Guide commented, 'may necessitate a quick detour to the Isle of Whithorn or anchoring in Garleston Bay. All of this dries and is rather exposed – especially from the S–SE – where there is a fetch of a hundred miles from the north Wales coast.' I looked at the time. We should probably have to anchor off, take the ground as the tide fell and use the dinghy to get ashore. Decision time now. We were nearly equidistant from Garleston and the Isle of Whithorn. The Isle of Whithorn had much deeper water.

The place, anyhow, could not be missed out for it is wrapped in history. The pilgrimages here in honour of St Ninian were so popular they even survived the Reformation – a special Act of Parliament had to be passed to make them illegal. Garleston, by contrast, was built as a village for the tenants of Lord Garlies, 'for as long as water runs to perpetuate the name'. It was well planned, in the style of the mid-1700s, two crescents of houses surrounding a village green, and its trading ships ran to the Azores and the Mediterranean. My crew, however, were perfectly happy with a 90 degree change of course towards the homeland of Scotland's first saint, and though haze covered the coast ahead, we soon spotted the useful seamark – 'St Ninian's Tower, Conspic.' as the chart puts it – and entered the narrow inlet leading to the harbour pier.

We would not reach the village pier as the tide was still ebbing, and when the echo sounder showed ten feet below us, Patrick lowered the anchor and I went astern for a moment to dig it in. The weather seemed settled and there would be very little pull in the tide. At high tide we should be in twenty-two feet of water. I settled for three times that, sixty-six feet of chain.

'It's a lot,' said Patrick, flexing his fingers.

'No, it's the minimum – four or five times the maximum depth is normal. The anchor only digs in and holds when the pull of the chain is along the sea floor. If a wind is heaving the boat around you should have six times the depth.'

I peered over the guardrail. 'Can you see the bottom?'

'Yes. Sandy, I think.'

'Good. One doesn't want kelp. An anchor can dig into seaweed and you think you're secure, then it drags in a gust of wind – probably when you're ashore. Joan and I anchored in a Brittany harbour once,' I added, 'and after we went ashore we saw *Sarakiniko* a hundred yards out, perched on rocks off the beach. It was sitting seven feet above the sand.'

'Was it smashed?'

'No, not even the rudder, though that was only about a foot from a rock. All four-and-a-half tons of her was perfectly level on the twin keels. It was quite amazing.'

'But what did you do?'

'We dug two of our anchors well into the sand on long lines from the bow and the stern, and waited for the tide to come back. I think it had a rise and fall of twenty-eight feet that day.'

'And then the tide came in?'

'We climbed aboard and waited. Joan made coffee and said we could have brandy later. She was very confident. Then *Sarakiniko* began to stir, so we tightened the anchor lines every few minutes, one of us at the bow and one at the stern. It was quite a moment when she began to ease sideways. We got off without a scratch. So, always watch out for weed. Do you think you can raise that anchor tomorrow?'

He grinned. 'No problem.'

'Good. I'll tell you then how *Sarakiniko* looked after us in a big gale in the Bay of Biscay. It was called Hurricane Charlie. You get very attached to a boat,' I added, glancing down the neat, uncluttered deck, 'but now we have a date with St Ninian, and your mother and Joan are beginning to look impatient.'

'I'm not.'

'I know that.'

What can one really say about St Ninian? Was he Scotland's St Patrick? All we have are probabilities, at best. It is probable that St Ninian died in about 432 AD, which makes him to some extent a contemporary of St Patrick, who may have died around 461. But St Ninian remains a shadowy figure because there were no written references to him until the eight century, and the first real biography was not written until 1164 when Ailred, Bishop of Rievaulx in Yorkshire, came to Galloway as a missionary. He wrote that he based his work on an older biography 'written in a barbarous tongue' – that, perhaps, was Gaelic.

What seems likely is that both Patrick and Ninian came to

countries where Christian communities already existed. So argues the classical scholar, Professor E. Thompson, in the *Scottish Historical Review* for 1958. Thompson wrote that there was no evidence that the early Popes made active efforts to spread Christianity outside the frontiers of the Roman Empire in the lands regarded as barbarian. Missionary work was left in the hands of individual bishops, and very few of these ventured outside the Roman borders. St Augustine was not a bishop when he was first sent to England – he was later summoned to Arles to be consecrated, having established a Christian community. The dispatch of a bishop meant that a Christian community already existed, so St Ninian's coming here as a bishop makes it likely that Scottish Christianity predates his arrival.

Of course, by the time the Romans left Britain, many of them were Christians – their emperors had encouraged the growth of the faith after Constantine made Christianity the state religion in the early fourth century. It is likely that many Celts, especially in Wales, followed Roman example in those earliest Christian centuries. It is also likely that the new faith waxed and waned in its early years, with some settlements slipping back into paganism. Professor Thompson cites an epistle said to have been sent by St Patrick to the soldiers of the King of Dumbarton, referring to the Picts who had relapsed. It cannot be dated but may have been written between 455 AD and Patrick's death in 461.

We can speculate, but certainty is elusive. The origins of Scottish Christianity, Thompson concluded, 'is impenetrably obscure'.

The tops of masts were visible above the pier when we beached the dinghy at a fringe of sand and climbed up the ladder at the pier to a tangle of old nets, discarded oil drums, broken lobster pots and the humped shapes of a few upended boats. We walked along the village street, surrounded by the creaking calls of seagulls, and dutifully crossed the causeway up the sea-girt slopes to what is called St Ninian's Chapel. The building dates probably to the thirteenth century. On a bright sunny day it lacked, I think, the magic of Iona, but it sat just above a small sheltered beach, and I had no doubt pilgrims would have landed here.

Ninian – we are now back to probabilities – was apparently the son of a chief from the shores of the Solway. He studied in Rome and on his return stayed a time with Bishop Martin of Tours. Some say that a white house, in Ninian's biography the 'Casa Candida', was built here as a missionary centre with help from Bishop Martin, who may have sent masons from France to do the work, for the Picts had no tradition of building in stone. If so, we could be looking at stones in this chapel which builders had first used in a sacred edifice fifteen centuries ago. Here, set among the scented clover of a small sea-washed promontory, is probably the oldest Christian site in Scotland.

St Ninian did not leave us. On a walk beyond the village we spotted a tiny roofless chapel on another promontory. St Ninian's Oratory is exposed to every wind that blows around Burrow Head – Scotland's Land's End – typical of the uncomfortable places hermits chose to find peace and fulfilment. Three miles inland, the ruins of St Ninian's Priory lie in the small town of Whithorn. It was a pity we had no time to visit it and the remarkable archaeological dig under its medieval graveyard which has revealed much about the Norse occupation in the eleventh century, and, digging deeper still, the Christian buildings and graves of the fifth century.

A last memento of St Ninian appeared next morning as we cleared around Burrow Head. Here he is supposed to have cut himself off at times from the sinful world by finding solitude in a cave standing above the beach. Early Christian crosses have been found carved into the rock here, and a number of stones have been moved for safety into the Whithorn Museum. Patrick, however, saw little point in focusing the glasses on a large hole in the cliffs, but we were too far out to find him a more interesting target, the large monument of an otter overlooking the sea, erected in memory of the writer and naturalist Gavin Maxwell whose family home was not far away.

A few miles further and we could have observed the foundations of another ancient chapel just off the coastal road at Whithorn. It is marked as St Finian's Chapel and was probably a landing point for pilgrims. By the mid-fifteenth century, monasteries were coming into use in Britain (in Ireland about a hundred years later), and Whithorn may have been the earliest foundation in Scotland. However fugitive their lives or elusive their relics, holy men travelled widely, as teachers, administrators or pilgrims. St Finian, who founded the big teaching monastery at Clonard in Ireland and was influenced by Welsh reformers like Cadoc and Gildas, is said to have been educated at Whithorn. The Irish connection is also marked by St Edna. She was almost certainly educated here and went on to found a monastery on the largest of the Aran Islands, Inishmore. Bangor Abbey in Belfast Lough, founded by St Comgall, was of course not far away and must surely have been in contact with Whithorn too.

For much of Ireland, communication with the great centre of Lindisfarne at Holy Island on the North Sea coast would have been most easily achieved by a sea crossing to Galloway, and perhaps a further short passage to the upper reaches of the Solway Firth. At a later date the hospitality of the famous Abbey of Jedburgh, about half-way to Lindisfarne, would ease the pilgrims' trek through the Cheviots.

IT IS strange that the triangular peninsula of Wigtown, shaped like a flint axehead, was not only the birthplace of Scottish Christianity but, a millennium later, the scene of official religious persecution on a scale which left the period a chilling name: the Killing Times. At Garleston a boardwalk leads across the marshy shore to a replica of the stake to which two women, Margaret Lachlan and Margaret Wilson, were tied until the rising tide covered them. In that year, 1645, they were just two victims of a struggle over church government when Protestant mauled Protestant as eagerly as ever Protestant mauled Catholic or Catholic Protestant.

This indelible cleavage in Scottish life dates from the sixteenth century, when the Reformation of 1560 (much later than in England) severed ties with Rome and ended the 'auld alliance' with France. When James VI of Scotland found himself now also James I of England in 1603, his personal agenda was to achieve the anglicisation of the church of John Knox and maintain his own notions of divine-right kingship – not for him Presbyterianism and its democratic, anti-monarchical sentiments.

He even suggested that the names England and Scotland be substituted by the name Great Britain. It was a move that faced opposition at all levels. Ships' masters felt that the Scottish flag would be insulted by having a design that would superimpose St George's Cross upon the banner of St Andrew. The use of the new title, Sir Francis Bacon wrote in the House of Commons *Journal*, had 'no cause; no precedence, several Confusions, Incongruities and Mischiefs ... The contracted name of "Brittaine" will bring [into] oblivion the names of England and Scotland. The change of name will be harsh in the popular opinion and unpleasing to the country.' But the idea of Britain caught on, though the 1707 act establishing political union was still a hundred years away. (And of that, many Scots still say, the country was never conquered by arms but became part of the United Kingdom by a treaty made and perpetuated by venal leaders for their own profit.) Do things come full circle? Some now say that Britishness is dying and the English identity is reawakening.

James' plan to introduce bishops to the Scottish church and arrange liturgical innovation met with fierce opposition from the Presbyterian Kirk, and led to riots in the reign of his stubborn successor, Charles I, whose new prayer book on the English model roused Scottish anger. Charles proved so unpopular, in fact, that he deferred his Scottish coronation until 1633, eight years after his succession.

The creation of the Covenant in 1638 proved a turning point. It called for the total abjuration of popery, outlined a list of statutes safeguarding the reformed Church of Scotland, and its signatories promised to defend the King while he was defending 'true religion and laws'. Thousands signed it. But what if defence of the King and the Kirk became incompatible?

In the event, it was the King who fell, executed in the English Civil War. The Covenanters were dismayed at the execution, despite their difficulties with Charles I, but worse was to follow. Cromwell, who now took control of Parliament, invaded Scotland by land and sea and achieved bloody victory at the Battle of Dunbar in 1650. Scotland was now an occupied country.

When the Crown was restored under Charles II in 1660, he promised to support the Scottish Covenant, but instead actually annulled the laws of earlier Scottish parliaments. He restored bishops, revived patronage, declared Covenants unlawful and forbade non-conformist religious services. About one-third of Scottish ministers refused to accept the new church settlement; pastoral Galloway was a hotbed of dissent. Troops were used to search out unlawful services and arrest Covenanters, some 1,200 of whom were sentenced to penal servitude in the West Indies. A true peasant revolt, the Pentland Rising, began in 1666, but in the years that followed state terrorism intensified. A Test Act in 1681 required all to recognise Charles II as Supreme Governor in all matters civil and ecclesiastical. The English Privy Council decided that all who failed to take the Test Oath should be shot. Provision was made to execute women who refused the oath by drowning them.

Thousands of Scots Presbyterians fled across the channel to the North of Ireland. Counties Down and Antrim had 7,000 to 8,000 people of English and Scottish descent settled there since the early years of the seventeenth century. Though Ulster was also being deliberately planted with settlers at this time, further settlement came simply from the tradition of crossing to and from Scotland informally. The Ards peninsula was, after all, part of Stranraer's hinterland, a day crossing for merchants to trade with their kinsfolk.

After 1660, large-scale immigration got underway and continued as Crown forces defeated the rebel Covenanters, who faced banishment to Barbados or hanging. Hundreds of refugees fled to Ulster. Scots clergymen hoped for asylum and understanding there, but found instead the Oath of Abjuration, the 'Black Oath', demanding they abjure their faith – the Irish authorities' response to the Covenanting Movement. The Crown had come to see Presbyterianism as being an equal or even greater danger than Catholicism; and both were equally objectionable to the Anglican Church of England, as by law established.

The community of interests which developed between Protestant Dissenters and Catholics dissolved, of course, as history moved on. But surely today the story of our relationships in these countries – which has given us the conflict in Northern Ireland and much else – can be looked at with some understanding and a willingness to accommodate the ambiguities and paradoxes of history. Let us have a little less cultural defensiveness and a little more pluralism, for that too is implicit in Irish history. People see, and have seen themselves, as Irish in different ways and experience that Irishness through more than one fixed cultural identity.

SUCH WERE the thoughts that came to mind as we passed the gentle shores of Galloway on a windless day, *Sarakiniko* painted on the ocean, its wake a V of ripples disturbing the silky water. A haze was developing. We had given no thought to the potentially severe sea that can build up beyond Burrow Head if a west-going tide confronts strong westerly winds. 'Then,' the pilot book declared, 'there will be a dangerous race insufficiently shown on the charts.'

We had eighteen miles to go across the mouth of Luce Bay, most of which is shut to unauthorised navigation, for it is used as a bombing range by the RAF. The chart showed how intensively these waters were used for bombing runs, pinpointing eight Target Floats or Target Barges anchored at intervals across the bay.

'Tell me about Hurricane Charlie,' Patrick said, as the skipper brooded on history.

'Hurricane Charlie?' The storm had arrived after a beautifully calm evening just like this. 'It was in 1986,' I said. 'We were coming from Spain to Portsmouth, and we had the big headland of Ushant to get around before we could turn into the English Channel. Then, on Sunday – the 24th August – life got exciting.

'We had done well, 139 miles in the last twenty-four hours, but the wind fell light by mid-morning. Then we heard of south-east winds of Force 6 to 8, and the next forecast, near 1800 – that's six o'clock – was about a vigorous Atlantic low coming north-east. That gave our sea area, Biscay, probably Force 9 by lunchtime next day, Monday. We were about 150 miles from Ushant Island, and it was still a beautiful, calm sunny evening.'

'So what did you do?'

'We checked and tightened up lots of things. The compass light had failed – we had to fix that; and I remember spending a full hour dismantling and drying out damp connections – using the oven. Frustrating Murphy's Law, Patrick, is an endless job on a boat. Then we put in the third reef in the mainsail to make it really small, and we rolled along very slowly.

'The four of us were awake for the dawn forecast that Bank Holiday Monday. It was Force 9 in the Plymouth Area, and they called it a possible Force 10 in the sea areas to the south and west. That is described officially as high waves with long overhanging crests and great foam patches. All around Ushant, you know, are rocks and reefs and, of course, passages through to the English Channel which are safe and very interesting in fair weather, but in bad conditions it is the very last place to be. Shallow waters mean big seas, and a gale can close down visibility. We wanted to get well west of Ushant, and lumpy seas were building up behind us now.

'The afternoon forecasts on Monday,' I went on, 'were just as depressing. I got a radio fix on Ushant lighthouse, and after I transferred the bearing to our chart we cheered up a bit because we were putting it a little to the east; it had been due north of us.'

'Were the waves big?'

'About every twenty minutes, two or three seemed to double up. But the ones that slapped dollops of water aboard were usually the silent beasts; not the growlers and hissers. At dusk I managed to give the crew the distracting excitement of a hot meal from a tin of lasagne.'

'And were there other ships around?'

'Yes. Their lights showed up in the dark – but intermittently, because of the big swell. Days later we heard thirty-two people had been lifted off a Polish freighter that sank near Ushant. It was a rough old night. One of the crew, James Newman, took over at 1200 and was thrown across the cockpit by a wave that smashed our sprayhood. His safety line held him. The wave spun *Sarakiniko* round and set us sailing west instead of north-east. Anyhow, by now we had achieved Sea Area Plymouth. The wide-open spaces of the English Channel were ahead. We were doing six knots on a scrap of sail, and the seas were as big as railway embankments. We managed a bacon sandwich for breakfast.

'Sea filled the cockpit once during my morning watch,' I continued. 'Think of the weight of just one bucket of water. It took two minutes to empty the cockpit, and the boat felt sluggish in the water. That was Tuesday. In the afternoon the BBC told us that the Channel winds would be Force 6 to 8 and that the deep depression had moved on to East Anglia. Thankfully, the big seas hadn't followed us into the Channel. By 0700 on Wednesday morning we actually saw Alderney in the Channel Islands away to the south-east. We got into Swanage in Dorset that night; four and a half days for the 485 miles from Spain.'

'What did you do then?'

'We ate. Your cousin, Bernard, made a Spanish omelette. Then we found a fruit cake, so we soaked it in brandy and covered it in double cream and ate that too. I remember someone saying: "I wouldn't have ordered that for anything, but I wouldn't have wanted to miss it either."'

'It was a strange meal,' Patrick laughed.

'Yes, but actually he was talking about the voyage.'

Patricia emerged with plates and cutlery. 'Have you put my son off sailing for life?'

'Never,' I said, pulling at the ring on a can of beer. 'He knows now how *Sarakiniko* looks after her crew.'

'ROCKS ON the bow,' Joan called, 'a few miles ahead.' These were 'The Scares', reefs that really qualify as islets – one is seventy feet high – and they rise most improbably from the centre of Luce Bay. We would leave them a mile to starboard. The tide had at last turned against us, and the long finger of the Mull of Galloway was still far ahead, a smudge between sea and sky. I suppose the sea teaches patience. I went to my bunk with a paperback.

I was half-dozing when I heard the slight 'cheep' from the engine; it called again a minute later. That was the solenoid, either repeating its antics off the Welsh coast or giving true warning of an overheated engine. We stopped the engine and slowed gently to a halt. I turned off the seacock and extracted the small tube of wire mesh to check the water intake. Clean as a whistle.

'Perhaps we'll be here all night,' someone said in a resigned voice. 'There's not a breath of wind.'

One has to do something. I removed the panels giving access to the engine. Black oil shone at me from the bilge. I got the torch beam on the dipstick area: dipstick missing. I had failed yesterday to give it the usual quarter-turn to clip it secure – I saw the top sticking out of the sludge – and oil had been discharging ever since. At least I had a spare can, and as the engine resumed its cheerful thudding, the splendid crew rallied round their skipper and eased his self-disgust.

The foul tide eased as the Irish Sea refilled itself from the Atlantic. The angular silhouette of the Mull of Galloway grew closer. The whole peninsula, the Rinns of Galloway, is about four miles wide and projects some twenty miles down from Portpatrick. The forecast suggested the weather was set to remain fine, so we would tuck ourselves into a sheltered corner of the Mull this evening and use the inshore passage to sail close around the 300 foot cliffs in the morning and avoid the race. An early start would give us a favourable tide all the way to Portpatrick. Most headlands are supposed to have an inshore passage – a ribbon of water close to the cliffs where a boat can sneak past a race without getting trapped in it. You need the right weather, and even then the narrow passage between tide-race and cliffs can make the heartbeat quicken.

When wind blows against the tide, this is a dangerous place. Even on this windless afternoon, we could see stretches of water rippling on each side of us, and we slewed and tumbled through some upwellings and eddies as we approached the cliffs. We could pick out the white-towered lighthouse now. It has a light range of twenty-eight miles, but they built it too high, and during a dark and windy night its light can be hidden by low cloud.

We closed up on the beach and anchored at 1830. An extract from the log sharpens my memory. 'Patrick, rather squeamish, stays on deck as Joan and Patricia boil the four small lobsters bought from the tank at the Smugglers' Lair at the quay of Whithorn. Cooks at critical stage of whisking up home-made mayonnaise. Ashore and climb past black Galloway cattle we had seen in skyline silhouette as we passed the cliffs. Later; one star out as we eat in cockpit.'

On the high bare hilltop, we had found a massive circle of earthworks and sunken ditches. It is called Double Dykes and may have been the site of the Picts' last stand against the Irish who invaded from Dalriada in Co. Antrim. They set up the rulership of that name, making the west coast of Scotland up to the Isle of Mull a colony founded from Ireland. The name of those Irish people, the Scotti, eventually spread so that Alba became Scotland, the 'Land of the Irish'. The Irish leader, Fergus Mór, became the founder of a Scottish dynasty, while St Columba made Iona the spiritual seat of the Dalriada government and a base for evangelising the Picts.

The sun set in a dazzling track of silver to the west. We could see Ireland over there, and to the south, far off like the rim of the world, was the shadow of the Isle of Man.

'THE FEROCITY of this race cannot be overstated,' the pilot book declared, 'and this is supported by the Admiralty Pilot, which states that the race of the Mull of Galloway is violent and may be dangerous to small vessels. The Admiralty,' the author added, 'regards minesweepers and destroyers as small vessels!' But in the morning the inshore passage round the Mull served us well. It was a broad, sluggish channel, its seaward bank marked by a ragged line of froth on the tide. Out there the dreaded race was gurgling happily, a gentle morning breeze stroking it into submission. Orange sunlight lit the cliffs a hundred yards away to port.

Eventually we turned due north and were about a mile off the coast when we lost the high blue sky and the curlicues of morning mist gave way to fog banks. We were swaddled in thick fog, impossible to tell how deep it was. The coast was littered with rocks too, and at five knots – maybe seven, given the flowing tide – we were covering a mile in about eight minutes. We cut our speed, sailing through a wall of fog which sometimes seemed several hundred yards away; at other times the bow was cutting a hole in the swirl. I watched *Sarakiniko* seeming to spin slowly around the lumps and ridges of these grey banks, an illusion of turning in circles which happens in fog, and I went to get the GPS unit, pressed a request for satellite help and plotted the certainties of latitude and longitude on the chart with a sense of relief. We were on course: Portpatrick was three miles ahead.

Fog breeds an anxious hyper-alertness; the continuous danger of grounding or collision wakens you to powers and instincts you hardly knew you had; eyes peeled for any movement, alert for the slightest darkening in the wall of grey. We dared to close the coast a little. The old broken pier at Portpatrick or its white-gabled houses should show up soon. Patricia saw them first, spectral houses shrouded in drifts of fog. We swung past boulders and rubble and, now almost upon the beach, went sharp to port and saw the high walls of the dock.

Portpatrick, the only place between Wales and the Clyde with adequate water at all states of the tide and only twenty-one miles from Donaghadee, was crucial for travel between Britain and Ireland. Before regular services were set up, people waited for enough travellers to arrive to fill a large flat-bottomed vessel. Then their animals were hoisted into the boat by derricks and pushed into the water to swim ashore when they arrived on the other side.

Portpatrick was an important military harbour also. The great Irish fortress of Carrickfergus was not far away, and in Elizabethan times the 'post bark' was kept ready for the urgent dispatches of mounted couriers. When the Irish rebellion broke out in 1641, some 10,000 troops were dispatched to Ireland from this port. Now only Barrack Street and Colonel Street recall that past.

Attempts were made to supervise civilian traffic after the Lord President of the Scottish Privy Council wrote to King James I in 1615 requesting that travel be controlled because men were crossing from Ireland in support of agitators in Argyll and the Western Isles. The landowner, Hugh Montgomerie, who held land in both Donaghadee and Portpatrick, agreed to employ a clerk in Donaghadee to register people arriving from Scotland: anyone arousing suspicion was to be asked to swear allegiance to the Crown. The scheme may not have worked, for in March 1625 Charles II was asking the Border Commissioners to overhaul the regulations – Kirkcudbright and Ayr were being used 'by fugitives and malefactors'. New rules sought to limit travel to authorised harbours such as Whithorn, Kirkcudbright, Portpatrick, Ayr and Glasgow.

Portpatrick's communications and its trade with Ireland

improved when the Military Road, or Irish Road, was built across Galloway in 1766 and the 100-year-old prohibition on the import of Irish cattle was lifted. Imports grew to around 10,000 animals a year, though in 1784 some 18,000 cattle and 1,200 horses crossed the channel, and 17,000 animals were recorded in 1790. They left from Donaghadee, where that cheerful young Breton emigré, de la Tocnaye, wrote in 1796: 'The number of cattle taken from here to Scotland is something inconceivable, and the farmers are obliged to submit to the impudent impositions of the owners of the boats which take the cattle. They ask as much as twenty guineas for a crossing and, as they hold the farmer in the hollow of their hands, he is obliged to pay what they ask. This means that the cost of transport for horned cattle is as much as one guinea per boat.'

There ought to be, he felt, 'a regular tariff as is done in many places. Here the distance is scarcely twenty miles. On the day I crossed there were 400 horned cattle taken over to Scotland and, in the six weeks previously, there had been transported nearly 3,000.'

De la Tocnaye himself was carried across in two and a half hours 'to salute anew the coast of Scotland'.

There was trouble about landing cattle on the Sabbath in Presbyterian Scotland. The local minister realised that it was useless to insist on full observance of the Lord's Day, but told his congregation that anyone who helped unload the beasts would face severe censure and every ecclesiastical penalty in his power unless the cattle owners could swear before a magistrate that the cargo's arrival on a Sunday was due solely to bad weather.

Things seemed more easygoing in matters of marriage, for Portpatrick was the Gretna Green of Ireland. On declaring that you were legally free to marry, you could get the necessary proclamation in church on your arrival and the ceremony completed without delay. In 1776, for example, 198 gentlemen, 15 army officers and 13 noblemen, the majority of them crossing from Ireland, achieved happy hasty unions. Church courts suppressed the process in 1826.

The connection across the North Channel persisted down the years, as did the conditions for passengers, which were slow to change. Their destination was just across the water, pinpointed by peat fires at night, but all depended on wind and tide and the disposition of the boat they sailed on. An actor, Williamson, wrote of his passage in an open boat in 1764 – 'all drunk, twenty pigs and sows and horses and a Methodist preacher'. Was he referring to John Wesley, who crossed the Irish Sea forty-two times to preach his new gospel? In 1765 the preacher wrote that on the crossing from Portpatrick 'The waves ran high. I was a little sick till I fell asleep. In five and a half hours we reached Donaghadee, but my mare could not land till five hours later.'

By now the mail coaches and mail packets were well established, and a coach would leave London every night except Saturday on a three-day run up to Carlisle. Then, according to a poster dated 1779, 'to accommodate passengers travelling to Ireland, a new Post Coach, which connects with the above, sets out on Tuesday and Thursday mornings at 6 for Dumfries'. A diligence took the traveller on to Portpatrick. The marathon mainland trek cost just over £5, excluding food and accommodation.

Edinburgh and Dublin were linked by coach by 1831. The Erin go Brágh (Ireland for Ever) was a green vehicle decorated with badges of shamrocks and thistles intertwined, and with four passengers inside and ten outside undertook the 280-mile journey, resting overnight at Portpatrick's Gordon's Inn. The passengers were roused early next day and aching – if not half crippled, I imagine – would hope for breakfast on the packet boat to Donaghadee.

The development of Portpatrick was hampered by its harbour entrance, which mariners complained was difficult to see. Entry and exit was further hampered by the prevalent onshore winds and frequent swell. Sailing ships sometimes had to haul themselves out of the harbour, anchoring a cable 700 feet offshore and hauling the ship along the line until she could safely raise sail. Two new piers with hauling points were eventually built. 'Some 700 to 800 labourers must be imagined digging, building and quarrying,' the local paper reflected in 1830, 'but we regret the loss of a number of antiquities which time has rendered sacred – the rock called the "Old Kirk" or "St Patrick's Kirk", with the impression of the saint's feet three inches deep, having yielded to the merciless attacks of boring irons and barrels of gunpowder. Also, his pole on St Catherine's from which he unloosed his barge when he set sail for that land, not of milk or honey, but of potatoes and buttermilk, must soon give way to the same sacrilegious powers.'

The railway arrived finally in 1862, but it was not long before Stranraer, in sheltered Loch Ryan, replaced Portpatrick as the port for Ireland. Storms eventually smashed the piers, which still lie derelict and dangerous beside the town.

Cheerful tourists peered down on us as we edged in to lie beside a Carrickfergus yacht, *Wee Intombi*. Whenever Irishmen meet, their first objective is to find out who they know in common, and almost before our lines were secured we were talking of mutual friends over the water. Pub tables were serving coffee in the emerging sun, and presumably customers would later fall for a menu offering 'Haggis with Tatties and Neaps and Creamy Malt White Sauce'.

Hope triumphing over experience, I went off to visit a curio shop, and in one of its dark corners I made a real find: an advertisement for the 'Buddy Jock', the Scottish golfer's secret weapon. The old poster showed it fitted to a semi-clothed sportsman. A wide elasticated belt incorporated a jock strap, the whole 'guaranteed not to chafe'; it sold for just one guinea and promised to 'give you a comfortable stance to improve your game, give greater distance to your drives and greater accuracy to your putts'. Can Tiger Woods be the man who has everything?

I went up to the churchyard by the old kirk, mounds shaggy with vegetation, gravestones bearded with moss. Presbyterian reticence ruled: most had just a name with dates of birth and death. One family had broken ranks and lavished on the departed the adjectives 'respected and lamented'. Was he not loved?

A little subdued, I moved towards the gate and became strangely pleased as I noticed a fraternal greeting, half-obscured by the lichen on the headstone, from John McCormack, Master Mariner.

Brother seaman, pass not by
My shattered hull lies here.
My anchor's cast, where rests its weight,
I new-rigged shall appear.
But though my shipwreck is my tomb,
My hull thus cast away,
I only wait to know my doom
Upon the Judgement Day.

TEN

To the Middle Passage

*S*ARAKINIKO WOULD SAIL south from now on. It seemed appropriate to change my Scottish family crew for an Irish one. Tony O'Gorman, returning to us for this leg of the voyage, had once served in the RAF in Anglesey and looked forward to seeing the coastal airfield of Valley again – from a suitable distance off. Anne Baily, who like Tony was from Co. Tipperary, had learned to sail with her father racing Dragons around the buoys in Belfast Lough and had crewed with us when we had circumnavigated Ireland. She was taking a short leave of absence from her cottage garden and had to return to Ireland as soon as we reached Holyhead.

The barometer had dropped a fraction, and we decided to wait another night at the anchorage near the Mull. We sheltered off the beach under the high cliffs, but the wind shifted to the south-east during the night, and before dawn *Sarakiniko* began to jerk and curtsey to her chain. The barometer had fallen further. The wind was rising. After some bleary-eyed calculations, we decided that the small fishing harbour of Drummore, four miles up Luce Bay, offered the only shelter in what the shift of wind had made a lee shore. For another hour it would have enough water to float *Sarakiniko*; then it would empty. We dressed quickly, clumsy fingers pulling on sweaters and oilskins, and lurched on deck. If we failed to enter Drummore, we would be forced into a wide diversion around the race and a long day's flog towards the Isle of Man.

An hour of dull motoring brought us to the little harbour, and we squeezed in among some small launches, allowing space astern in case a trawler returned on the afternoon tide. Two were already nesting on the muddy ooze of the foreshore. No life stirred in the sheds crouched along the shore or the houses of the village. I saw

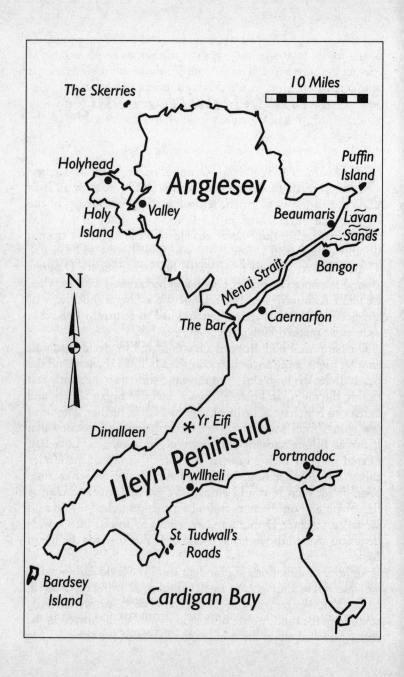

10 Miles

The Skerries

Holyhead

Anglesey

Puffin
Island

Holy
Island

Valley

Beaumaris

Lavan
Sands

N

Menai Strait

Bangor

The Bar

Caernarfon

Yr Eifi

Dinallaen

Lleyn Peninsula

Portmadoc

Pwllheli

St Tudwall's
Roads

Bardsey
Island

Cardigan Bay

two pontoons, their steel decks gashed and peeled open: target barges for the bombing ranges out in the bay, each one as large as a tennis court. It was still only 0730. We shut out the scene of rust and dereliction, shut in the delicious aroma of bacon and eggs, and went back to our bunks. Next morning we cleared into deep water, heeling to an east wind, bouncing and crashing through the outer edges of the race.

'Why do they use white lobster-pot buoys?' cried Anne. 'They're so hard to see. There's another one.'

Suddenly there was a buoy ten feet away, speeding at us through the tumble. Just in time we swung our stern clear. This was no place to be tied by the tail.

The central maelstrom of the race can shift with the changes of the tide, and it was a relief when its serrated waves-tops finally sank astern. A few hours later the perverse wind shifted south to head us, and as we were anxious to enter Peel while there was still adequate water to reach the inner harbour, we got the sails down and closed on the Isle of Man under engine.

We passed through a 'Submarine Exercise Area' as we approached the island. Our chart marked several in the Irish Sea and warned us that we should 'keep a good lookout at all times' as exercises can be either on the surface or submerged. How do you look out for a submerged submarine? I had asked a friend, Wallace Clark, about this. His wartime duties had involving bomb and mine disposal, and as a yachtsman he had circumnavigated Ireland five times, but he offered little solace when he wrote in *Yachting Monthly*: 'Bear in mind that, if you are hit, the submarine is unlikely to render any help as it will probably be under orders not to surface under any circumstances.' It may not even realise that it has struck a small vessel.

I have seen a nuclear submarine coming from its Scottish base through the Clyde approaches. It was a striking sight, the huge hull displacing such a massive amount of water it seemed to ride on a dome of sea. Wallace recounted how at least one yacht and several fishing boats had been sunk in the Irish Sea by submarines from various navies, and many more damaged. The crew of an army yacht, *Dalriada*, sailing off the Antrim coast some ten years ago, collided with what looked like a periscope and sank in five minutes. The crew were left in the water when their liferaft failed to inflate and were lucky to be rescued by a passing ship. A few years later three men in a small trawler, *South Stack*, out from Holyhead for a few days fishing, never came back. The wind was light, the sea calm. A week later a yacht on passage from the Isle of Man found a liferaft part deflated and the flares intact; it seemed to have just surfaced. Though the official inquiry was inconclusive, one view was that the trawler had caught its gear on an obstruction and overturned. Catching gear on an obstruction must be fairly commonplace, but to cause a capsize in good weather, an obstruction would surely have to be moving fast. In the last year or so speculation has also surrounded the loss of the *Tullaghmurray Lass* from Kilkeel.

Sarakiniko, at any rate, safely entered the attractive harbour of Peel once more, but then the weather broke, and for two days we trudged around the streets of the town, until a fair morning finally arrived and we resumed our attack on the forty-mile journey to Holyhead, that frustrating wind still on the nose. By mid-afternoon a grey island was beginning to take shape on the horizon. It was Anglesey.

To the Romans, Anglesey was Mona, traditionally Mother of Wales, Mam Cyomru, and so fertile that some have claimed it once grew enough corn to feed the whole of that country. It is cut off from the Welsh mainland by the Menai Strait, a turbulent, tidal narrows bordered by cliffs, hanging woods and pastoral farmlands, and at each seaward end miles of treacherous sands and shifting channels. Rome's legions finally reached the Menai Strait in 59 AD and looked across a mile of shoals and mud-banks at the massed Druidical warriors on the other shore. 'Our soldiers were gripped by fear' at the sight of their forest of weapons, Tacitus records, but swimming their horses, wading bodily and using rafts, they made a successful assault under General Suetonius. The Romans remained for about three centuries, and when they departed left Anglesey to the raids of the Irish from the west, the Saxons from the east and eventually the Vikings – Porth Swtan on Anglesey, the 'Cave of the Swedes', may refer to them.

We could continue down the Irish Sea by using Holyhead as a staging post or, by bearing to port a few degrees, run along the north coast of Anglesey and go south through the Menai Strait. But Holyhead was nearer and would enable Anne to catch her ferry home; we also hoped to contact our next crew, Julian Smith, at the Holyhead Sailing Club bar.

'I suppose we could have anchored or even picked up a spare mooring off Beaumaris or Bangor,' I said, still pondering the Menai Strait route. 'They are both busy sailing places. Have you heard of the Swellies?'

'Swellies?'

'Yes, the narrow bit between the two bridges, Telford's road bridge and the Brittania railway bridge.' I knew it of old. At the fortnightly spring tides, the current there can run at eight knots, racing over rocks like a mountain stream. 'Even if the tide's in your favour, it's too fast for safe steering. There's a tiny island there where a family once made a living out of fish traps, the only ones in Britain that could just use tidal pressures to keep fish from escaping from the net.

'It's best,' I went on, 'to aim to arrive at high water slack, and that lasts only about fifteen minutes. If we went that way we would be held up tomorrow until about lunchtime. It's a pity. Caernarfon, at the south end, is quite a sight.' There was a fortress from the age of Edward I soaring above the water, I remembered.

'Was it years ago that you came through?' Anne asked.

'Yes, many years ago. We chartered a twenty-four footer in Holyhead for a week, sailed to Dun Laoghaire, down to Wicklow and then back around the north of Anglesea and down the Menai Strait. We found a lovely mooring spot under the castle. Then we went out across the Caernarfon Bar and continued clockwise back to Holyhead.'

Actually the Menai Strait had seemed to us not Welsh but English Victorian. Anchored off Beaumaris as we waited for the tide, we had taken a stroll along the Tudor-fronted High Street and the Victorian terraces overlooking the green and a grand hotel, hefty in a gentleman's club sort of way. We had also absorbed the aura of that statement of alien power, Beaumaris Castle, the last of the twelve castles Edward I built in north and west Wales after crushing the defiant Prince of Wales, Llywelyn the Last, in 1282. Built on sites personally selected by Edward himself, several were built by the sea to facilitate provisioning and were designed brilliantly to be held by a small garrison – in 1294 just thirty-seven men held Harlech. Edward I used Ireland as a base to support his conquest of Wales – timber and stone could be fetched more easily across the Irish Sea than from the English midlands. He also provisioned his new strongholds from Ireland, ordering the Lord Deputy and officials at Irish ports to ship over wine and cheese, wheat, oats and hay, shoes and even tubs to hold bread. The records say the roads to Irish ports were crowded by hogs and cattle.

In the later English Civil Wars, much of north Wales and strongholds like Beaumaris and Chester remained Royalist. Again they were supported from Ireland. The Duke of Ormond landed thousands of Irishmen on the Welsh coast – 4,000 into Chester alone, and its fall in February 1646 proved disastrous for Charles I. Nor could Anglesey hold out. As a fertile island, sparsely inhabited, far from the centres of power and government and protected by the Menai Strait, it was seen for centuries as a potential beachhead for invaders. Even in Queen Elizabeth's time, the Crown feared that the Spanish might land there or that local gentry might make common cause with forces from Ireland. By the seventeenth century, there seemed to be a panic every decade. In the following century, the descent of John Paul Jones on northeast England and the French landing near Fishguard in 1797 kept these fears alive.

I recalled Caernarfon rather well. It has provoked two anxieties in my life. I have only once injured my crew, when I caught Eugene Byrne with the end of a boat-hook as I probed to catch a mooring buoy under the walls of Caernarfon castle. The injury was alarmingly close to his eye, and we three unshaven, oil-skinned figures, one with a bloodied face, went hastening through the town in search of a surgery to stitch our friend. Eugene still carries a small memento of our friendship.

The second anxiety was the Bar. You cannot get southward out of the Menai Strait without crossing the Bar, negotiating the shifting channels through sandbanks – 'a very hazardous task in onshore winds', the pilot book said solemnly. Next day, our week's charter running out and the yacht needed in Holyhead, Eugene still looking like a pirate with his bandaged eye, my big anxiety was whether the wind out in the delta was – or would become – a southerly Force 5 and more. It was difficult to gauge from our sheltered anchorage, and I made the error of asking opinions from the visiting yachts. Naturally they were all different, so I lay sleepless in the bunk that night trying to reason myself out of nervous fears, sick of the wind and the need to get on.

On that voyage we had agreed that the worst shipping forecast was for a wind which is strong but suitable for bold men. Once we confessed we were craven cowards, we could relax and even tolerate the smugness with which a BBC announcer would hail us from his warm studio: 'Good night, gentlemen, and good sailing.' I woke at 0500 to the drumming of rain on the sprayhood, but the wind had stopped shaking the rigging, and a local fisherman I met offered lots of reassurance. One can be duped by one's fears. By the time we set sail, the burgee at the masthead was limp in the breeze, and as we made the two-mile run through the channels of the Bar, we even enjoyed rounding the buoys in the pelting rain.

PRESUMABLY SNOWDONIA has always been a rain factory. Following an afternoon of warm sunshine, Anne, who was on watch, called down, 'Very black cloud ahead.' Tony and I struggled into oilskins and seaboots and once we reached the cockpit saw we were in for torrential rain. I took a quick fix with the handbearing compass on Holy Island as the coast dissolved in murk. It was a remarkably fast transition – seven o'clock on an August evening, and suddenly we were in semi-darkness. Presently a light flashed off to port, two every ten seconds. It was the Skerries; Holyhead harbour was five miles south.

We kept sharp lookout now, for here on the watery tip of Wales we were crossing the sea-lane where vessels bound for Liverpool do a turn to the east as they come up the Irish Sea. As in most busy waters where traffic may converge, each charted sea-lane is two miles wide, with a similar width for the separation zone between. The Skerries, this famous turning point, is actually a group of seven rocky islets a few miles off the mainland. The tidal streams which run across the rocky patches surrounding the islets provoke heavy overfalls, even in quiet weather.

Rocks' names, I find, resonate with history, invite speculation. Why was the West Mouse so called? There is a legend that St Patrick was wrecked on the Middle Mouse islet – and, indeed, when I looked at the chart I found the words Ynys Badrig (Patrick's Rock). And the Africa Rock? Did Coal Rock wreck a deep-loaded collier? The two Coal Beacons could refer to the pre-lighthouse age, when a brazier of flaming coal, kept ablaze by a lightkeeper and his wife, warned all sailing ships to stand well clear.

William Trench, a merchant of Dublin, got a ninety-nine-year lease of these reefs from the Crown in 1714, together with a patent to build a light tower and authority to charge one and two pennies a ton on passing cargoes. His Crown rent was only £5 a year. Erecting a light was dangerous work; it claimed the life of his son. By 1717 the job was done and 'on ye 1st of November a fire was kindled there and ever since supported'. But not by Trench. Vessels which passed failed to pay dues when they arrived in port, and Trench died a broken man. His daughter sold the balance of the lease for a nominal sum. In later years, following the expansion of American trade to and from Liverpool and other northern ports, Trinity House paid £445,000 for a renewed lease in 1836.

The rainstorm continued, cutting visibility to a few hundred yards, but the chop in the water had moderated, so the breakwater must be close ahead. A buoy appeared, marking the line of a channel. For safety we edged to port into shallower water. The ghost of a white Ireland-bound ferry appeared briefly out to starboard. It seemed to be turning, for we glimpsed three cascades of spray from its great engines as it vanished. We hoped that the radar unit on our crosstrees would signal our presence to anything coming up astern. Then, as so often happens, Neptune relented, the tropical downpour ceased to pockmark the sea, the breakwater appeared, and soon we could see dozens of moored yachts a mile away, down at the south-west corner of the huge harbour.

The Holyhead Sailing Club has the best kind of bar: nobody pays much attention to what is being said; they just like making conversation. Tony, who had come ashore white-faced with cold as his oilskins had developed a leak, gave priority to a hot shower before a large whisky. In the meantime I had become involved in conversation with a rather earnest man who bore a slight resemblance to the former Prime Minister, John Major. He told me of an army of Welsh workers who were waiting to commute across the Irish Sea and cash in on the Irish jobs boom. The 'Holyhead and Dun Laoghaire Link Group' was trying to match Welsh job-skills to thousands of vacancies around Dublin. 'It's only an hour and a half across,' he said, waving a forefinger, 'and we have 3,000 jobless in the Holyhead area alone. People are thinking of leaving on the ferry on a Monday and returning on Friday, or even daily.'

It was a neat reversal of the traditional traffic of workers across the Irish Sea, which made the phrase 'taking the boat' a byword for Irish immigration. Holyhead was not always the primary port of contact between Dublin and Britain. Geography put this fishing village on Holy Island at the back of beyond, water almost cutting it off from Anglesey, and that island itself cut off from mainland Wales by the Menai Strait. Northern Wales in turn was a mountainous region with roads little better than tracks, where packhorses were the only practicable means of shifting goods.

Chester on the Dee, that border estuary river between England and Wales, was for centuries the natural port for Dublin, even if it was double the sea distance of the Holyhead route. In the twelfth century, Lucian, a monk of Chester, could describe the town as 'keeping the keys of Ireland'. By the start of the sixteenth century, two-thirds of Chester's imports and almost all its exports were with Ireland, mostly Dublin, and this in spite of shifting sandbanks and silting in the tidal estuary. In Roman and Norman times, ships probably did have direct access to Chester's town quays, but the progressive silting of the channels across the sands of the Dee caused the deep-water anchorages to be moved further downstream. Small villages grew up along the muddy shores, and one, Parkgate, about eight miles down from Chester, became the embarkation and arrival anchorage for Dublin in the late seventeenth century.

As an anchorage it was not ideal. Perhaps it was the best of a poor lot. 'Vessels must lie aground on the beach below the houses to be safe,' a chart warns in 1794, 'for, though there is two and a half fathoms in the channel off the town ... the stream of the tide is so strong and the anchor-ground so weak that the strength of the stream would make a vessel drag her anchor.' Merchant ships were best lying afloat at anchor rather than beached, so they could be watched to achieve a correctly balanced hull while the cargo was being put aboard. Yet there were some deep-water anchorages within the estuary, like Hoylake, and from here King William's army left for the Boyne in 1689, some 10,000 strong. The expedition needed 300 ships, and the troops and about 400 horses had to be embarked from small boats on to the larger vessels.

Despite these difficulties, the village of Parkgate had the great advantage over Holyhead of a regular coach service from London. From the 1650s, the stagecoach left Charing Cross for Chester three days a week on an 182-mile journey which took four or five days, depending on the weather. It was one of the earliest long-distance routes and well organised in nineteen post stages.

There were risks en route. There were robberies at pistol point on the short run down from Chester to Parkgate. The Bishop of Chester sent his own coach in 1687 to fetch the Lord Chancellor of Ireland, Sir Charles Porter, and his family who had landed in the Royal Yacht *Portsmouth*. A search found Porter's children 'set in a stage coach and broke in the quicksands' three miles from Chester. Another traveller, ten years later, forded the Dee at the wrong point 'while riding to Parkgate to embark for Ireland and was drowned trying to return'. The sands and tide channels of the Dee estuary were a place of great danger. Charles Kingsley's poem tells of Mary, sent to call the cattle home from across the Dee, but 'Rolling mist came down and hid the land, and never home came she.'

Holyhead could not easily compete with Chester until it got a better road system in the eighteenth century. But for the individual traveller the trek along the coast road was difficult and dangerous. A ferry crossing had to be arranged at Conwy, where the mountain-fed river often flooded, and a few miles further on, where the train today enters a tunnel, were the looming heights of Penmaenmawr. They rise so close to the sea that, until a carriage road was built after 1757, the cliff-hanging track was too narrow for two horses abreast. Bangor, on the Menai Strait, is ten miles further on, and from here yet another ferry led on to Anglesey and the twenty miles of lonely road to Holyhead harbour.

The ferrymen were said to be insolent and dishonest, and their boats dangerous: 'Ill-contrived and dirty and, to strange horses, a service of great hazard,' said one traveller, 'for they are obliged to leap out into deep water.' The crowded Bangor ferry sank in 1726; years later another was blown on to a sandbank in a gale, drowning all but one of the people on board. The expanses of the Lavan sands which lie around Bangor stretch for miles away to the north and separate the mainland from Anglesey; a watery desert, modern charts show it speckled with the black symbols of many wrecks. The only buoyed channel past Beaumaris and on to the Strait is marked by a thin blue line.

The Earl of Clarendon left an account of crossing north Wales in mid-winter 1685, describing it as 'the most heathenish country ever man travelled'. Approaching the Penmaenmawr cliffs, the Earl put his wife in a litter and 'the rest of us on horses, though I confess I went on foot'. They climbed above the sea and then descended to Bangor, having had the Earl's coach taken to pieces on the mountain 'and carried by strength of hands'.

On reaching Holyhead, a traveller held up by gales found it an uncomfortable spot. 'We await passage,' wrote one, 'but the weather is so bad that the packet which started yesterday was forced back. If I stay any time in this miserable place I shall not know what to do for contentment.'

Even provisions could be scarce. 'All the bread used here comes from Dublin,' another wrote in 1770. 'Thirteen sixpenny loaves to the dozen, but a supply has frequently been wanting for a week in bad weather and there is no fresh water in the village except for rain.' Jonathan Swift was here in 1727, fretting at 'Holyhead with muddy ale and mouldy bread'. He fell off his horse riding in from Parkgate, 'though without hurt, the horse lying quietly until I got up'. Some years before Swift had ridden from London to Chester in six days and just missed his ship at Parkgate. Undeterred, he set out for Holyhead, riding a further three days to get there.

Sometimes a vessel bound to Dublin from the Dee ran into Holyhead for shelter. That was probably why a traveller, in 1748, found Holyhead 'swarming with labouring men from Ireland who are returning there from harvest, and among them their wives and children and many other poor passengers, computed at above 700 souls, who would starve but for a collection we were obliged to make and thereout buy provisions to distribute among them. New passengers are coming in every day from Chester and Beaumaris, which has enhanced the price of food very much.'

Roads improved, and soon after the mid-eighteenth century a tolerable highway over Penmaenmawr was able to take a daily coach service from Chester. But a coach ride on these roads could be as tiring as a journey on horseback. A letter from Thomas Moore mentions how 'poor Hobart was almost shaken to death during 97 miles on the outside of the coach'.

Once at sea, the greatest risk a traveller faced was shipwreck, and the scale of this danger in the Irish Sea was startling. The treacherous banks along the Irish coast south of Wicklow became known as the 'Graveyard of 1,000 Ships'. Some 600 vessels were lost there in the nineteenth century, over 200 more in the twentieth. And these are only the known and recorded losses; they omit the tragedies of scores of small fishing boats. *Hunt's Magazine* for 1869 estimated that 2,594 ships had been wrecked on the coasts of Britain and Ireland in the previous decade, tragedies incurring the loss of 933 lives, and concluded that the largest loss of life was 'in the Irish Sea and on its coasts'.

An unknown shore could hold greater dangers than just rocks. In 1751, a passenger on a Dublin ship driven on to the beach near Colwyn Bay declared that he was 'alarmed on account of country people coming down to plunder us'. Two years later, the *Charming Jenny*, sailing from Dublin to Waterford with a cargo of rum, brandy and geneva, was blown far off course by a gale and crashed on to the Anglesey coast. Captain Chilcot, who had sailed with two seamen, an apprentice and his wife, who had come as a passenger, was the sole survivor. When he recovered consciousness on the beach, he saw his wife's body near by, and as he lay 'exhausted and speechless' he saw a man approach, armed with a knife. The man cut the silver buckles off the captain's shoes, his wife's body was stripped and her clothes looted. A crowd arrived with 'carts, boats, drags and horses' and began collecting whatever cargo was strewn on the beach, while Captain Chilcot lay 'disregarded and unpitied'.

Later, three men were charged with 'feloniously plundering,

stealing and taking away' – though not with piracy as the depredations did not take place on the high seas – and two were sentenced to death.

A Shrewsbury newspaper had reported that local people had lured the ship ashore with 'false lights', but Captain Chilcot specifically denied this. There was a general belief – there still is – that 'wreckers' would fix a light on an animal or a cart and move it along the shore to mislead ships at sea and draw them on to the rocks, but no case of this practice has ever been proven in European waters. In his definitive work, *Ireland and the Irish in Maritime History*, John de Courcy Ireland failed to trace a single conviction of a 'wrecker', though he trawled through the records of countries as far afield as France and Denmark.

THE BRITISH NAVY attempted to soften the discomfort of crossing the Irish Sea for officers of state, the gentry and high civil servants, and of course the aristocracy. These arrangements, a little-known corner of Irish history, introduced the first yachts on the Irish Sea.

From the 1660s to the 1830s, a special vessel was made available for the Lord Lieutenant of Ireland and his staff. Accommodation was excellent, the ship well maintained, and instead of the half-dozen men you might find on an ordinary merchant ship, here was a crew of forty or fifty. Their success, as well as their vice-regal status, made their captains very conscious of protocol and ceremony. There was a social cachet attached to getting a passage on a ship where the nobility were saluted on board with the appropriate number of guns.

These, really the first vessels to be known as yachts, had two further attractions. They were relatively small, some seventy or eighty feet long, with a shallow draft, and therefore could get well up estuaries like that of the Dee. And, as possessions of the Crown, their captains had no obligation to convey vagrants being repatriated to their Irish place of origin under the English Poor Laws, especially the Vagrancy Act of 1744.

There was a further, practical reason for using an armed vessel with a large and competent crew under naval discipline: they could carry coinage, maybe thirty to fifty chests at a time, in considerable safety. Indeed, long before these Royal yachts were introduced, Queen Elizabeth had a warship stationed in Irish waters – Her Majesty's Irish Galley – and Lord Deputy Sidney is recorded in 1576 requesting one of Her Majesty's ships 'to lie upon the Irish coast for the safe conduct of treasure'.

But it was the Dutch who filled the need for light, fast, man-oeuvrable vessels, when the City of Amsterdam in 1660 presented King Charles II with a vessel whose design was an immediate success – the Royal yacht *Mary*. Samuel Pepys thought her 'one of the finest things I ever saw for neatness – and in so small a vessel'. Thirty men and guns were crammed aboard her fifty-two-foot gilded hull. It was the first genuine yacht to be used in England, and when Charles's enthusiasm for this gift had cooled a little, he handed her over to the navy for service in Ireland.

She was first recorded as lying at Parkgate in 1666, about to sail to Dublin carrying over £11,000 in coins. Chests of money were too valuable to be entrusted to Post Office barques at Holyhead and too heavy to be carried on lonely hill tracks across Wales. The *Mary*'s main task, however, was to fetch important passengers between Dublin and Holyhead or Parkgate, and, occasionally, Milford Haven. She so impressed the Post Office agent at Holyhead that, after he lost a packet ship in a storm, he asked for a 'Holland ship' as the fittest for a sea usually 'so short and broken'.

However, the little craft was not immune to the dangers of the Irish Sea. Sailing from Dublin for the Dee on a foggy night in March 1675, wind and tide took her through the fog on to the rocks of the Skerries. Four of the crew of twenty-eight, including the captain, were lost, as were thirty-one of the forty-six passengers, including the Earl of Meath. The wreck of the *Mary* was discovered on 11 July 1971 by the British Sub Aqua Club, and the many artefacts which were found on her are listed in the 1973 *International Journal of Nautical Archaeology*.

Samuel Pepys was Secretary of the Navy when the *Mary* was lost. He sought a replacement which would be suitable for the Irish Sea; in particular she should have a keel that would permit the boat to remain upright when the tide ebbed from anchorages such as the Dee. They did not want any 'rankness' in the keel, they said.

The next Royal yacht, the *Monmouth*, served the Dublin run for several years and was followed by the richly carved and gilded *Portsmouth*, painted by the great Dutch artist Willem van der Velde when he was at the summit of his career and his country at the height of its prosperity. These vessels were much bigger than the little *Mary*. The *Portsmouth* served through the first half of the eighteenth century and its successor, the *Dorset*, through the second half and on to 1814.

The Royal yachts had the additional task of offering safe convoy to merchantmen. As early as 1702, the City of Chester had petitioned Queen Anne for naval protection: 'The prosperity of the said City doth chiefly depend upon trade at sea and particularly to and from the City of Dublin and other parts of the Kingdom of Ireland. That in the time of war the Irish Channel is greatly infested with privateers invited thereto by the prospect of intercepting the coal fleets and other ships carrying persons of great quality and valuable goods.'

'Infested' may have been a suitable word. Mrs Freke, the lady we met earlier, wrote that in May 1707 'my cousin, John Freke, landed safe at Dublin after he had been four days at sea in the packet boat from Chester. Whilst he was crossing the sea eleven ships were taken by privateers from Holy Head.'

The Royal yachts became well known. On the way down the estuary from Chester to Parkgate, there was an inn 'commonly known by the sign of the Dublin Yacht', and in Chester itself the Dublin Packet Inn had long stood on Northgate Street.

A Royal yacht might have many passengers. When the Lord Lieutenant of Ireland, the Duke of Devonshire, embarked at Parkgate in 1738, he had a retinue of thirty-eight: the Duke and Duchess and their two children, two ADCs, two secretaries, a gentleman of the bedchamber, two chaplains, four pages, four gentlemen for His Grace, Her Grace's four women, a steward, a cook and fourteen footmen.

The yacht's sailing orders were granted by a warrant of the Lord Lieutenant, the names of warrant-holders being entered into the vessel's roll and listed as supernumeraries (i.e. extra to the vessel's complement). They were 'borne for victuals only', entitled to meals and free transport but not to wages. Yet there was spare capacity on most voyages, when no 'warrant' passengers joined the yacht. Fare-paying passengers, and there could be 100 or 200 of these crowding aboard at short notice, made a private arrangement with the captain. It was a perk of the job, though strongly discouraged officially if the captain was still a serving naval officer.

The celebrated Mrs Delaney, wife of the Dean of Down, gives a description of crossing from Parkgate aboard the *Dorset* in June 1754. 'We have good reason to think that we shall sail this evening; the wind is turning about and is very temperate and pleasant and we have secured our passage in the yacht. She is a charming, clean, new ship and reckoned the best sailor on the coast. The Dean went on board her yesterday to fix the best accommodation he could and, had we not come to Parkgate as we did, we should not have found room. People come every day and the place is crowded.'

In a long account of a voyage in the Royal yacht *Dublin*, George Pakenham tells of meeting Lord and Lady Buttevant at Parkgate before embarking: 'We were received with kettle-drums, trumpets, etc ... No other company of fashion ... Ship commanded by Captain Walter and very fine accommodation aboard.'

Bad weather struck, and they put into Beaumaris on Anglesey, where the captain decided to run back the forty or so miles to Parkgate and wait for better weather. 'We chose rather to go ashore here, which we did to the number of 200 people in all, in order to go overland to Holyhead, there to take the Pacquet. Lord and Lady Buttevant and I came in a boat first and, at going down from the ship's side, were saluted with eight guns.' The hardships of sailing could be mitigated for some by 'company of fashion'.

The quality travelled in some style. Joshua Wedgewood described the Royal yacht *Dorset* in 1782: 'The cabin is red velvet with silk flowers, very grand indeed ... As soon as we got upon deck we went down a few steps into a cabin where there were two or three nursery beds for the children and their nurse. There were two doors out of this, one of which led into a closet where the captain slept and the other into the state cabin, which has two beds in it, one for the Lord Lieutenant and Lady. That is a crimson silk bed and the other is for someone else, I do not know who ... Each man has a small cabin and bed to himself. The crew is half

English and half Irish. When she is in Dublin the Irish stay ashore and when she is here the English stay ashore.'

The Royal yachts faded into history as the nineteenth century brought more efficient transport by sea and land. The packet ships were offering better accommodation, and there were more of them, and in any case Dublin lost much of its social sparkle after the Act of Union in 1801. The role of the Royal yacht passed away when steamers began to provide a service from Holyhead and Liverpool in the 1820s. The last Royal yacht on the Irish station, the *Royal Charlotte*, was decommissioned in 1832.

COMFORT VARIED greatly on Post Office packets and merchant ships. With luck – and cash – one might secure a share in a cabin, and some packet boats might have several. 'Twenty beds in two rooms fitted up with mahogany and every convenience a traveller could desire' runs one account in 1795. Another traveller struck a more disenchanted note: 'when I entered, my fellow passengers were seated around a large table in the cabin. We were fourteen in number ... To do them justice, they exerted themselves zealously for the common entertainment. As for my part, I had nothing to say; nor, if I had, was anyone at leisure to listen to me, so I took possession of what the captain called a bed.'

Occasionally the well-to-do, coming aboard with a post-chaise or a coach, brought their accommodation with them. With its wheels removed and the carriage secured on deck, the coach made a useful shelter during the day and a snug place at night. That assiduous traveller, John Wesley, always hid away in his coach to read in comfort while his ship was at sea.

The most numerous cross-Channel passengers in the seventeenth and eighteenth centuries were migrant labourers, for whom comfort was simply not a consideration. Large numbers travelled to Parkgate and walked from there to the south of England looking for work, especially at haymaking and harvesting, which were a little earlier in south-east England than in Ireland. The poor seasonal migrant preferred to walk towards London on the busy road from Chester than walk through Wales

– there was the prospect of work and a better chance of begging bread or buttermilk or shelter in a stable or shed. Migrants seeking work tended to go to the big farms in East Anglia rather than the small family farms of the west.

Migrants who failed to find work and took to begging were classed as vagrants. Under the Poor Laws – which, in Queen Elizabeth's time, penalised 'Mansyke [Isle of Man], Scottish or Irish rogues' – a vagrant was liable to be returned to his original place of settlement in Ireland. A magistrate would order that the vagrant, and his wife and children be conveyed by a constable to a port of departure such as Parkgate, and that a warrant be then obtained directing the captain of any ship bound for Ireland to take them on board.

These unfortunate people awaited deportation in Parkgate's House of Correction, which, like other coastal townships, complained at the expense. Between 1750 and 1800, over 25,000 people were detained in Parkgate, an average of some 500 a year. The vast majority were single men, though there were couples also and many children, some of them orphaned and left on their own.

They were put on board a ship as soon as possible, though ships' captains, despite being obliged by the law of Queen Anne to take them under pain of a £5 fine, were generally reluctant to have passengers who could not pay their way. They complained that the passage and food allowances were quite inadequate and in 1787 resolved that no more vagrants would be taken at 2s 4d a head freight 'except what the law compels them to take, as [the allowance] is often devoured before the vessel gets over the bar, and the passengers would starve if the captain did not relieve them'. The food allowance was subsequently increased to 6d and the passage money to 2s 6d a day.

There were instances of generosity, too. The *Chester Chronicle* wrote in 1789: 'Not less than 140 haymakers, natives of our sister country, last week, after embarking twice from Parkgate, had each time the mortification of being driven back by adverse winds. The benevolent inhabitants of Neston opened a subscription for them, when the sum of £20 16s was immediately collected by Captain Heird.'

The unfortunate migrant workers were received with less charity when they reached Dublin's dockside. There was no Poor Law in Ireland. Though Dean Swift, Berkeley and many others had argued in vain for a constitutional Poor Law as a very necessary measure of social welfare, the first legislation was not passed until 1838 – so the destitute had to rely on voluntary bodies to help them reach their homes. Some people, such as Earl Temple in 1799, used this deplorable fact to support the suggestion that the Irish poor might welcome the coming Union of Britain and Ireland.

Poor travellers crossing the Irish Sea were also vulnerable to the activities of the press gangs. Slater's *Dublin Chronicle* reported in August 1790 that twenty-seven Irish haymakers, waiting to take ship to England, were seized by a press gang at Dublin's Pidgeon House terminal. A few years later, when an army sergeant escorting a party of soldiers to England spotted on the same boat fifteen Irish migrants bound for haymaking, he stood them enough whiskey to persuade them to exchange their clothing for a soldier's uniform. His scheme did not pay off, however; the magistrates in Chester discharged his victims.

When King James II fled Ireland after the Battle of the Boyne, he and his son, James Francis Edward – otherwise James III or The Old Pretender – kept court in exile in Rome. There the Old Pretender received a letter sent from Naples from one Patrick Sarsfield, who complained: 'They pressed me in Parkgate when I went over to make the harvest. I come here to you to get some money to buy Cloths and victuals and Carry me to Leghorn and depend I will love you forever.' The letter, today in the Royal Archives in Windsor Castle, has a postscript: 'My grandfather fought for your father in Ireland against King William.' The writer, who may indeed have been a grandson of Patrick Sarsfield, was given £10 for his troubles.

In the 1770s, the traffic of Irish people to England began to switch towards Liverpool. Before then the road to London was not very good, while heavy winds also endangered the ferry services across the Mersey. Daniel Defoe, in his tour through Britain in the 1720s, recorded that 'the ferry at full sea is more than two miles across. We land on the flat shore on the other side and are contented to ride through the water for some length, not on horseback but on the shoulders of some honest Lancashire clown who comes knee deep to the best side to truss you up and then runs away with you, as nimbly as you desire to ride ... I was shaken by him,' Defoe complained, 'more than I cared for and much worse than a hard trotting horse would have shaken me.'

By the 1830s, of course, Liverpool had become a major port for Ireland, with hundreds of ships offering emigrants cheap fares across the Atlantic. Emigrants fleeing the Famine from the late 1840s onward used direct transport to Liverpool in huge numbers, whether to seek work in this and other expanding cities or to board ship for America. Records show that 296,231 people landed in Liverpool from Ireland in the first eleven months of 1847. Of that number, some 130,000 went on to the United States.

THE FIRST commercial steamship service in Europe began in 1812 when the engineer Henry Bell started a passenger service on the River Clyde aboard the *Comet*. Sir Walter Scott was an early passenger and in sonorous prose described the ship sailing at 8 knots 'with a smoothness of motion which probably resembles flying'.

Steamer services received a major boost when in 1819 a House of Commons Committee suggested that a steam vessel should be used to tow vessels in and out of Holyhead harbour – Isaac Weld's report of his voyage on the first steamship to cross the Irish Sea had probably made an impression. The age of steam, which quickly halved the journey time across the Irish Sea, had begun in earnest.

A group of Dublin businessmen, including two sons of Mr Wye-Williams, Secretary to the Bank of Ireland, established the Steam Packet Company to serve Holyhead, and their ship, the *Hibernia*, sailed from Dublin in 1818. The younger son, Charles, later founded his own company, the City of Dublin Steam Packet Company (CDSPC), which had a paddle steamer crossing the Irish Sea by 1823. The CDSPC was a major success. Buying up weaker enterprises, it extended its services for passengers, goods and livestock to several ports around the Irish Sea and even on the River Shannon and the canals. The company's boats travelled overnight from places such as Ballinasloe, Dromineer (Nenagh), Portumna, Killaloe, Limerick and Shannon harbour with cattle for the Dublin markets. The company built up a large fleet and pursued innovations in shipbuilding, such as watertight bulkheads, from the yard of Lairds of Birkenhead, later the great engineering company Cammel Laird. In 1829 the Dublin company gave Lairds orders for large barges which were the first iron vessels to be built on the Mersey, and in 1833 Lairds built the first all-iron paddle steamer, the 130-feet-long *Lady Lansdowne*, which was delivered in sections to the Shannon where it was to act as a ferry.

The CDSPC received a further boost when the British Admiralty sold two of its paddle steamers to the company in 1849 and granted it the valuable contract to convey the mail. The London and North Western Railway Company bitterly resented the move, but ten years later, after a round of acrimonious tendering, the Dublin company won a renewed contract at an annual fee of £85,900. In a lesson perhaps for a future age, they agreed to a penalty clause of £1 4d for each minute of avoidable delay in their sea service.

The CDSPC now ordered four new paddle steamers. Prospects were rosy, for Robert Stephenson's great rail bridge had been opened across the Menai Strait in 1850, completing the last section of the railroad from London to the coast. The bridge was an engineering marvel, the first tubular structure and designed to support the weight of a train. Raising the immense weight of its sections high above the water with quite primitive lifting appliances was an astonishing achievement in itself. Three of the new paddle steamers were built by Lairds, and the fleet was named after Ireland's four provinces: the *Ulster*, *Munster*, *Leinster* and *Connaught*.

In 1895 the Dublin company ordered four more ships, again carrying these names and now of twin-screw design, having once again got a twenty-year contract for the mail. These would be Laird's most advanced designs, each able to carry 1,400 passengers and with sorting facilities for up to 250 bags of mail by thirty postal workers. After a lavish launching ceremony at Birkenhead, the *Leinster* broke the Irish Sea crossing record on her maiden voyage.

The company's mail contract saw them through the difficult years following the outbreak of World War I, but in 1917 the Ministry of Shipping requisitioned the *Connaught* for 'trooping' in the English Channel. Within months the *Ulster* and *Munster* were also requisitioned. The company still received revenue, but difficulties arose, such as when the Admiralty ordered guns to be fitted without consultation. Then came the disaster of 10 October 1918 when two torpedoes sank the *Leinster* within sight of Dun Laoghaire, killing 501 people out of the 780 on board. Trading by the Dublin company was unsustainable after that disaster, and a few years later this fine Irish enterprise was wound up.

ELEVEN

Coastwise Wales

A QUESTIONING FACE appeared around the door of the sailing club bar. 'It's Julian,' I cried, waving my beer mug, 'he's made it!'

Introductions followed. I had selected Julian as crew although I did not know him well. Though not a lawyer himself, he had been a guest at a dinner for judges in London which I had a small part in planning. The Lord Chancellor arranges an annual reception where members of the European Union judiciary meet the English legal world. One fallout from this occasion is that London's Irish lawyers offer further hospitality to judges from Dublin and Belfast. They lure them over with the suggestion that they may find a dinner party of fifty more convivial, if less colourful, than the din produced by 500 bewigged figures gathered like a flock of sheep in the Great Hall of Edward I at Westminster.

Ever since man made a dugout canoe big enough for two people, I am sure he has had to face up to crewing problems. The qualifications for an ideal crew are obvious. The boat engine needs an engineer, a steady practical type who can bleed the diesel fuel line when bubbly air gets into the system. Such a crew will also be more ready than the skipper to clamber about a wet cockpit at dawn and get the sails up. He or she will be a trusted navigator and a willing cook when the oven is rocking on its gimbals. A certificate in First Aid is useful too. The ideal crew will rarely have all these qualities, of course. Indeed, I compromised when I married one.

Sailing can be pleasant, calm and peaceful, but you really cannot judge the calibre of crew until the stakes get high. To be avoided at all costs are the worried crew and the jovial crew. The first will cause nerves to vibrate soon after coming aboard. The second will never understand that the life and soul of the party should occasionally turn down the emotional temperature.

There are as many variations on crews as there are on skippers. For the latter, it is easier to advise on what to avoid than on what to accept. All I can say is that one should think twice before going sailing with me because I probably combine the worst elements of all of them. I once crossed to France with a good companion on a chartered twenty-five-footer. He brought his girlfriend. It was an inclement crossing, grey skies and sodden winds while daylight lasted, and in the dark a few interesting moments among the confusion of ships' lights. The moment we arrived at Cherbourg, the girlfriend telephoned a Parisian aunt, who apparently developed an ailment which required her niece's immediate attendance. There was little I could do to console my crewman, torn between romance and his responsibility as a sailor.

Perhaps temperament is more important than skills. Already I felt that Tony would hit it off with Julian, and as our dinghy bumped against *Sarakiniko*'s hull and we climbed the short ladder to the cockpit, I noticed Julian's ease and dexterity from the way he attached the painter to a cleat as surely as one recognises a horseman the moment he puts foot to stirrup. As we waited with Anne next morning for the taxi to fetch her away to the ferry terminal, it must have been the black mantle of rain over Holy Island which prompted Julian to tell us that he planned to settle down in Co. Kerry. We did not try to put him off. We simply said that, though it had more rocks than you would otherwise see in a lifetime, it was now a glamorous destination, a haven for upmarket tourists and English expats, where plain and genuine pubs were being gutted and refurbished to conform to a notion of Irishness that would astonish our fathers. We must have been unconvincing. A year or so later he was helping to run a successful sailing school over there and loving every moment.

We waved to Anne's departing taxi from the shelter of the sailing club porch. 'There's a wall chart inside,' I said. 'Let's look at our prospects. We ought to reach the anchorage called Dinallaen halfway down the Lleyn peninsula tonight.'

'Dinallaen,' said Tony.

'That's what I said.' I turned to Julian. 'Tony knows these parts. His wife, Wendy, was born in Anglesey, so I have to take instruction in Welsh pronunciation from this Tipperary man.'

We studied the layout of the Lleyn peninsula. If you put your right hand palm down on a table, pulling the thumb back as far as painfully possible, your fingers would be reaching over Anglesey, the tip of the forefinger being approximately over Holy Island and Holyhead. The root of the forefinger would be the shallows that lead from the bay up to Caernarfon town and the Menai Strait. The thumb would then represent the Lleyn peninsula, pointing towards Ireland.

Off its tip is Bardsey Island. You may see it from a starboard window on an aircraft flying from London to Dublin. In fact, Bardsey is a few miles closer to Ireland than is Holy Island and Holyhead, and from a port-side window one might at the same time see the shoals of the long Arklow Banks, where at low tide the tumbling white waves there glitter like the blade of a knife.

Porth Dinallaen, where we hoped to anchor tonight, was some thirty-five miles away, a crescent beach between two green headlands about halfway along the Lleyn peninsula. It is well sheltered as long as the prevalent south-westerlies do not shift into the west, blowing around, so to speak, the tip of that thumb.

As the chart showed, beyond the Lleyn peninsula the great sweep of Cardigan Bay runs south to Fishguard and St David's Head. Looking at it I had a sense of our voyage around the Irish Sea as an entity, not a circle of course, but now some distance on the way to completion.

The thrusting land masses of Anglesey and the Lleyn peninsula halve the width of the northern Irish Sea. Because of this, they generate tumbling races of water, especially when the fortnightly spring tides ebb and flow to the increased pull of the moon. The flow around Holy Island can run at up to six knots, creating, as our Cruising Guide declared, 'fierce tide rips extending one and a half miles to the north-west'. In a comment that explains why ferry services are often suspended during heavy gales, the author went on: 'in severe conditions the tide rips extend over six miles to the Holyhead Deep and seas in excess of fifty feet have been reported'.

A glint of sunshine out to sea eased the wrench of leaving the friendly arm of Holyhead harbour. As we hauled the rubber dinghy off the slip, I fell to talking with the club boatman, who had once fished all round this coast.

'Keep right under the cliff, boy, and you haff no problem. An eddy will be against you there, so keep the engine on, because the wind can be all over the place between the North Stack and the South Stack.'

These cliffs buttressing the Welsh coast are offshoots of Holy Mountain, which at 750 feet is really just a hill, though by far the highest ground in Anglesey. The cliffs disgorged an inexhaustible supply of gulls as we thudded around the headland. A few hundred yards to seaward the race broke white. The Dublin-bound ferry left white plumes of wash in its wake a few miles away, but if Anne was looking back from a window at the stern, we were probably invisible against the cliffs.

The two Stacks, set about a mile apart, are familiar to thousands of travellers. The southern one – actually an island with a short pedestrian suspension bridge – carries the lighthouse. On the high ground between them are the mounds of an ancient hillfort, and further south are the relics of the 'Irishmen's Huts', the circular stone foundations of primitive village dwellings. The experts date them back some 1,700 years and say they belonged to workers in wood and metal. The layout of the massive stone slabs shows where the inhabitants placed their fires, their seats and their beds. The name of the settlement suggests ancient migrations. In clear weather you can see the mountains of Ireland from there.

We came around Holy Island, passing by a cove called Abraham's Bosom, which, I may say, we thought far from snug, and looking astern at the distant sandy beaches of Porth Dafach. It is a surfing area now when the westerlies blow, but before the great breakwater gave Holyhead shelter from the north, this was an anchorage of refuge for the sailing ships coming in from Dublin. You could land here and walk or ride the two miles across the island to Holyhead village.

Presently we were passing RAF Valley, so long a training school for jet pilots and a base for search and rescue helicopters. Its name has a prosaic origin. It comes from Thomas Telford's decision to create a deep cutting along the mainland near here as he built his great road – now the A5. No aircraft streaked above us, but as we passed RAF Valley by I though of my search, many years ago, in the files of the Dublin *Freeman's Journal* for details of the first aerial crossing of the Irish Sea.

It was in a balloon piloted by Richard Crosbie of Wicklow. He had begun to experiment with balloons less than four years after the first paper bags of hot air had been shown in France by the famous brothers Montgolfier. In 1783 they put a sheep, a dog and a duck into the basket of a balloon which drifted across Versailles, and soon after that a scientist called de Rosier remained airborne for a few minutes in a tethered balloon and then made a free flight, heating the air in the envelope from a brazier beneath its neck. An Italian, Lunardi, achieved the first real balloon flight in Britain in 1784 when, after making his will, he bade farewell to his friends and drifted across north London accompanied by his cat and his dog.

Crosbie's 'aeronautical chariot' went on view in Dublin later that year. It was fitted with sails, a rudder and a hand-operated 'windmill' which, the airman claimed, would make it almost independent of the wind. Early in January 1785, waving a speaking trumpet and clad in garments more exotic than practical – 'quilted satin breeches, morocco leather boots and a leopard-skin hat' – Crosbie ascended from Ranelagh in full view of some 40,000 people and drifted across Dublin Bay to land by the shore at Clontarf.

After another trial he was all set to tackle the Irish Sea, but he had a rival, the French Dr Potain. Potain had built a balloon under the useful patronage of the Duke of Leinster, Lord Edward Fitzgerald, Dr Usher and some other Dubliners, including the playboy Buck Whaley whose enforced move from Dublin to live on Douglas Head we had noted on our voyage past the Isle of Man. In June, Potain rose from a site near the present Connolly railway station. Canon boomed. Crowds cheered. An hour later he was floating over the parklands of Powerscourt in Co. Wicklow when a wooden hoop splintered and pierced the envelope of gas. The craft drifted across hedges, struck a mound, and the brave occupant, tangled in ropes, was dragged along the ground before he fell free. Perhaps wisely, Potain seems to have turned to writing, and forty years later published a book on balloons which he dedicated to the Irish nation.

Crosbie carried on in the meantime, and in a craft arrayed with bladders rose from the garden of Leinster House in July. He had

300 pounds of ballast on board and chucked some fifty-six pounds of it overboard just to clear the garden wall. Crosbie climbed to the east through the afternoon, suffering from cold and earache, but the balloon could not maintain its flight, and he eventually descended into the sea.

He tried another ascent in 1812 at Limerick, the same year that James Sadler built a balloon some fifty-five feet in diameter which he felt might reach Wales. An old print shows him standing in the gondola waving a flag, high above what was probably the pier of Howth harbour. He rose from Belvedere House in Drumcondra at noon on 1 October 1812 and sailed over the Irish Sea until he sighted the Isle of Man, but the wind then shifted. By four in the afternoon he was near Holyhead, but the wind would not allow him cross the coast. He released gas, hoping a fishing boat would be on hand to rescue him, and when none appeared he climbed again, 'surprised to see once more the sun, which had already set, appear above the horizon'. Then he sank, a recklessly brave man, rescued by a fishing boat about forty miles north of Llandudno.

His son, William, became the first man to finally cross the Irish Sea. His elderly father helped inflate the balloon at Portobello in July 1817. On the 22nd William was airborne, and a light wind took him over Howth. He kept close to the water, though at one stage he recorded that 'an egg I dropped took twenty-eight seconds to reach the sea'. Surely this must have been at a height which would prevent him from observing its impact. Nevertheless, he could soon see Wales and in the end made a gentle landfall near Holyhead. The flight took five and a half hours. Sadly, in 1824 the balloonist was thrown from the basket of another craft and killed. It would be very satisfying to have an airport or ferry terminal displaying a mural or plaque commemorating his historic achievement.

During the First World War, airships crossed the Irish Sea regularly, mainly between a base on Anglesey and one at Malahide, Co. Dublin. There were, in all, five airship stations. Their job was to escort the mail boats and other shipping, and the force grew to twenty-four craft armed with machines-guns and small bombs. They were also supposed to be able to lower a sonar unit into the water to help detect U-boat engines, but this was not usually very effective. These airships could fly for about seven hours, enough to accompany a ship across the Irish Sea. A craft could also operate around the Irish Sea to its mileage limit of about 270 miles and then return to its home mooring. The landing area at Malahide Castle was close to trees, and photographs show that it sometimes took the efforts of several men to haul a blimp to the ground.

There were many innovations in this early air defence system. The late Air Marshall Sir Thomas Elmhirst described how he used a hydrogen-filled gasbag to support an aeroplane fuselage from which the wings and tail had been removed. A seventy horse-power Renault engine turned the wooden propeller while the airman operated the rudder using foot pedals. The craft carried a few twenty-pound bombs which could be dropped on a submarine – 'but it would have dived deep before we got to it,' Elmhirst admitted.

As a nineteen-year-old sub-lieutenant based at Luce Bay in Galloway, Elmhirst made what was probably the first ever aerial crossing of the Irish Sea from east to west. He took off in an east wind on a summer's day in 1915, but after an hour in the air the line to the rudder frayed and broke and the craft descended rapidly – the propeller even struck the water. Elmhirst cast out the bombs, sand and even the compass and radio transmitter and rose in hope of the east wind taking him across to the distant Antrim coast. The grapnel and long trail rope went overboard to help get above the 300 foot cliffs on the Irish coast, and ship and crew eventually collapsed into a hedge. An hospitable farmer gave the airmen a meal and helped them unrig the ship so as to make it back to base.

Three years later, during an Armistice Night dinner at Holyhead, Elmhirst's senior officer and host, Captain Gordon Campbell VC, wondered if he could fly an airship under the Menai Bridge. This was flouting strict orders, but Elmhirst was not one to flunk a challenge and made his attempt a few days later, trailing a small sack of sand along the surface of the water as a guide. He managed to keep the top of the gasbag just below the road surface, and having got the craft into equilibrium and exact trim, he 'shot' the bridge at forty miles an hour. Of this balloon 'first' he said, 'it was the same feeling as riding a good horse over fences – nerves, excitement and thrill'. The army authorities turned a blind eye.

Valley has a political resonance with the Welsh. Of all the Celtic peoples, they have fought the most successful campaign to preserve and restore their native tongue. One battle in that campaign was led by Saunders Lewis, man of letters, playwright and critic; the Rev. Lewis Valentine; and the schoolmaster author D.J. Williams, when they set fire to one of the huts being built for the new RAF bombing school as it was being set up in 1934. Then they went to the police to inform them that the arson was in protest at the physical and cultural damage this military station would inflict on their traditional farming community.

After a Welsh jury failed to convict them, the Baldwin government made the crass decision that there had to be a retrial at the Old Bailey in London to avoid jury bias. The decision led to uproar. Lloyd George wrote to his wife of 'a craven appeasing government that cringes before Mussolini in Abyssinia but wantonly bullies gallant little Wales, and is the first government that has tried Wales in the Old Bailey ... an outrage that makes my blood boil.'

The three men, who refused to give evidence in an English court, were duly convicted and sentenced to nine months in Wormwood Scrubbs. After serving their sentences, they returned home to popular acclamation. Saunders Lewis, however, had been removed from his lectureship at University College, Swansea, even before the trial. He subsequently retired from public life, studied in a Roman Catholic seminary and then taught at schools in remote parts of Cardiganshire. He became a standard-bearer of Welsh identity. 'We are in this dock of our own will, not only for the sake of Wales, but also for the sake of peaceful and unviolent charitable relations now and in the future between Wales and England,' he said.

Sarakiniko slipped on through the afternoon, her pyramid of white canvas describing slow curves against the sky as the boat rolled gently. We were on a slantwise course, closing on the peninsula. Snowdon emerged in the east, dim in haze. Closer to us rose the twin-pronged mountain of Yr Eifi (The Rivals), its summit at near 2,000 feet soaring directly and superbly barely a mile from the sea.

We were much too far out to spot the southern end of the

Menai Strait, far less its guardian castle of Caernarfon, but I thought of a sailing ship called *Albion* which offered passage to America from here in the 1800s. Many accounts have recorded the ugly realities of the Irish victims of famine, taken in 'coffin ships' across the Atlantic from ports such as Liverpool. But emigration by communities around the Irish Sea long preceded those mid-century horrors, when so many people, exploited and near destitute, could be more truly classed as refugees than emigrants. In 1818, one Peter Lewis read a poster in Caernarfon announcing that the *Albion* was sailing, and he took passage on 21 May bound for America. He kept a diary – translated from Welsh only in 1958 – and records that their exit from the Irish Sea was frustratingly slow; after three days the crew claimed that they could still see the Welsh hilltops. The ship's routine was organised by an elected committee of church elders on strict chapel lines. Swearing and blasphemy were met with punishment – miscreants received only a half ration of water and were obliged to wear a badge of shame; proven liars had to clean the privy for three days. One should add that the diary does not contain even a hint of mutiny.

They met their first icebergs on 13 June. No one had seen such things before, 'but,' wrote Lewis, 'we decided that one looked like the head by Garn where Gabriel Davies grazes his sheep'.

Few would ever see Garn again, but perhaps those Welsh farmers would have understood why, in years to come, the Fastnet Rock out from Co. Kerry would become known to other emigrants as the 'Teardrop of Ireland'.

A FLEET of small yachts and dinghies defined a crescent of shallow water. 'Dinallaen Bay,' I said.

'Dinallaen,' Tony corrected me.

I turned to Julian. 'Isn't that what I said? We have a linguistic perfectionist on board. Let's give up and call it Donnelly.'

'You should remember,' Tony grinned, 'that the Irish, like the Scots, are "Q" Celts, and the Welsh are linguistically "P" Celts, like the Bretons and Cornish.'

'And never the twain can understand each other?'

'Exactly. The Q Celts say *ceann* for head and the P Celts say *pen*. Kintyre in Scotland is *ceann tíre*, the head of the land, but the headland in Cornwall is *pendeen*.'

'Why, for Heaven's sake?'

'There is a theory,' put in Julian, with a very straight face, 'that the Welsh and Bretons have differently shaped heads from the Scots and Irish, so their tongues and palates are different.'

'Obviously,' I said, 'watching their Ps and Qs, nations of Celts couldn't talk to each other until they all got some English.'

'Philistines!' Tony cried in mock horror. 'I'm going forward to check the anchor.'

I turned to Julian. 'In the Isle of Man we found the local radio giving lessons in spoken Manx. You can buy the cassettes, too.'

'But didn't the last Manx speaker die years ago?'

'Yes, in 1974 I think, at the age of ninety-seven. But Manx is more than pretty names on gate posts there – they use it ceremonially in the Parliament, the Tynwald.'

'Welsh is supposed to be the language of Heaven,' Julian mused.

'I can believe that; it would take an eternity to learn it.'

I stood and called to Tony: 'We'll go close in and anchor in about eight feet. The tide is rising now.'

We anchored *Sarakiniko* facing a handful of gentrified old fishermen's cottages, holiday homes almost touching pristine sands. It was a two-mile walk to the village of Morfa Nevin if we needed any stores, but fortunately ours were ample. Joan and Anne had even insisted on a stock of bottled water despite *Sarakiniko's* thirty-gallon tank. Our supply of diesel also seemed adequate to deal with any likely headwind on the way to Fishguard.

We rowed ashore, hoisted the dinghy on to some rocks safe from the rising tide, and found ourselves in National Trustland, a neat and discreet place with signs asking non-residents to park on the main road – about a mile away – and others warning us not to climb on the rather crumbly cliffs. Sun-tanned parents in smart leisure wear, whose accents had none of the soft Welsh lilt, watched over children on the spotless sand. In seaboots and frayed sweaters, we felt ill at ease among people who chatted as do those who come back year after year to the same much-loved place.

'We're just grockles,' said Julian, 'the waterborne version.'

We wandered around for a while, obediently resisted any temptation to clamber about the cliffs, and by sunset found ourselves back aboard, where we set up our own snug society by getting gin, tonic and cushions into the warm cockpit, until, affected I think by the neat atmosphere ashore, Tony began tidying up every coil of rope lying around us.

It was this lovely spot that the local and affluent MP, Alexander Madocks, had in his sights long ago as a replacement harbour for Holyhead. Friendship with the poet Percy Bysshe Shelly did not stop him from setting up the Porthdinallaen Harbour Company in 1806 to spoil its beauty.

Holyhead did have disadvantages as a terminal for Ireland. It did not then have the huge breakwater which would, after thirty years of building, provide 700 acres of sheltered water for shipping. Access had not yet been improved by Telford's high bridge across the Menai Strait or his causeway to Holy Island. Steam power lay in the future, and in the meantime few imagined that it would achieve navigation independent of the wind.

This was important. Holyhead lies east of Dublin, so the prevailing winds from the west and south-west often frustrated skippers of sailing craft trying to reach Dublin Bay without tacking. A harbour thirty miles further south would allow a better point of sailing – often on a comfortable beam wind.

Such were Madocks' submissions to the British Parliament. He was helped by a Statement of Facts signed by many captains and pilots on the Irish Sea. 'Holyhead is two points to leeward of Porthdinallaen,' it declared, 'and the prevailing winds are south-west, so Porthdinallaen has the advantage and vessels could go to and from Dublin upon a stretch without making a tack, whereas, when the wind is south-west with a fresh gale, packets from Holyhead cannot fetch Dublin at all but are obliged to run for Carlingford or Newry.' Heading the scores of names on the document is that of a Welsh skipper, Captain William Jones, master of the trading brigs *Suir* and *Union*, who gave his address at Waterford.

But not only did ships' masters from Welsh ports like Barmouth, Pwllheli and Cardigan support the scheme, so did others from Chester and Liverpool and Appledore, and the High

Sheriff of Caernarfon received a forceful letter from one Thomas Owen who described himself as 'Agent to the London Underwriters' and the 'British Postmaster General in the Port of Waterford'.

Madocks planned a road from the new port around the top of Cardigan Bay, curving inland at the village of Tremadoc and running on to Shrewsbury and the familiar turnpike to London. He aimed to build up Tremadoc as a major halt for post horses and improve the highway with a mile of new embankment running across the salt marshes. By 1807 Parliament had given approval to that scheme and the causeway was built within six years. Today that causeway, the Cob, shortens the road and rail route to the Lleyn peninsula. Vehicles pay a toll to use it, but a regulation still in force adds a gracenote to history, stipulating that there shall be free passage to any 'conveyance by any minister or lay preacher crossing to conduct a service in a church on the other side'.

The Lleyn peninsula, some twenty-five miles long and five miles wide, had been one of the most remote areas of Wales, its people a law unto themselves long after Henry VIII annexed the country to the English Crown. Even into the eighteenth century, when the rise of Methodism began to transform the nature of Wales, it remained one of the places loyal to the forbidden Catholic faith. Through it went the pilgrim road along to Bardsey Island, legendary resting place of 20,000 saints.

The peninsula had few natural resources, and like Ireland and Scotland was often pushed to the edge of famine when the harvest failed. There were riots against the export of corn in 1752, and in the 1840s Lleyn suffered potato blight, as Ireland did. Its relative remoteness made it a convenient resort for smugglers and privateers, and it was grateful for the regular bounty from ship-wreck along its rugged coast.

Its traditional port was Pwllheli, tucked up in the north-west armpit of Cardigan Bay and a bare six miles across the hills and farmlands from our present anchorage. Pwllheli is a major sailing centre now, a favourite weekend destination for Irish pleasure boats. Jam-packed in summer with cars, its local beaches studded with portable windbreaks, its bay alive with windsurfers and inflatable boats, it has come a long way from the medieval village of '36 households or cottages with barkes or vessels but none belonging to the same'.

Pwllheli had close links with Irish vessels, which would come into Cardigan Bay to trade their cargoes when wind and the markets served. A record of 7 July 1587 mentions '*Le Grace* of Weshford [Wexford], master John Keale' sailing from Tenby in the Bristol Channel and aiming for Pwllheli or, alternatively, Aberystwyth, with 'coal and 56 quarters of English malt and 40 quarters of other malt'. Another document gives us a glimpse of the *Mary Fortune* of Wexford leaving Milford Haven for Pwllheli on 22 July 1603 with '100 barrels of oaten malt, 20 barrels of barley malt and 20 barrels of wheat'.

As raiders or traders the Irish would always have known this coast. Lleyn really bears the same name as Leinster. In clear weather the mountain summits of Wicklow are visible on the horizon, greatly aiding navigation. Through later centuries, especially under the Tudors and Stuarts, west Wales, with its many small ports and isolated coves, was seen as an obvious point for a hostile invasion of Britain. As long ago as 1485, exiled Henry Tudor landed at Milford Haven to begin the march which would lead through Bosworth Field to his reign as Henry VII.

In the aftermath of the Reformation, the chief danger came from France. By 1560, there were many Catholic exiles from Wales at the missionary centre of Douai, including a William Morys of Clynnog and a William Lewis of Anglesey, both Oxford graduates. In 1570, Morys, who was later to become head of the English College in Rome, made a detailed plan for a Catholic rising in Wales, supported by ships landing troops in the Menai Strait. Owen Lewis, who became Bishop of Cassano, Naples, hoped to become Bishop of St David's if the Spanish Armada invaded England and restored the country to Catholicism.

Some eleven of the fifty-two priests sent into Britain in the four years after 1574 were Welsh, and in old Catholic regions like Lleyn, priests were protected by the gentry, men like Owen Thomas who had two brothers exiled in France. Hugh Owen, the younger son of another local squire, who had been educated at Lincoln's Inn in London, was suspected of being actively involved in plans for a Spanish invasion when he was found taking soundings in the channel approach into Pwllheli harbour in 1560.

Fears of an Irish incursion were commonplace in the seventeenth century, when it was feared that if Wales were overrun the towns of the English midlands would be open to assault. Potential alliances between local Welsh subversives and invaders from Ireland continued until the Irish threat diminished after the Williamite wars, but subsequently there developed the fear of Catholic invaders from France making alliance with Welsh Jacobites, supported by the Welsh gentry. These were not idle fears. Later we would sail past the cliffs near Fishguard where French troops under the Irish-American William Tate would briefly achieve the last invasion of Britain.

Dinallaen did not replace Holyhead as Wales' major port, but the advent of steamers in the 1830s and the railways three decades later transformed life on this Cambrian coast. More piers were built, and smacks no longer had to ground themselves on the beaches while horse-drays toiled up the shingle with their cargoes, while village women walked down the strand to buy directly from the boats. I could see the remains of a pier from where we were now anchored. It lay under a sheltered slope where no doubt Lleyn would once have received its imports of lime and coal and dispatched to market its butter and cheese and salted herrings. Paddle steamers brought the first changes, linking harbours like Pwllheli and Aberystwyth along Cardigan Bay and expanding the agricultural markets. Portdinallaen also acquired a connection with Liverpool. As a result, a town meeting noted in 1834, not only would a passenger coach collect passengers from Caernarfon three times weekly to connect with a steamer at Pwllheli, but livestock would now reach the English city markets in prime condition. Droving herds through the hills – 'highly injurious to the flesh, especially of pigs' – would now be almost eliminated.

'The extraordinary agency of steam navigation,' declared one enthusiast, a Mr Rice, was 'a mighty power acting on both sides of the Irish Channel and would draw Ireland and Wales closely into union and make them know each other the better.' That would come 'from the connection of their mutual wants'.

Economic development pitted much of Wales with quarries, be they for granite to pave the streets of industrial Britain, or roadstone, copper or limestone. As the nineteenth century advanced, coal-mining dominated south Wales, slate-quarrying the north. It not only roofed the growing cities in these islands, but huge fleets of sailing ships, and later steamers, transported the smooth stone as far as America and Australia. The development of Portmadoc as one of the great export harbours depended on transporting slate from the huge mountain quarries at Ffestiniog, a dozen miles away in the hills, by some means more efficient than lines of horses and mules. It meant building a narrow-gauge railway. The Dublin company which undertook the work placed the line along Madocks' embankment, up daunting mountain gradients, through woodlands and groves of rhododendrons, past lakes and over streams and through a long tunnel in the slate to Blaenau Ffestiniog station and the loading points. The line was opened in 1836 and still exists today, a fascination for tourists. Portmadoc flourished. Its narrow, twisting approach channels were dredged so steam tugs could safely tow the great sailing ships into open water, new loading quays were built, and chandleries and ship building yards developed, the last becoming famous for the Western Ocean Yachts, fast schooners which were built there up to the start of the First World War.

'WIND'S SHIFTED,' called Tony, pouring the early cup of tea next morning. I yawned and wriggled from the sleeping-bag and stuffed it behind the bunk.

'I'm afraid it's going into the south,' Tony added as we opened the chart across the navigation table.

'Going down the coast we should be all right,' I said. 'The peninsula points south-west – towards Wexford really – so in a southerly it's almost an offshore wind.'

'Yes, and then we come to Bardsey Sound and need to plug into the southerly. Another Irish Sea gateway.'

'It's near spring tides. The flow from about mid-morning on should whip us through it.'

'Not so good in a strong south wind.'

'No,' I agreed. 'We might prefer to keep on round the humpback of Bardsey Island, staying well out.'

We turned to the much-thumbed Cruising Guide. 'An evil reputation,' it said of the Sound, 'earned by its particularly vicious tide rip which has caused many a ship to come to grief in past centuries. Horror stories aside, however, the route through the Sound is viable when conditions of tide and wind are at their best, though the more conditions deteriorate from this ideal, the worse the passage becomes. A Force 8 against a spring tide makes the water in the Sound look like hell itself.'

'We shall have nothing approaching a gale-force wind,' I said. 'You know we have the *Cruise of the Nona* on the shelves? Belloc nearly lost his life there, but he had hit at least Force 7, if not Force 8.'

Helped on by an ebb tide, Hilaire Belloc had come down from Holyhead a little late and found that the ebb had petered out as he approached Bardsey. With no lull between tides, the Sound, he wrote, 'turned into a confusion of huge tumbling, pyramidal waves, leaping up, twisting and turning and boiling in such confusion as I have never seen, not even in the Alderney Race'.

The wooden dinghy which he was foolishly towing broke loose and was lost. The adverse tide grew stronger. Suddenly the jib 'blew out with a noise like a gun' and his boat, unbalanced, became more difficult to steer, slewing around and losing the speed it needed to combat the tide. After being set back into the maelstrom three times, it edged finally into a weaker eddy and safer water.

Julian emerged from the forepeak, zipping up his sailing jacket. 'It kept me awake last night,' he said, catching the end of our conversation. 'You should read it, Tony. But perhaps tomorrow.'

A few hours later *Sarakiniko* was thrusting south-west along the shore. Then the southerly wind freshened and a sliver of sea gradually widened, detaching Bardsey Island from the mainland. As we turned towards the south, the mainsail fluttered and crackled, losing wind and drive although we tightened in the boom. It was time to start the engine. The perverse headwind was growing stronger as we continued to open up the Sound, the ebb tide, blowing against it, throwing up white water. Wind against tide, the sailor's curse.

I decided to steer back to starboard. That would keep the sails drawing, and some vigorous motor-sailing across the tide should take us north around the island into more comfortable conditions than the Sound now seemed to offer.

Looking out to port, I could see Bardsey lighthouse with its two red bands peeping up over the northern slopes. How was it bearing? What were we doing over the ground? It was now in line with a corner of our sprayhood. Five minutes later I felt uneasy: the bearing had hardly improved and the black teeth of Bardsey's reefs, extending a fair way into the Sound, were distinctly closer. We seemed to be crawling crabwise towards them. I pushed the throttle lever down. We were dashing through the tumble now, but the building tide, I could sense, was pulling us towards those acres of rocks that lie off Bardsey and constrict the passage through the Sound. Still, they were about a mile off, and ten anxious minutes later the lighthouse was definitely moving along our quarter. Julian had fetched up the chart, folded small against the wind.

'The biggest rock is marked,' he called. 'It sticks up about fourteen feet at low tide.'

'Yes, I can see it; well off the island.'

'Maen Bagail,' Julian said. 'I wonder how it translates into English?'

'You could make a guess,' I said, 'but we're passing holy ground. Actually,' I added, 'the island's name is Ynys Enlli – Island of the Tides.'

'Very suitable.'

'Good to have twenty-seven horsepower under the cockpit all the same,' Tony said, contemplating the western slopes of Bardsey, which was at long last coming into view.

TWELVE

Closing the Circle

J EREMY HAD THE binoculars trained on the island. 'A scatter of
buildings but no landing place, I think.'
  'It's very exposed here,' I said, 'but there's a small cove
marked on the other side.'
  This was a waiting point for pilgrims planning to cross the
Sound to Bardsey, many, I have no doubt, having voyaged as
pilgrims from Glendalough in Co. Wicklow. There was a little
church close to the village on the mainland, said to date from
around 600 AD, and a medieval building called the 'Big Kitchen'
with massive walls and a low ceiling.
  There were several staging places for pilgrims. Near our
anchorage last night was the hamlet of Pistyll, which had a sixth-
or seventh-century church dedicated to St Beieno set in a grove of
trees with a stream flowing past on to a long shingle beach.
Remains of the fishpond which served the pilgrims' hostel are still
visible. Seven miles further inland was another stopping place, and
a church founded by St Beieno himself. A church was founded on
Bardsey too, of course, and through the Dark Ages the holy and
mystic island was a refuge from the lawlessness of the mainland
after the fall of Roman power.
  Every account of Bardsey, even the carved inscription on a
nineteenth-century Celtic cross in the old burial ground, claims
that up to 20,000 people were buried on the island, whether
carried there for burial or arriving to die as pilgrims. Three visits
to the island were regarded as being the equivalent of one to
Rome, and a roll call of 20,000 was probably a dramatic device to
emphasise how many thousands actually came. The thirteenth-
century tower of the Augustinian Abbey of St Mary is the only
relic from the distant Christian past now remaining.
  A century ago about one hundred people made a living here

from farming and fishing. Earlier it had been something of a private fiefdom, but in the eighteenth century the owners, the Wynn family, though suspected of dire deeds themselves, took steps to discourage pirates from using the island. Maria Stella, having married into this family, satisfied a romantic whim by crowning the island's oldest inhabitant, John Williams, as King of Bardsey. He was adorned with a crown – admittedly made only of brass – and offered a casket as a symbol of his treasury, and one of his functions was to settle islanders' disputes. The length of his reign is unknown, but he died tragically only one day after the birth of his son and heir.

Preoccupied by rearing sheep and fishing lobster, Bardsey played no great part in the modern world, although its last monarch, King Love Pritchard, declared it neutral in World War I. This may have been his riposte to the Crown after having been turned down as a recruit to the British Army because of his mature years. After the war, in 1925, he was welcomed as 'an overseas king' to the national Eisteddfod in Pwllheli by David Lloyd George. King Love Pritchard died two years later and the monarchy became defunct, but I have a copy of a photograph of the bearded king wearing his quite ornate crown, shaking hands with a lighthouse officer on his way to meet Lloyd George. His crown was put among the artefacts acquired by the Liverpool Maritime Museum in 1986.

The Wynn family sold Bardsey in the 1950s. Today the Bardsey Island Trust administers the island with the support of about 400 members. Its summer population is expanded by holiday-makers who come to sail among the seals and watch the island's seabirds. Some of the old farm buildings have been turned into hostels. There are a few goats and Connemara ponies, there is a tractor and electricity comes from a generator, but nobody can guarantee that visitors will be able to leave on the day they would like.

Sad that we had missed landing on Bardsey, I later managed to telephone Ernest Evans of Pwllheli. 'I was not only reared there,' he said, 'but I was the last pupil in the school!' He still returns for the lobster season and tries to deliver the post every week to the island's six year-round inhabitants.

Shortly after I spoke to Mr Evans we heard remarkable news of a Manx shearwater on Bardsey. Our western coasts and islands have most of the world's population of this black and white seabird, who probably got its name from the colonies on the Isle of Man. They winter in South America and return to breed, safe from predators, in sandy burrows near the sea, sometimes dug out by the birds themselves and sometimes borrowed from the rabbits.

This particular shearwater had been ringed when it was about five years old. That was in 1957. It was netted and ringed again in 1961 and 1977 and had now been found and ringed for the fourth time. And as a result it was estimated that in fifty years, gliding on the ocean winds in migratory flights to South America and feeding flights on American and European coasts, the shearwater had covered some five million miles – about ten times to the moon and back.

'I don't know which impressed me the more,' reported Chris Mead, advisor to the British Trust for Ornithology, 'its extraordinary longevity or the fantastic distance it has travelled.'

I will no longer shout rudely to these summer visitors, who bob cheerfully in the water and wait until the very last instant before taking off before the thrust of *Sarakiniko*'s bow.

SO BARDSEY slipped astern, its hips and hollows looking like a sculpture by Henry Moore. We were entering that great watery recess of Cardigan Bay, which cuts deep into the mainland like a half moon. For much of our bow-string course across that bay it would prove a bouncy afternoon and evening, as we made our way over forty miles towards the shores of Pembrokeshire.

It is a bay of shoals, long claws waiting to snatch any vessel which loses sail or engine power and is driven towards the crescent-shaped coast in heavy south-western winds. The most notorious is Sarn Badrig (St Patrick's Causeway) where at low tide sweeping white rollers crash around sandbanks and rocks just inches below the surface. The buoy signalling the outer limit of that long reef sits some twelve miles out from the shore.

I expect one would find at least a dozen locations on the east coast of Ireland which carry the name of St Patrick, but he is commemorated throughout the Irish Sea and even beyond, in places like St Ives in Cornwall. His name occurs in Anglesey and in mainland Wales, such as at St Patrick's Chapel in Pembrokeshire. He is at Portpatrick in Scotland and at Peel in the Isle of Man. At Old Heysham in north-west England is the ninth-century Chapel of St Patrick, the sole example of a Saxon single-cell chapel in the country. Padstow, in the Bristol Channel, was originally Petrockstow, in honour of one of his disciples.

'A mariner meets him everywhere,' Cowper wrote in his *Sailing Tours*, 'and no other name has so impressed itself on these western shores…. One grows more and more convinced that Patrick, worthy man, was an excellent sailor.'

We were now passing well offshore from Sarn Badrig and taking a last view of the receding coast of Lleyn, where Tony claimed he could still see the line of the sands. Our tourist volume, *Britain's Coast*, advertised a three-mile-long beach and promised 'spectacular surfing conditions'. How perceptions alter. In the early nineteenth century, sailors saw this place of marching billows as 'bare and bleak, exposed to all the storms which rush up St George's Channel…. In the season of danger its protection is fallacious and an underdraught into it irretrievably fixes upon the shore any vessel compelled to fall under its influence.' They named it 'Hell's Mouth' on the charts.

Yet if a vessel, driving ashore in peril, had but some daylight and could get five miles further along that coast, it would reach St Tudwall's Roads. Two small islands off St Tudwall break the run of the seas to give ships an anchorage, one of the only really secure storm havens on the entire west coast of Wales once Milford Haven is left behind. 'Tudwall's Roads,' Lewis Morris wrote in a survey in 1746, 'is one of the best roadsteads in Great Britain…. It would contain the whole of the Royal Navy.'

Facing an unremitting headwind, we had lowered the mainsail but left the jib aloft in the hope that it would fill from time to time and steady us. The day had grown grey and nasty, and our conversation fell into intermittent smalltalk. The south-flowing tide, which we had planned to use for a fast run into Cardigan Bay, was breaking raggedly, and the petulant, choppy waves set *Sarakiniko* on a jerky, stilted motion.

Some tea and biscuits might help. Personally I favour ginger biscuits. I do not think they have any medicinal value against seasickness, but I came to like them, especially when I heard someone say that they can seem to make a boat go faster. I braced myself at the stove – simple operations like getting a packet of biscuits out of a locker, filling the kettle and putting a flame to the gas involves a great deal of physical effort in a short choppy sea, and at these moments I don't think much of *Sarakiniko* as a floating home. I got three mugs slopping tea into a plastic bowl and up to the cockpit in time to see the only other sign of human life we were to encounter today. Revelling in a beam wind, a yacht a mile ahead was threshing across our bows on a course for Arklow or Wicklow – 'And an evening in an agreeable bar,' Tony muttered. We watched the craft fade into the distance and then disappear.

'A boat always seems so small against the sea,' I said.

'Relatively speaking,' Julian suggested.

'Yes. Take this forty miles from Bardsey to Fishguard.' I was doing hasty mental arithmetic. 'At 2,000 yards to a sea mile that's 80,000 yards. A smallish yacht may be ten yards overall so, at 1 to 8,000, something just a touch smaller than *Sarakiniko* is no more than equivalent to a foot ruler navigating across four miles. So, we're a pretty small object,' I concluded.

'Especially from the sky,' Julian agreed, 'and especially if there are white horses tossing around a white hull.'

We flogged on, wondering if sailing was a mad, mad sport.

None of us felt at our best. One should never feel ashamed of seasickness: everyone feels queasy sometimes, and then kindness and patience are all. I have not actually been sick for many years, but if the dread moment should arrive, I will retire to my bunk with a bucket to hand and call up to those in the cockpit to stop this madness, steer for the land!

Julian checked his watch and moved carefully across the bucking cockpit to take the tiller from Tony. We had adopted one-hour watches. A structured routine helps enormously to speed the hours.

By late afternoon the tide had eased off, the wind itself was dropping fast, and the sea had lost its surly mood. The faintest stroke of grey in the south-east suggested the headlands around Cardigan. Then Fishguard began to define itself, and the higher ground to the south-west had to be Strumble Head. I had the binoculars trained on what might be the breakwater some four miles ahead when the engine gasped, recovered, gasped again and died. *Sarakiniko* rocked on the swell as we began checking oil and water and fuel. The tank was one-third full. Tony pressed the ignition. Our reward was a healthy burst – for five seconds.

'A fuel blockage,' said Julian, and nobody disagreed.

We reassured each other that an engine is only an auxiliary. *Sarakiniko*'s function is to sail.

'If it had happened earlier ...' Tony began.

'Well, we could have followed that yacht to Arklow on a fair wind,' I said. 'You'd be in Tipperary tomorrow.'

Tony and Julian cast off the ties securing the mainsail, which snaked slowly aloft as Julian wound the winch handle. Just as *Sarakiniko* began to move, porpoises came swimming around us, diving under the hull, cutting ahead in twos and threes and leaping from the sea so that we caught a glimpse of their beady eyes and grinning faces. They plunged in unison so close to the hull that a gobbet of water spattered the side deck. I hurried down for the camera and heard an occasional squeak communicated through the resonance of the hull. Who could fail to cheer up in the face of this display of energy and enjoyment, this feeling of being assumed into the community of nature? The sea has the power to take you out of the workaday world to a place dominated by nature, by wind and waves and sea creatures which signal how far you've travelled from your ordinary lifestyle.

Presently dusk closed in. The tide was against us, urging us off the coast, but tack after tack against the gentle headwind drew us closer. Off to the west Strumble Head began to flash, and a ferry for Rosslare came round the half-mile-long breakwater, its red and green navigation lights challenging ours until it swung to port for the open sea. We crept past the pierhead in the dark, the confusion of lights from buildings and cars threatening our night vision. We held on for the shallows of Old Fishguard harbour. When the flicker of the depth finder recorded two fathoms and the outline of cliffs seemed to put us a few hundred yards from shipwreck, I spun *Sarakiniko*, spilled the wind, and Tony lowered the anchor.

'The shore always seems so unnervingly near when you close it at night,' I complained as we scrambled into the dinghy and

Julian's torch pin-pointed an ancient jetty.

We were pleased to find many members still at the bar of the quayside sailing club. Our great need was food, and a sailor detached himself from the lamp-lit clamour to tell us of the many restaurants which would not be open now or would have shut by the time we climbed the five hairpin bends to the town centre. They were not bored with people coming in from the sea, as many might be in the south of England, but when we heard of an Indian restaurant that would be open up to 11 PM we set off at a heart-stopping lope along the wharf, past rusty hawsers and piles of old fishing nets and up the cliffside road where houses dipped to the water like a Continental harbour. We found a relaxed staff waiting for us in an empty restaurant and enjoyed a good meal. Right to the bitter coffee stage not a single waiter started to flick unnecessarily over the empty tables with a rolled napkin.

We warmed to Fishguard, especially to a man who spotted us coming ashore and, hearing of our engine problem, put his fishing line aside next morning and drove us nearly three miles to Goodwick harbour, but neither there nor in Old Fishguard did there seem to be an engineer free to come out to *Sarakiniko*.

'Maybe tomorrow,' called the manager in one yard as he beat hell with a mallet on the deck of a plastic dayboat to show a new customer how solid it was.

'We'll try Lewis; he does an odd job for me,' said our friend, who drove us to a suburban garden where a man in black overalls crouched over the parts of a motorcycle. Yes, he would meet me at the jetty later, but he didn't hold much with going out in rubber dinghies, he added a little grumpily.

We parted from our friend, whose kindness in driving us about had been memorable, and started down the hairpin bends to find a large truck stuck at the sharpest one and its English driver standing on the pavement in heated discussion with two motorists and some ladies looking on from their front garden. No, he had not read any notice suggesting that this road was unsuitable for large vehicles – in Wales all road signs are in both English and Welsh, and I do think the eye's message to the brain can sometimes cause confusion. But the truck driver's assertions that English was good enough for him had begun to widen the scope of this debate, so we edged quietly past and kept our own counsel.

When Lewis arrived I had to coax him into the rubber dinghy, and as we reached *Sarakiniko* his foot slipped and trailed in the water as he grabbed for the boarding ladder. He was weighted with a belt of heavy tools, I noticed. Down in the saloon we removed the companionway, and mostly after that I spoke to his bottom. He had to work entirely by feel, probing for taps, unclipping fuel lines. Sometimes an oily hand appeared to ask for another spanner. 'Got some plastic tubing?' came a muffled call. Amazingly I had. Later I passed him a bucket into which he chucked a mouthful of diesel. Then the engine thumped sweetly, running smooth as a sewing-machine. When the fuel had run low in the tank, the very bouncy seas had stirred years of accumulated silt into action. *Sarakiniko*'s winter overhaul would require some serious siphoning.

Tomorrow we should close the Irish Sea circuit. A sixteen-mile run would take us past Strumble Head and St David's Head and through the excitements of Ramsey Sound. It was only a few weeks ago that I had gazed across the Sound from Whitesands Bay and speculated about the mound covering St Patrick's Chapel and the mystery of Porth Mawr.

Sadly I did not have time now to climb to Fishguard Fort. It was a simple structure, but it justified its cost and upkeep during the Last Invasion of Britain – even if it fired only one shot in anger, and that possibly a blank.

WHEN THE French Directory sent 12,000 battle-hardened veterans to attempt a landing at Bantry Bay in south-west Ireland in December 1796, their plan was not only to expel the British from Ireland with the help of Wolfe Tone's United Irishmen, but to build on this as a platform for invading England. Tone was aboard the flagship of the fleet as they reached the Irish coast, and when the Commander-in-Chief, General Hoche, became separated from the main body, they decided to await his arrival. It was a fateful decision. An east wind developed, blowing squalls of rain and snow, and the cumbersome ships could not beat east against it up the long, relatively narrow inlet of Bantry Bay. By Christmas Eve, the gale had become a storm, leaving the ships no option but to cut their cables and run back to Brest.

Though the expedition ended in failure, England, Tone remarked, had not been in such peril since the Spanish Armada. Indeed, the needs of the French war had meant that perhaps no more than 5,000 regular infantry and cavalry and fewer than 10,000 troops of any sort were available in Ireland to muster against the French, had they landed.

The French at Bantry is a familiar page of Irish history, but it is strange that a further French invasion has been little noted in Ireland, though the invasion of west Wales had Irish support. Just seven weeks after the Bantry debacle, some 1,400 troops were landed on the Welsh coast under the command of an Irish-American, General Tait. Several Irish emigrés took part, for Tait, who had come to live in Paris in 1795, knew many of the Irish community there and indeed lived just a few doors away from Wolfe Tone. A young Limerick-born officer of the Irish Brigade, Barry St Leger, led the platoon of twenty-five grenadiers who secured a bridgehead on a headland just around the corner from Fishguard harbour.

Landings continued through the evening of 16 February 1797, and by the next day a substantial force had scrambled up the low cliffs with supplies and ammunition and moved inland to occupy the strongest position in the area, a line of high rocks overlooking the approaches to Fishguard town. Among the many Irishmen in the force were Robert Morrison and Nicholas Tyrell, both captains. They had wanted to be on the Bantry expedition, but General Hoche had ordered them to stay and act as interpreters for this invasion of Wales.

The French plan was ambitious, if not reckless. Tate was to sail up the Bristol Channel, capture Bristol and march through Wales, gathering support from the Welsh people, and then destroy Liverpool. Another French fleet was to attack Newcastle on Tyne. The French saw Wales as a subject country, backward, poverty stricken, the prey of absentee landlords and, like south-west Ireland, remote from central government. But Wales was no hotbed of revolt. Industrialisation had begun to alleviate poverty in the towns, the Dissenters in Wales were not as oppressed as the Catholics in Ireland, and the people were not avid to join with an invader. The second French error was that the landing force held only some 600 trained troops. The balance of about 800, many released from French jails, thirsted for plunder and were difficult to discipline.

Surprise was vital, but an east wind had made a rapid descent on Bristol impossible, so the fleet of four ships sailed west and north around Pembrokeshire until Fishguard lay before them. It was then a remote town, a hundred miles from Cardiff, with excellent landing beaches and defended by no more than 285 soldiers. The Fishguard Fensibles were enthusiastic but ill-trained part-time volunteers, and on this February day many were working in the fields or out in their fishing boats.

Fishguard did have a fort, however. In 1779, during the American War of Independence, the town had been bombarded by the privateer Patrick Dowling, who, like the notorious Luke Ryan, was a native of Rush in Co. Dublin. In fact he was on board Ryan's former ship, *Friendship*, now renamed the *Black Prince*. The population was greatly alarmed, all the more so as they believed they were under attack by the daring John Paul Jones, but still they refused Dowling's demand for ransom money, and eventually he was driven off by canon shot from a vessel in the harbour. Fishguard learned a lesson from the encounter, though, and the local gentry decided to build a small fort to defend the harbour. In 1797, however, it was in a parlous state, manned by three invalided gunners, and the shot from its eight guns could not even reach the western areas of the harbour, the Goodwick sands around the site of the present Irish Ferry terminal.

However, the fort fired on the first French vessel to enter the harbour, and though this was probably a blank – the governor of the fort, Gwynne Vaughan, later wrote to the Home Secretary that there were just three rounds of live ammunition in the whole armoury – the French vessel turned tail, reported that Fishguard was defended by a fort, and so the invasion troops made their landing instead on slippery rocks under the cliffs a few miles away. Valuable time was secured for British forces to be collected from nearby towns such as Carmarthen and Haverfordwest.

Now outnumbered by British troops and with their original plans all awry, at 9 AM on 24 February the French surrendered. Six or seven people had been killed and several injured, and houses destroyed or damaged in the fracas, but hostilities ended at the Royal Oak in the centre of town. Apparently it was then a private house, but it is now a pleasant pub where tourists ask to see the table where the document of surrender – since lost – brought the last invasion of Britain to an end.

What of the prisoners? Tate was an American citizen, and it was against American law to engage in acts of war against a state with which America was at peace. The three Irish officers were in an even more dangerous situation, for they had waged war against King George III and faced the prospect of trial and execution for treason. However, they were treated as prisoners of war and subsequently repatriated to France, except for St Leger, who escaped from confinement in Portchester Castle. Some twenty years later, a record states that the widow of Sir Edward Mansell, a soldier of Pembroke, had married Colonel Barry St Leger. It is not certain, but this was probably the idealistic twenty-year-old who had led those grenadiers up the Careg Wastad cliffs and thereafter behaved with great courage, attempting to control his marauding troops. Perhaps he found a happy life in Pembrokeshire.

The French soldiers were held in different prisons, and most were later exchanged for British prisoners held in France. But in one gaol near Pembroke Castle, a remarkable love affair developed between two of the foreign officers and local girls, who smuggled tools into the prison to help the Frenchmen escape. Twenty-five prisoners got out through a tunnel they dug under the prison's walls and made their way to a nearby quay where, by remarkable chance, they slipped aboard the yacht of Lord Cawdor, the Commander of the Castlemartin Troop of Cavalry who had negotiated their surrender. They reached St Malo, where the Welsh girls married their men, and years later during the Peace of Amiens one pair returned to set up a public house in Merthyr Tydfil.

NEXT MORNING we slipped past that invasion site at Careg Wastad Point. The 200-foot cliff is really a steep hillside cut by gullies and clefts in the rock, and it must have been a difficult climb for heavily laden troops, especially as it began at five o'clock on a February evening and continued through the night in the fitful illumination of camp fires. Seventeen boatloads of troops and stores had followed St Leger over the rocks. Now, a cautious distance from the white-bearded surf, we marvelled that only one boat had been lost, after capsizing in the dark. We scanned the clifftop to see if we could spot the memorial stone to the French landing, then turned to concentrate on Strumble Head looming two miles to the west, a black towering presence crowned by a squat lighthouse and white-walled enclosures. We came around this northern point of Pembrokeshire close in, skirting the tumble of a race offshore and occasionally dodging a lobster-pot buoy half-submerged in the tide-rip.

Our easy assumption that it was all downhill now was abruptly challenged at Strumble Head, where an unexpected eddy got us in its grip and slowed our speed over the ground to 2 knots. We twisted through it for half an hour, unwilling to ask the engine for help, but St David's Head and the entrance to Ramsey Sound were still eleven miles down the coast, and we simply had to carry a favourable tide through there.

'At the narrowest part,' declared the pilot book, 'the stream is charted at six knots, which means one-way traffic only.... When a yacht is firmly committed to the two-mile-long narrows of the Sound the features are unwinding more rapidly than they can be taken in.... With the exception of Solva harbour [in St Bride's Bay] there are no worthwhile harbours en route – only a few small bays with partial shelter.'

Standing in the shadow cast by the forenoon sun, the cliffs and small beaches along this coast seemed unwelcoming and difficult to reach. No golden sands here but stark shadows where the coastline was measured vertically. Our eyes strayed from the cliffs up to wastes of heather, gorse and stunted bushes, or down to caves, fissures and sea-stacks in the water.

At Strumble one must make a drastic change of course to the south-west; more than a right angle. Could we afford to stand on under sail in this splendid wind, which had now, I fear, veered just a touch to the west of true south? Repeated calculations at the chart table showed that we could not, without increasing our distance to St David's Head and the Sound and risking our date with the tide. We were running out of time.

With a large scale chart and a day in hand, we might have been tempted to enter one small artificial harbour which broke this wall of cliffs – Porth Gain, built in Victorian times to export granite and slate extracted from the local quarries. But it might have been difficult to find space for *Sarakiniko* amid the harbour's small fishing boats, so we turned on the engine and thrust for St David's Head.

By 1340 we were in a big swell off the corner of Wales and in the full grip of the ebb. Whitesands Bay emerged over to port, windsurfers bouncing in the creamy waves, while we fed *Sarakiniko* into the swirl, engine growling. It felt as if we were being poured downhill. We had to identify the Horse Rock quickly: it is not visible except at low tide, but the eddies and white water show what must be avoided. Then we faced The Bitches, the long reef running out from Ramsey Island; a prominent rock, permanently uncovered, conveniently marks the end of the reef in mid-Sound. The sea gathered us up and tossed us two miles down past lines of intimidating standing waves two or three hundred yards to starboard. The relative shelter of St Bride's Bay, all eight miles of it, now lay ahead.

We breathed easily again, the danger of the moment over. Our circuit of the Irish Sea was over too, and we were left with an end-of-term feeling, half satisfaction, half sadness. *Sarakiniko* would be on home moorings in Milford Haven tonight. Mundane, practical life was awaiting us. Yet the voyage had challenged our preconceptions, stirred and subverted our views as we traced the lines of our interdependence, moulded by the sea around us.

No land is an island. In this shrinking world, we depend more than ever on co-operation – for the management of fish stocks, the control of drugs trafficking and terrorism, the handling of migration and asylum, and, of course, the protection of the environment. Nowhere is this fact more relevant than in and around the relatively confined waters of this sea, especially from pollution by hazardous waste and oil spillage.

I thought of New Zealand, with a smaller population than Ireland, which confronted France for using the Pacific as a nuclear test site and – despite Britain's objections – won Commonwealth support for its campaign. I wondered if Ireland might ever rejoin that body. There may have been an historical explanation for Ireland's departure half a century ago, but the Commonwealth is no longer 'British' – of its fifty-four sovereign states, thirty-three are republics, five have their own monarchs and two, Mozambique and Cameroon, were never within the British Empire. Queen Elizabeth acts now in a personal capacity as its symbolic head, not as a personification of the Crown. And I felt that Asian and African countries, appreciating the educational and pastoral work of Irish professionals, lay and clerical, would surely rejoice if Ireland were to join them.

I was riding a hobby horse, I knew. Still, there is another body which may be even more appropriate as a way of giving the communities of the Irish Sea a new chance to express and build on their common concerns. This is the Council of the Isles (a pity it is being called the British-Irish Council) in which the sovereign parliaments of Westminster and Dublin will share deliberations with lawmakers from less-than-sovereign Scotland, Wales and Northern Ireland, and with the Tynwald of the Isle of Man and the elective states of the Channel Islands. It emerged from the affairs of Northern Ireland and was apparently the brainchild of Ulster Unionists, who felt that the prospect of having simple cross-border structures would put the Protestant Unionists in a minority position within Ireland. More room for manoeuvre would exist, they thought, if several regional interest groups could consult together. The Council of the Isles is meant to provide a multilateral setting where each voice is to be equal – and it must be remembered that the devolution of power to Scotland and Wales will hardly remain static. Devolution has a long history ever since Gladstone intended Scotland to have Home Rule as well as Ireland.

The cynic will call the council just a talking shop, but it is wise to talk. Surely the chances of co-operation are improved by listening, and we need to look at ways of overcoming the strains caused by our shared history. Let us give the Council of the Isles, and the idea of sharing our forums, a run. It may well prove more likely to soften and dissolve difficulties within our islands than any international gathering.

On board *Sarakiniko* we were in a mood for optimistic reflections as our boat crossed the notional line of her outward voyage to Arklow and closed her circuit of the Irish Sea. Our journey had enriched us, teaching us about a world we could never fully understand just by looking out from land.

Bibliography

Anderson, E. *Sailing Ships of Ireland*, Dublin, 1851
Atkinson, T. *Southwest Scotland*, Luath Press, Edinburgh
Bardon, J. *A History of Ulster*, Blackstaff Press, 1992
Birch, C. and Jones, G. *The Lake Counties 1500-1800*, MUP, 1961
Booth, J. *Antique Maps of Wales*, Blackmore Press, 1997
Bowen, E.G. *Britain and the Western Seaways*, 1972
Bradbury, T. *The Battle of Hastings*, Phoenix Mill, 1998
Brian, J. *Pembrokeshire*, David and Charles, 1976
Brunicardi, D. *Seahound: The Story of an Irish Ship*, Collins Press, Cork
Burke, J. *A Traveller's History of Scotland*, John Murray, 1990
Byron, R. 'Social Anthropology of an Irish Sea Fishing Community,'
    The Irish Sea, Institute of Irish Studies, Queen's University Belfast,
    1989
Carradice, P. *The Last Invasion*, Village Publishing, 1992
Chadwick, L. *The Smalls Lighthouse*, Dobson Books, London, 1971
Cowper, F. *Sailing Tours*, Ashford Press, Southampton, 1985
Cullen, L.M. 'Privateers fitted out in Irish ports in the 18th century,'
    Irish Sword Journal, 1957-58
Davies, N. *The Isles*, Macmillan, 1999
De Courcy Ireland, J. *Ireland and the Irish in Maritime History*,
    Glendale, 1986
— *Wreck and Rescue on the East Coast of Ireland*, Dublin, 1983
— 'Survey of Early Irish Maritime Trade,' *The Irish Sea*, Institute of Irish
    Studies, Queen's University Belfast, 1989
Defoe, D. *Tour Through Great Britain*, Dent and Sons, 1974
De la Tocnaye, *A Frenchman's Walk Through Ireland*, Blackstone Press,
    1984
Driver, J. *Chester in the Later Middle Ages*, Chester Community
    Council, 1971
Dudley Edwards, R. *An Atlas of Irish History*, Methuen, 1981
Eames, A. *Ships and Seamen of Anglesey*, Cardiff, 1981
— 'Shrouded Quays,' Welsh Heritage Series, No. 2, 1991
Enoch, V. *The Martello Towers of Ireland*, Dublin

Erickson, C. *Bonnie Prince Charlie*, Robson Books, 1993

Fitzgerald, W. *Historical Geography of Early Ireland*, London, 1925

Forde, F. *Maritime Arklow*, Glendale Press, 1988

Fox, C. *Skerries Harbour*, Three Candles, 1970

Froude, J. *The English in Ireland*, 3 Vols, London, 1877

Gavin, C. *Royal Yachts*, Rich and Cowan, 1932

George, B. 'Pembrokeshire Seafaring Before 1900,' Field Studies Council, 1964

Harbison, P. *Pilgrimage in Ireland*, Barry and Jenkins, 1991

Hawkins, E. (ed.) *Brereton's Travels in Holland and Ireland 1634-5*, Chatham Society, 1844

Heaton, P. *The History of Yachting*, Batsford, 1955

Herbert, Dorothea, *Retrospections from 1770 to 1806*, Gerald Howe, 1929

Hill, C. *A Galloway Venture*, Dumfries and Galloway Museum Service, 1999

Hughes, H. *Chronicle of Chester*, MacDonald and James, London, 1975

Hughes, L. and Williams, D. *Holyhead: The Story of a Port*, Gee and Sons, 1967

Johnson, G.W. *The First Captain: The Story of John Paul Jones*, Coward-McCann, 1947

Jones, M. *American Immigration*, University of Chicago Press, 1969

Jones, P. *Memorials of Rear Admiral Paul Jones*, Edinburgh, 1830

Lawlor, B. *Dublin Bay*, O'Brien Press, Dublin, 1989

Lewis, S. *Topographical Dictionary of Ireland*, Dublin, 1837

Lloyd, L.W. *The Port of Caernarvon: 1793-1900*, Harlech, 1989

— *The Port and Mart of Llyn*, Gwasg Pantycelyn, Caernarfon, 1991

McFee, W. *The Law of the Sea*, Faber and Faber, 1951

MacHaffie, *The Short Sea Route*, Preston, 1975

McKenna, D. *The Maritime History of Ringsend*, Dublin

McLeod, J. *The Highlands: A History of the Gaels*, Hodder and Stoughton, 1996

MacLysaght, E. *Irish Life in the Seventeenth Century*, Irish Academic Press, 1979

Mahon, J. *Kate Tyrrell: Lady Mariner*, Basement Press, Dublin

Marcus, G. *A Naval History of England: The Age of Napoleon*, Allen and Unwin, 1971

Maritime Wales, Vol. 15, Gwynedd Archives and Museum Service, Caernarfon, 1992

Mason, T. *The Islands of Ireland*, Batsford, 1936

Maxwell, C. *Ireland Under the Georges*, Dundalgan Press, 1949

Moody, T. and Martin, F. (eds.), *The Course of Irish History*, Mercier Press, 1984

Morris, J. *Wales*, Viking Press, 1998

Morrison, S.E. *John Paul Jones*, Faber and Faber, 1950

Mourne Local Studies Group Journal, Vol. 7, Kilkeel, 1996

Nolan, W. and Power, T. *Waterford: History and Society*, Geography Publications, Dublin, 1992

O'Faoláin, S. *The Irish*, Penguin, 1978

O'Neill, T. *Merchants and Mariners in Medieval Ireland*, Dublin, 1987

Place, G. *The Rise and Fall of Parkgate*, Preston, 1994

Powell, R. *The Navy in the English Civil War*, Anchor Books, 1962

Power, E. and Poston, M. *Studies in English Trade in the 15th Century*, London, 1933

Raggetts, P. *Solva*, Haverfordwest, 1990

Rees, J. F. *The Story of Milford*, Cardiff University Press, 1954

Reid, A. *The Castles of Wales*, London, 1973

Reilly, T. *Cromwell*, Brandon, 1999

Robinson, A. and Millward, R. *Illustrated Guide to Britain's Coast*, Basingstoke, 1983

Roche, R. *The Norman Invasion of Ireland*, Anvil Press, 1970

Rowlands, J. (ed.) *Welsh Family History: A Guide*, Association of Family History Societies of Wales, 1993

Shields, J. 'Captain Luke Ryan of Rush,' Dublin Historical Record, 1970

Stammers, M. *West Coast Shipping*, Aylesbury, 1976

Stenning. E. *Portrait of the Isle of Man*, Robert Hale, London, 1978

Stokes, G. *Ireland and the Anglo-Norman Church*, Hodder and Stoughton, 1989

Stokes, R. *Death in the Irish Sea: The Sinking of the Leinster*, Collins Press, 1998

Sweetman, R. and Nimmons, C. 'The Port of Belfast,' Belfast Harbour Commissioners, 1985

Westropp, T. 'Early Maps: 1300–1600,' PRIA, 1913

Wilkins, F. *Dumfries and Galloway's Smuggling Story*, Kidderminster, 1993

Williams, E. *Packet to Ireland*, Caernarfon, 1984

Wilson, T. *The Irish Lifeboat Service*, Allen Figgis, 1968

Winbolt, S.E. *Britain Under the Romans*, Pelican, 1945

Young, A. *A Tour in Ireland: 1776-79*, Shannon, 1970